LOVE BROKE THROUGH

Odilie M. Bagwell Portocarrero Au.D.

WESTBOW
PRESS®
A DIVISION OF THOMAS NELSON
& ZONDERVAN

WestBow Press books may be ordered through booksellers or by contacting:

WestBow Press
A Division of Thomas Nelson & Zondervan
1663 Liberty Drive
Bloomington, IN 47403
www.westbowpress.com
844-714-3454

ISBN: 978-1-6642-7525-6 (sc)
ISBN: 978-1-6642-7526-3 (hc)
ISBN: 978-1-6642-7524-9 (e)

Library of Congress Control Number: 2022915114

Print information available on the last page.

WestBow Press rev. date: 10/29/2022

TODAY IS THE DAY

LOVE CAN GET THROUGH ANYTHING FOR YOU.

"I HAVE LOVED, YOU MY PEOPLE, WITH AN
EVERLASTING LOVE; WITH AN UNFAILING LOVE
I HAVE DRAWN YOU TO MYSELF." NLT JER 31:3

LOVE BROKE THROUGH YOUR
PAST TO GET YOU HERE.

LOVE BROKE THOUGH YOUR PRESENT
STRUGGLES TO REACH YOU.

LOVE REMAINS ALWAYS AND WILL BREAK
THROUGH FOR YOUR FUTURE.

LOVE TRANSFORMS.

LOVE DELIVERS.

LOVE GIVES YOU THE LIFE YOU LOVE.

THERE IS ONLY ONE YOU. LET LOVE SAVE YOU!

ONE LOVE

ONE PEOPLE

ONE LIFE,

LIVE IT.

LOVE IT.

SHARE IT.

LOVE IS WHAT YOU DO.

The Story Line
The Main Idea: How Love Broke Through
to a Desperate and Wounded Girl.
Love Broke Through the Past to Give the Present
Life, and It Sealed My Blessed Future.

If You Allow It, Walk through the Details of How a Love Can
and Will Break Through Anything to Save You and Bless You.

No Worries; All That Has Ever Concerned
You Will Serve You Well.

Tired Of Being Tired? Are You Tired Of Going
Through The Duties Of Life In Discontentment?
Love Is The Answer.

The Plot:
Identify the Real Threat on Your Foundation
Your Identity
Your Role
Your Purpose
Your Future
Your Legacy

The Setting:
For Such a Time Is This In Your Life, Now. Your Call Is
Outside of Time. It's Never Too Late to Answer Your Call.
Love Is Outside of Time.
Love Is Eternal.

The Ending:
When You Line Up with What Is Absolute and Infallibly True.
Love Never Fails.
When Love Wins! You Win!

CONTENTS

PROLOGUE

Do You Know Love?

Unhappy but don't know why? That's how I felt.

Burned out, but not knowing what or how to quit? That's how I felt.

Do you want different, but don't know how? You are not alone. Everyone would benefit from reading this book, if you have made mistakes and want peace with yourself and what happened, this book will help. Or if you just love a good story and want to learn from people so you won't make the same mistakes, this book will help. Even if you just like to read stories, let this book get you thinking, maybe even tenderize your heart.

In this book, I hope to point you to your next most needed step. This book is a call to action on your call. Everyone has a call. Not everyone answers. As you let yourself be real and honest with yourself, you will break through your barriers and into your purpose. Everyone thrives in a wholesome environment of belonging, safety, nourishment, purpose, direction, encouragement, and love—and best of all, the push of a good coach! Allow me to share what God has done for me, and you might come open to allowing God to see what His might can do through and in *you!*

Love really did come and break though my very desperate situation. How? I will later reveal. Love redeemed me and gave me that word, when I really didn't even know what redemption meant.

Love cleaned up my dirty sin and self-centered perspectives. Love identified wounds and brokenness I didn't even know I had. Love walked me through the frightening dark closets and caves of pain, shame, and guilt. Love lifted me up from the mire and muck where I was stuck in my mind.

Love restored hope. Love overflowed in me for me to receive love and then give it from overflow. Love forgave and *forgot.* Love blessed me for all my wrongs. Love helped me accept forgiveness for others and—the hardest—for myself. Love shared an unconditional kind and lavish love, the kind I never saw or knew existed. Love freed me to be who I always wanted to be. Love filled me so much I'm compelled to share it with you.

I wrote this book … just for you!

You are the *one* I must share with.

I hope and pray that you are ready for an adventure of a lifetime and lessons you too will pass along.

With an open mind, an honest heart, and a willing resolve, you will allow *love to break through for just you!*

Do You Need to Know?

I have been diligently studying the Word of God alongside Bible scholars and just ordinary people. With God's spirit, I can convey to you what you *need to know, now.*

The answer to all our pains and problems is this: *fix it* with *love—God's real love!*

Tried and true, the answer for any life crisis or question is God's love, His name, His words, and His breath.

Since the beginning, God's breath and love create. Love makes whole or complete, it flourishes, it abundantly fulfills. When there is good, there is *God,* and it always occurs in uniquely complex and yet complementing ways.

Do You Need an Answer Now?

Well, God's love directs and gives answers. I don't know anyone who doesn't want God to text him to her on what is right for them. This book holds the promise and perspective to help you hear God's good plan for you. As you grow, you will know which way your next step is. You will grow in confidence and courage to step into your hope and a good future.

Do You Need Faith?

If you're wondering or have questions or so desperately want faith and a love for God, but don't know how to awaken it, just keep reading. This is for you.

If you have faith and just want to live in faith more fully, keep reading. By fully accepting this amazing gift of God's free love, you can and will conquer all previous obstacles in your life. You will experience freedom from the self-tripping hazards and entanglements that keep you from reaching your happy place. Your happy place has more than you involved. It is your calling, the very reason for your existence.

You can rise above the daily grind and find divine connection in the everyday mundane. If you use the practical applications made available to you in this book you will live in peace instead of questioning. You'll live on a curious quest instead of cynical doubt. You can live life in blessed assurance instead of dread or fear of the future.

Most of all, you can learn to experience God's power in His holy presence. In His strength and favor, you will experience courage to conquer your biggest giants. Then, as you see them fall before your eyes, you will raise your arms in true gratitude. You can finally defeat what has defeated you for so long! Once you see faith really works, you will put it to work. As you experience more battle wins, you will learn to keep trading in your shortcomings for His sure-win victories. As you notice all the progress you are making, you'll be happy to trade your sorrows for the joy of the Lord.

You can and will learn how to live in a sacred and daily exchange with your active and living God. You will finally learn to recognize a pitfall or that same old trial or temptation that comes to trip you up. You will know how to send it packing and bind it so that it can be "gone for good." All this "good living" comes from *God's good loving!* All because *you let* God's massive love break through and make you altogether new!

Want to Know More God?

In this book you'll start to see that no matter what the outcome of the trial you are in—sad or happy, pain-filled or joy-filled—when you give up the need to know and understand, you can experience the peace of God in the midst of your trial. In that surrender, God deposits faith in exchange for your doubts. This graceful exchange yields a blessed trust in Him that is unshakable and undying. In wonder and awe, you will experience God in *real* love in everyday types of ways.

Do You Need a New Way?

God will make a way when there is no way. He is in relentless pursuit to have you know Him and receive His amazing love and grace for you. Even if you have deep emotional, psychological scars or wounds, even if or in addition you have major trust and commitment issues, just read on. *God* has a plan and a way for you. God's love can make a way when there is no way. He brings water in the desert out of rocks. No amount of dead and dry can stay that way when Jesus gets involved. He is about you, and no amount of rebellion or denial can push Him out of His pursuit for you. His love is so strong, it broke through the grave's ginormous tombstone. Jesus walked out of His grave a victor who defeated all that hell had to offer, all so that you could live too.

Mediocre or just making it is not what God died to give you.

Enough is enough. The cycle of just barely surviving that theoretical mountain is finished! No more repeating mistakes. Your God is about to break you out! God, who is *love*, is coming to break you out. I ask you again: Where are you closed off? Stone cold? Where won't you allow love or God to come in? He is ready to do the great, miraculous work for you if you just give Him access. A Breakthrough for you? Yes, a powerful one can defeat even lifetime old mindsets. The Savior of your life knocks at the door. You, open the door; just a crack is enough. Glory and thanks be to *God*, you'll never be the same again.

ACKNOWLEDGMENTS

Thank you to my Lord and Savior, Jesus Christ. He chose me to let you know he has chosen *you*.

Thank you to Ruach Elohim—the Breath of God. When we don't understand the complexity and pains of this life, bring it back to the basics. What could be more basic than our breath? So when the heat of life sears, and the pose I must hold gets too intense, I bring the center of my soul back to "the Breath"; there you can connect to the very Breath of Life. In this holy connection with my creator and giver of each and all of my days, this book was developed.

I can with all honesty tell you that each time I sat down to write another chapter, you specifically, as a reader of this book, were prayed for. I prayed each time for all the priests, pastors, and prophets who teach, lead, and encourage the church body of today. I thank the saints and host of angels who do the work of our Lord. I give thanks and praise to God for the heavenly hosts. They champion our progress personally and bring forth the purpose and help us progress in the kingdom of God.

I give thanks and praise for the generational curses broken by God in your and my family lines. A chain of sin breaks every time we have the courage to allow God to do His great work in us. Transformed by His love and grace, we can step into our life's purpose. Our Rabbi, AKA Jesus the teacher, will bring us into courageous, free, and abundant living. He will empower us to do His work and wait well and joyfully in His *hope* until He comes again!

Thank you to my mother and deceased father and our very loving Latin family. I'm grateful for your unconditional love and your honesty and grateful to know that I am fully known and adored as I am, a work in progress. You didn't want to cast me out when I failed the family. You believed in me and had faith for me when I lost mine. You never stopped believing God would save me. I'm grateful for all the love, support, prayers, and lessons you have given me and continue to give. I am eternally grateful to God that He chose you all as my family. We are learning together that we are perfectly imperfect. I love us as we are. Thank you for staying in faith and relationship together; we must not stop making the commitment and priority to gather. We as a family are richly bonded in love and support for each other's success and purposeful living.

Thank you to my husband. Your love gave me a hope and a future, and an endless love filled with adventure. With you, Brad, I am inspired to the greatest heights. Thank you to my four God-given children. God speaks through each of you every day! You are my greatest love and teacher. Sofia, because of your love and asking me to be there for you, I had the courage to move where God called. Alana, because of your believing and your love, I'm healed or fixed as you said I would be! When I didn't know what to do in brokenness, you at the age of eight said, "Fix it with *love*." Alana, with your love I am strong and aspire to God's greatness.

Isabelle, because of your *love* I am tender and energetic. Your love activates the box of love and joy inside all of us. You refresh all with your kindness and joy, especially me. I love that you are known for your giggles; they lift my countenance immediately.

Bo Alan, because of your *love* I am filled with belief, generosity, and hope. Giants fall in my life with your positivity. You comfort me, you believe in me, and you hope big with me. You are skilled and completing excellent work, and you ground me with the confidence that anything is possible, with God.

To my tribe of godly women in my community, to everyone who has ever prayed with me, studied the Bible with me, or taken my little Bible workshops, I made it here to share God's Word, bold and unashamed because of you. Your love and prayers have been and continue to be fierce. You fought for me when I could not for myself. I am eternally grateful. I thank you for giving me the strength to embrace the unknown deep living waters of *God's* love. Together we learned how to fight for the kingdom and our purpose in it. In united and shared faith, we take what Jesus died to give us all, His love, protection, and provision. I love ~~walking~~ running the faith race with you all. Let us not grow weary. We pursue His leading. Time is of the essence. He is doing a new and mighty thing in each of us!

Thank you to the people of social media. You each gave me courage to speak of the things of God. Together we have "liked" what God has done to grow and inspire us and propel us.

A special thank-you to the pastoral and worship leading community, both live and online, all over the world. Your faithfulness and commitment to faithfully teach and spread the "good news" literally freed me. With each sermon, worship song, and series of teachings on biblical truths God has given you, you freed this prisoner! Pandemic or no pandemic, you choose to remain faithful to pointing up to Jesus as the hope and answer and cure of all. You tirelessly shepherd the Lord's flocks. Day and night you each deliver the beautiful and powerful Word of God through the flavor of your unique you. Because of you, I step into the hope and courage I need to cast out fear and fulfill my calling.

All together, in humble faith, we as the body of Christ have the keys to success in life. By trusting and practicing the living and active Word of God, we are given godliness for this life and unto the next. You alone, God, are the great antidote to all my self-defeating thoughts. You, O Lord, freed me to speak of Your power and goodness to all the world, so here I go …. Let all the stories of Your love be told to set all the captives free.

In a humble love, I present to you the love of Jesus poured out through my heart to yours. I'm not too shy to ask you again: Won't you allow *love to break through—just for you?*

ABOUT THE AUTHOR

Odilie Marie Bagwell Portocarrero is passionate about getting the believers of Jesus to be free of all that hinders them from living in their full expression of God in them. She herself has always been a believer but, like most, was just getting by the best way she knew how. Before she knew her true worth, she thrived on achievements and seeking perfection to feel good and loved. She ran her efforts almost into the ground. Her marriage of thirteen years was threatened to the point of divorce talk; her children were praying desperately she would quit drinking. Alcoholism ran in her family, and she had fallen into alcoholic and abusive drinking to manage all that she couldn't get free of.

Now more than eight years into sobriety and seven years in freedom, she can share with all people biblical truths and life applications that helped her. She hopes to help those caught up in the web of any abuse and addiction itself. Maybe, by sharing this real and raw story, someone can be saved from being caught up in addictive behaviors. In seeking her purpose, passion, and potential in Christ, she found an anointing to free people as she was freed. By encouraging and energizing believers to live their best life, she is living hers. When you read through these real and raw stories in Odilie's life, you will see how God's love broke through her circumstances. It is her genuine hope to inspire change in your life. She with her whole heart believes that *you* can have the *real love of Christ break through* your same old same-old. You *will* break through, in Jesus's name! You win in your new story—in such a way that God is honored by revealing His glorious expression in *you*.

A NOTE FROM THE AUTHOR

My dear People,

I hope, as you read the contents of this book, that you make peace with your colorful past if you have one. If you are wise to read this before you go astray, thank the Lord for lessons learned softly and through others' experience of what not to do. Yet mostly I pray you come to see evidence of God's truth for yourself: that we were made to love Him because He first loved us. We are meant to walk and talk with God just like Adam and Eve did, intimately and all the time. We were made to reflect His goodness in active and living relationship. We are to live abundantly in God's love and power.

If you don't have faith or hope and want it, open your mind's eye, open your heart's desire, and let your soul connect with my deepest and most vulnerable stories. We as humans are much more alike than you think. When you read of the lessons and experiences that taught me experientially of God's real and powerful love, you will see that I have been redeemed. It is hard to show you what I've lived through and done, but I hope it serves as hope that what God does for one, He can do for all who are willing.

Love is universal and eternal. God's greatest gift is the gift of love. In this book you will see how *love broke through for me. My* question to you is *will you allow it to for you?*

Know this promise and truth: there is no situation too desperate or too wrong for *real love* to *break through.* If you let it, it will break through, *just for you!*

Read on with me, about this true and harrowed tale with death and paths of ruin that eventually led to the pleasant places under the protection of a *true King* and His *real love.* We can rise to be *royals*!

WestBow Press
Dr. Odilie Bagwell Portocarrero
www.lovebrokethrough.org
IG@drodiliebagwell
@Lovebrokethroughthebook

1

THE BACKSTORY

Shaken off the Throne of Me;
All False Will Fall!

A young queen took her platform. Though she had lost and suffered much to get to this place, it would soon be all worth it. Instead of a misplaced English as a second language immigrant or foreigner, she would soon be crowned a royal who belonged. At this point, she embraced the poise, grace, and confidence that the difficult upbringing had built into her. Roles were easy for her to play. This role would be her favorite—the recognition, the adoration, and the hope of a bright future ahead.

All the ugly and pain-filled generational dysfunction was dead and gone, so she thought. Without a blink, she resolved to leave all that behind. It was locked up and buried well. With perhaps the same fury, rage, fear, and disgrace of a scorned mafia woman, all evidence of dysfunction and hurt was gone from her memory. It was time finally to bury the pain-filled past and now embrace a new era. Now she would take her rightful place of distinction. As a newly appointed bright future royal, her reign of self and image promotion would begin.

There was no doubt she had the makings of a true queen. She was thoughtful and altruistic and cared for the common promotion of good, all while displaying her masquerade of false self-confidence. Yes, anything less than an intelligent, kind, and enthusiastic, beautifully packaged royal was not to be pondered. Anything that tried to stop her from taking her bright future was buried. In fact any pain, insecurity, or self-doubt that surfaced was quickly disposed of. Her tools for burying any negative emotions or fear were crowd-pleasing, achievements, and noble deeds. Those tools became a perfect model for rising to the top of her next kingdom goals. Each goal was easy for her to meet, and her kingdom and influence grew. She knew that she was unstoppable and would attain all her goals with her faith, positivity, and perseverance.

Until the enemy of her soul introduced her to her tonic: alcohol.

With her soon-enough betraying best friend, she conquered kingdom after kingdom. Her trusty allegiance with alcohol was easy to hide and the perfect comedown to her fast-paced life of working hard and playing harder. She did go far with this ally; much territory was gained, and recognition and dreams of her life came true.

Until one day, her ally swatted her off her throne like a fly and left her for dead—almost dead.

Her betrayer celebrated in a villainous way that that was the end of her. This kind, life-giving queen could no longer positively influence her kingdom. She was once known as exactly who she had aspired to be as a child: a trophy wife, supermom, *hostess with the mostest,* life of the party, altruistic fundraiser for good, lover of God, and frequent *churchgoer and Bible study attender.* She was adored by her family as she was the glue that gathered all of them together.

Yet the secret was exposed. Her vice and cocktail for success became public knowledge. So public that she was called into the principal's office of her children's elementary school. Neighbors and friends were trying to help, telling her of the problem, but they really didn't know how to help either. The snickering and rejection just caused more shame for her. The shame she carried was so great she went from self-consciousness or poor self-esteem to self-loathing.

After she crashed into a mailbox and ruined her minivan, it became harder and harder for her to believe there was any good left in her. Her children wrote her cards and letters begging her to stop the allegiance with this terrible influence: wine. Her husband would plead with her to stop and videotaped her under the influence so that she could see how foolish she was. Yes, at this point, she had suffered public disgrace that most would not survive. The internal battle was killing her soul, stealing her health, and finally casting a shadow on her family's love for her.

All the territory and valuables in her kingdom—faith, marriage, children, career, and positive influence—were pillaged. Her body and life were wasting away like a ransacked village after a bloody battle. Her life was a mess along with her thoughts and her eating and sleeping patterns. Her own people did not want or trust her anymore. It was looking all too familiar; her household castle had gone from a loving and fun little nursery school filled with love, dancing, and performances to frequent battles and fights—a few in front of the kids.

What this queen most feared came to be daily life, a polarized home with the kids and spouse aligned against the "drinker" or the one who messed things up. Her loving home became exactly like the one she had seen when she was little. Laughter and love were swapped for either excessive screaming or emotionally numbed hurting parents escaping to their internal worries. It was sad but true. The home environment became chaotic and unpredictable, just like her parents' home, just the way she swore she would never be. How could the vices and demons that she had already fought to escape as a child—yes, the same memories she killed, cursed, and buried as a child—come back? They had come to take her down as an adult, happy life and all. The same generational sins and patterns that took lives and marriages across her family line as victims had come to take her family, her legacy, and her purpose too.

(Beware, as this story in many families may entail different characters with different substance problems, but the ending is always the same: a family destroyed. Yes, without the Savior, Jesus Christ, at the very core of the family unit, the sad tale of death to the core family unit, along with its originally intended joyful future and generational blessings, will banish it.)

Until, that is, just like a great tale of a monarch kingdom, a saving King in shining armor came in on His white horse to rescue this royal. Oh yes, this queen's fairy tale was at its bleakest point, but this King was not of this world. He was and is a true and powerful Savior. His nail-scarred yet strong and beautiful hands met this queen late at night while I was sleepless and scared. There He pulled me up. I, the fool who almost lost it all, was pulled out of my swampy morass and murky pit. That was when *real love broke through* for me! Jesus, my King, said to me, "You, my royal, let Me show you a better way. Make Me the King of your heart, and I will show you what it is like to be a real royal." Jesus spoke life into my lifeless, sad eyes and said, "Now that you have been knocked off the throne of self you created, let Me teach you what *real* love, *real* life, and *real* confidence and achievement look like."

> Jesus said to her, "I am the resurrection and the life. He who believes in me will live even though they die." (John 11:25 NIV)

I of course said yes to Jesus. I had suffered enough. The never-ending cycle of overachieving to compensate for insufficiency had gone on long enough.

> I knew that if I kept doing what I was doing—drinking my sorrows and unresolved pains—I would die young like my dad had. Besides, King Jesus had really big and important plans for me to get to-*sober.*

I knew that if I kept doing what I was doing—drinking my sorrows and unresolved pains—I would die young like my dad had. The desperation of trying to change myself and failing so miserably put me right where the King of my heart wanted me: *empty of me* and dead to all that I had hung my confidence on. In this royal tale, I, as this queen, went down to a sackcloth wardrobe and turned in all her jewels. At the end of herself, she had to leave all that she had loved and built so long to have. Humbly and in a pool of tears, I made myself go to in-patient rehabilitation for alcoholism. For the first time in my forty-one-year life, I would be by myself. I left a big, loving family—including a loving husband of thirteen years and four healthy, funny, smart, and beautiful children—as well as my private practice small business and my faith family, to face all my demons and consequences to my bad choices. I said to myself, "Do it afraid."

I would give up abusing the substance of alcohol and swap it for faith. I had always loved the following verse of faith:

> Faith is the substance of things hoped for, the evidence of things not seen. (Hebrews 11:1 KJV)

I had relied on that verse before, to hope my children into existence. Now it was to be used to save my life, instead of creating a life. Since that day, God gave me a life-saving substance swap. That was the greatest substance swap of all. On that day, that was how love broke through.

Real love broke through my mess!

It broke through my stubbornness to do it my way.

It even broke through all my miserable alcohol withdrawal symptoms. Up ahead, I'll tell of that hilarious and sobering tale.

For now, let's finish this chapter and every chapter hereafter by walking into a sacred space: you meeting with your Creator, Savior, and Friend. Allow your heart and mind into the blessed and sacred space of God Almighty's heart for you. I love the truth of this being available to me and you. Jesus Himself encouraged us to honor and ponder His love and will for us. Step courageously and humbly into this space for some reflection. Allow yourself to be open and dedicated enough in stillness. How long? Long enough to wonder or marvel. Instead of resistance or doubt, embrace invitation and confidence. Take the objection "But I have to see it or understand it first," and replace it with exploration and investigation.

Allow continued exploration until you find some revealing details to God Almighty. Picture yourself alone within the sacred chambers of Jesus's Blessed and Sacred Heart. There you will step into the greatest love ever. Redirect your focus repeatedly until you find undistracted and patient stillness. You are not emptying your mind; you are filling it with the *One* who matters most.

I believe that God will draw your heart into *His* and His into yours. Picture the two hearts beating in synch. Just allow yourself to picture it. This heart is not like any others. Picture the Sacred Heart of Jesus, adored and explored with every sense of humanity stepping into pure and complete divinity. Here in your mind's eye and in united spirit you will be meeting with Jesus. In this mental and spiritual space you will learn to meet with Jesus. Here He puts the super into your natural! Miracles happen here!

If you are faithful in seeking, dedicated in the wait, and pure in heart by intention, you will meet the presence of God Almighty. Here you will develop your spiritual ears and eyes. Just like a newborn's seeing and hearing become sharp and clear at further distances with each day of life, so will you grow more spiritually sharp. With your enhanced spiritual senses, you will be able to see God's hand at work in your life from further away. You will know and trust His voice above all the background noise of life. Fully developed spiritual senses strengthen your trust for God, and you will be able to actually follow through with His will for your life.

At the end of each chapter I urge you to contemplate the scripture tied to the story, reflect a biblical point and then write out what the Lord's sacred heart leads you to. Is it in the form of a word that came to mind, a memory, a question? Write anything down and then take the time to explore what it means to you. God allows you to have that prompting so that you can discover something about Him, about you, and about what you are called to do and be at this moment in time. If you have breath in your lungs, no matter your age, you have an important purpose to play out. Is that not totally exciting? You are the main character in a riveting adventure with a mystery to solve. It totally has a big treasure at the end, a win, and your name will be known. I hope you are willing to follow the clues and get to your glorious finish.

I don't know your life story; and if you want to write me something, do. I'm in the middle of my journey of exploration and I have been taking notes, so I hope that through my story you will find out more about your *divine you*, for if you choose, God lives in you.

INTRODUCING A SACRED SPACE ... HIS SACRED HEART FOR YOURS

REFLECTIONS OF HOW TO GET YOUR HEART CLOSER TO JESUS'S HEART

After each chapter I humbly ask you to accompany me to a place that really helped me advance into accepting and understanding Jesus's love for me. As I allowed myself to explore the concept that Jesus already lived in my heart, I wanted to connect deeper to the divine living in me. I invite you to do the same. I know most of us totally ignore the questions authors ask us at the end of their chapters. But if you could, get to doing something different so that you experience something altogether different. Make yourself face the uncomfortable and respond with a pen, with an utterance of your voice somehow. Think on the reflections; ponder and ruminate on them, and marinate in them. Then jot down the spontaneous thoughts and words that come up. Take them to God, even if it does not make sense. It will eventually make sense. Answer honestly with what first comes to mind, even if it is a jaded or anti-faith perspective. Be honest and write down your questions, your doubts, and your wounded or jaded unbelieving thoughts. God is faithful to lead you to truth when you are completely honest with him.

So, for me ... How did I dare approach this sacred heart of my Savior? I was demoralized, devastated. I said to myself, *O Lord, how can I make it out of this?*

It felt like so many different feelings and thoughts. It felt insurmountably impossible. (Is that even a word?) It felt like epic proportions to leave the old way behind. I really even didn't want to. It may not be good, but it's familiar. Yet I knew. I knew that God was calling me to a new life. Quitting this time didn't feel like my previous attempts while trying to diet or fast or discipline my appetites. This time God was backing me; I could feel Him differently. It was an alluring draw to fearful and wonderful, made all the same. I finally could process that complex phrase. He spoke it into my being, and I knew it was time; it hit my soul differently. It resonated all over me in that in-audible but certain voice. It was an invitation to a better way. He was asking me to walk and talk intimately with our greatest-of-all living example, King Jesus.

I came to him fully surrendered. I said to Him, "I'm broken down and torn raw in my heart. I'm barely functioning, and I want to give up. Even with so many blessings. I've been told that You have a great plan for my life and my future. I want to believe this, but You know how often I fail. How will it work? I am tired of making the same mistakes. Take my life and make it Yours. I find it spectacular that if I really knew Your plans for me, I would never want to be anyone else. Help me live that way. I want to know You. I want to love You better. But it's hard for me to love what I can't experience, hear, or see. I know You love me, but I want to know this better."

After some more time with Jesus, I said, "I now know, Lord, that You aren't trying to squash the unique parts of me, but to highlight them with Your love! I have a great feeling and hope that I know You have given me. Your holy highlighter will make the substance of my character shine like the full expression of You, God in me! Your character and Your greatness expressed in me. Now that is worth highlighting. I now know that I alone am at best ordinary and typically a miserable failure. But at the end of me, is the beginning of Your best work in me. Lord, You at work in me becomes Extraordinary. All of that sounds so good, Jesus. How do I do this? How do I sign up?'

This is what God said to me: "My love in you—accept it, take it, unwrap it, play with it, give thanks, and then share it. It is the greatest gift of all. Odilie, I'll give you all of Me if you give Me all of you."

Let the truth be told to my heart and yours. At more than one ˙
time in my life, I have realized this: that something in me was not
right. I was most broken this time, and I have admitted to myself,
my Lord God, and all my family and friends that I am not okay right
now. "I've made it out of a lot of messes, God. But this one seems
to be the worst. You, God, only You can fix it." Only God can take
all my pieces and make something of me. This great restoration can
only start after my redemption.

My King Jesus became and still is my redeemer. Is he yours? It
is the best decision you will ever make. The best yes you will ever
say. It is for life now; it is for life in the future and forevermore. The
way to Jesus's heart is at the end of yours. It is the moment you are
awakened to the love of Him in you that has been there since before
your first breath. *Mind-boggling!*

A Glimpse at His Heart …

"That Not One Should Perish"
(adapted from Matthew 18:14)

Step into the sacred chambers of His heart. The holy
word says, "For God so loved the world that he gave
his one and only son, so that everyone who believes
in him, will not perish but have eternal life. God sent
his son into the world not to judge the world, but
to save the world through him" (John 3:16–17 NLT).

Let this settle into all of you! Every single cell in
your body needs to embrace this! If one cell believes,
the rest will know the way and follow. A saved,
Spirit-led life down to the cellular and even the
atomic level is magnetic; the rest will follow.

You, my dear, are HIS WORLD!

First order of business. You. Are you redeemed?

Let today be the day of your redemption. Make it official and without question. What does redeem mean? You are "born again," Jesus Himself calls it. It is a swap of sorts. You redeem a winning ticket, and you get your prize.

What are you redeeming? Your old nature that keeps falling into the same trap, for your new nature in Christ. This new nature is finally able to succeed at change. How? By way of believing in grace through faith.

There, the transformative power of Jesus Christ goes to work for you. You exchange the flopping efforts of self-goodness for real and eternal gains of good, manifesting in your life like never before.

Sometimes spiritual work and mental exercise can be exhausting! So I encourage you to take a break; I call it a praise break. It is just you listening to worship songs that can inspire you to talk to God in your own words, to give thanks to God, and to tell Him what you like and soon enough love about Him!

Something eternally significant and utterly amazing just happened. Heaven just broke out into song over your salvation—yes, literally and for real!

If you were already saved and ran away from your spiritual home for a bit, welcome back! Your coming home is like that of the prodigal son.

Finally, if you are already born again, a rededication will help you accept the call to go deeper, wider, and higher in your faith. There is no such thing as a plateau in faith; there is always a way to "be moved" by greater faith or—what I love imagining—to "level up" in your understanding about God's higher ways.

Consider selecting your own redemption song. Listen to "One Step" by Unspoken, released July 24, 2020. Select your own song, and write it down here to remember forever.

For a special throwback: My redemption song was by Big Daddy Weave, "Redeemed," released May 3, 2012.

A Guided Redemption Prayer for You

Father God, thank You for the opportunity to start over. I have heard that You will never let me down. I am sorry to admit that I have done things my way. I think I even made a mess of my life. Perhaps I have stopped letting myself dream big. I don't want to live my life apart from Your guidance, protection, and provision. I repent of my sins, and I give You my life along with all my heart and mind today.

I realize I am in need of Your salvation. You are the Lord over all, and I want that to include me. I ask You for the first time or once again to come into my heart and be my Lord and Savior. Make something of me that only You can do, all so that You can present me to Your Father in heaven one day. I'm ready to give You all of me, for all of You.

Thank You that You fully know me and still love me. Thank You for choosing me to save and give life abundant to. Thank You that from this day forward You live in my heart and that I am never alone. Thank You that I now have resurrection power in my entire body, mind, and heart to do what You need me to do. I'm so excited that You are all I'll ever need to be all that I'll need to be. Lord, You are now the very air I breathe. Help me remember that when I am weak. You are my redeemer, and with that, You will fill me with goodness and mercy all my days.

Write what you hear God wants you to know about you being His chosen.

2

SHAKEN INTO NEW

The Exodus; Delivered from Bondage.
Saved from Slavery and Straight into Rehab

Imagine you find out the home you built was all wrong. It must be torn down and rebuilt. Suddenly, there is a wrecking ball, and it's coming at you, Get ready. It's demo day. It's all gotta come down. If there is a crack in the foundation, nothing can be salvaged; all of it must come down. In the demolition, the lowest point will be identified and the weakest spot targeted. A new foundation will be used. You might ask like me, "Why does all of it have to come down and be exposed?"

I'll tell you what God's Spirit told me, because it's built on the wrong foundation. As the Home Depot says, "Let's do this." Would you believe me if I told you that's what my uncle and husband told me the day I flew to rehab? Yes, I was so scared that I needed my hand held all the way there. But my spirit knew that I can't be freed from whatever I won't face. I also knew in my "knower" that whatever God calls me to face, though it may scare me, I won't be alone.

God will either get you a companion to take you where you need to go, or He will strengthen you with His presence so you will have the courage to go on your own. So let us do this! In this chapter, I'll share how rehab was pitched to me and share parts of what it did for me. You will hear real-life stories of what life looked like in a rehab facility.

Hopefully, you could find some applications to your own life. What life compensation habit or quirk do you need to be free of? What does your new-natured self look and act like? Hopefully, in witnessing an account of my delivery from slavery, spiritually speaking, you will be able to pinpoint what your Exodus story is. What mindset are you a slave to? People-pleasing? Achievement-focused identity? Self-defeating cycles? What place, person, or habit has your Exodus freed you from?

DO IT AFRAID

I had every excuse in the book not to go. I had built a marriage of fourteen years, had made four little amazing lives, and was raising them in a loving and stimulating environment. We were always signing, performing, role playing, and playing when home. We had a great little Christian school to attend as well as dance school, tumbling, and soccer for all four of them. We attended church regularly. I had built a successful private practice as a doctor of hearing that was going on six years old now. Why was I feeling so trapped and needing to drink as my escape?

So about checking into rehab. All this crossed my troubled and shaky mind. Who would drive the kids to those places? Who would make them lunches? Who would make sure their uniforms were clean for the next day? Who would see my patients? Worst of all, I had never been alone in my forty years of life. As much as it pained me to leave the little lives I loved and help make, I couldn't live without them for thirty days. If I am bare-bones honest, they were the only reason I wanted to live. If I didn't have them, who knew whether I might crumble even more.

Besides that, I didn't want to be alone with myself. I hated myself. What thoughts would come up? What would God say to me when He had me alone and undistracted? I feared, greatly. Plus, on another level of honesty, I didn't even really want to learn to live life without drinking. I had been trying on my own for the last few years, and it was miserable. I was a dry drunk, they say. That's when you are not drinking, but you have not changed or addressed any of your character flaws or relationship hang-ups that led you to drink. In a nutshell, I was bitter, not better. This was the first time I seriously tried to quit drinking and "do life differently."

The deciding factor was this, God gave me a dream, clear, lucid, and vivid. I was in a natural freshwater pool with Jesus, it was dark, and I saw a foolish girl frolicking past us. She represented a morph between me and my guardian angel. So she was the foolish side of me and yet all at once the wise, protective guardian angel of mine. She knelt down to me and warned me that if I didn't stop behaving foolishly, self-centered and playing a pitiful "woe is me, life is hard" game, I would die young. Then she kissed me on the cheek, and off she went.

Jesus was in and with me in that earthy pool—it was dark waters. He held me close in my dream with that difficult news to swallow. Jesus tried to come into my heart more alive in the dream, but I backed off and left His presence.

The Holy Spirit helped me make sense of that dream. I saw that I had been foolish, passing up all the good that was happening in my life. I saw that I had to quit living a double life. I was called to live, love, and have my being in an intimate relationship with Jesus. I saw that I didn't want to die; I wanted to live well for my kids and husband. I wanted to live life fully present. I didn't want to hurt my family. Our family had suffered enough hardships. I also saw that I had deeply hurt the ones who loved me with my selfish self-medicating. My family when I was a young child had suffered domestic abuse, adultery, and divorce due to alcoholism, crowned ultimately with an untimely death due to the aftermath of alcoholism. Alcoholism robbed me of a happy mom-and-dad type of home. So I was not going to let alcohol have me or my marriage. I wanted to be better; so that I could live with and for the family God had entrusted me with.

For the greater good, I would do the hard things necessary to "get well."

THE JUMP

Within a few days of my arrival at the recovery ranch, I had a powerful experience with God's grace. At "the Ranch" or rehab facility, we had physical and mental exercises to help up face fear and push us out of denial and comfort zones. 'The jump" was one the most powerful ones for me.

We had to climb to the top of a thirty-foot telephone pole like an AT&T worker. We each took a turn tethering or climbing up to the tower and jumping off a tiny, rickety twelve-by-twelve-inch square landing. It was a free jump in whatever style you wanted. There was no soft-landing parachute, no beefy hunky type of person to catch you, no trampoline mat. Instead, you had to select five women to counter your weight and pull you into suspension until they let you down—one hoped, gently and carefully.

Can you imagine ever doing this? Let alone while grumpy because you have left your family, you are not taking medications or drinks because you are detoxing, and there is no sugar or sodas, again because you are detoxing? Oh man, really not easy to do with bravery and any grace. But guess what, where God leads you to, God gets you through. He did give me smiles every day, an internal peace, humility, and tremendous bravery and tons of grace to do this and much more!

So as I selected five caring, not necessarily athletic women to catch me, this was God's prompting to me, as He wanted me to break "judgments of strength" and truly rely on big-hearted people for strength in community and character. This helped me for my future growth in recovery, as I wanted God's strength, not what the world selects as strong. Sure enough, I trembled and shook my way to the top. I was terrified to jump off—but not more terrified than I was to face and fight what had taken my dad's life, alcoholism, and recover from it.

The detailed playback: I was about the tenth woman in the sequence of jumps. Everyone said nothing, quickly leapt off the tower, and "got it over with." Yet I knew how powerful this line in the sand was for me. I was going to milk every therapeutic and spiritual element out of this exercise.

I paused at the top, teetering on the twelve-inch-square very wobbly tower; it could barely hold my two feet. I looked up, out, and down at those ready to catch me, then back out to the skyline of the heavens and trees. With a shaking soul yet a smooth, loud voice, I sang a song to God, my Savior and my hope.

I sang a classic Catholic church hymn: "Be not afraid, I go before you always. Come follow me, and I will give you rest." Then I said a prayer to God, aloud: "I need You and I rely on You, God the Father, God the Son, God the Holy Spirit." Then right before I leapt out with flying open arms I said, *"En tus manos, Señor"*—"Into your hands, my God" in Spanish.

There, at the Ranch, for the first time in my life I stepped off the throne of self-image. I dove into and out with legs and arms sprawled out of that sinking ship of self-centeredness. I took that desperate dive into knowing what a true lover of Christ would be like. I was tired of being who I thought I needed to be to be liked and loved, that old image-managing beauty queen. I traded in the "homecoming queen and scholar" image and for the first time called myself *redeemed*.

A mighty God and King of all kings was now in charge of me. Only He could tell me and shape me into who I needed to be. Through the redemption and recovery process, I would replace self-hating, numbing, escaping, and barely surviving with acceptance, vulnerability, authentic love, honesty, caring, and serving from the heart.

I wanted to trade chameleon-type people-mirroring for an experience of unspeakable joy and thriving in authentic connection. I guess being the new girl so many times in my life made me want to be included more than being myself. So I played the role people wanted to see. I wanted to cast out that "survivor" hustling immigrant mentality to be a real and authentic person. I would identify with now living my life in redemption—meaning chosen, enough, known, and fully loved.

My true King and Most High God showed up to save me from me. In this new way of life and living as a freed me, the calling to greatness was always on point. It's just that the needle of greatness only goes one direction. It always point north, true north, like Our God Most High north and all around. So this former queen was not far off. I was to be a royal, just not in the kingdom of self-centeredness. Slowly, I learned how to be and behave in God's eternal kingdom. The greatness in me is Christ's. The calling to greatness was my heart's pure cry to step into my irreplaceable role in God's kingdom.

This irreplaceable role of a royal co-heir comes with our belief in one and only savior and king, King Jesus. God offers "sonship" to every believer; we are not left orphan on the only planet with life as we know it. No, I tend to ponder that the earth is a set-apart human experience to prepare us for life eternal. Imagine: eternity in a paradise teeming with life that we never imagined existed yet was there fighting and cheering for us all along. I know this seems unbelievable, but we are not alone.

As a restored Royal, I finally was living what my heart knew, but what my head would not accept. Everyone has a legacy and purpose that only they can live out. I was so determined to come to know of God, in a personal way. Not the way I had approached Him before, as a faraway God who was not involved in my day-to-day life. My new mission in life was to get to know the God who saved me so that He could be involved in all parts of my life. I was excited to create opportunity and openness for me to experience Him in real ways. I would soon discover what it meant to be in relationship with Him, what grace and mercy felt like instead of guilt and shame.

God wastes nothing. None of our pain or our history is in vain. It is all meant to be learned from and be transformed into a foundation for good. By facing my past and what I had come from, I found the geodes of my life. A geode is ugly, rough, and hard on the outside, yet when split open, it is bright and colorful and a multifaceted beautiful gem. In this chapter, I hope to show you time and time again that God is faithful to turn each of our ugly experiences in life into beauty. If you travel with me through repeated human stories of fallenness, you will see how God's love oftentimes comes through *His* people. He is faithful to save; that is what Messiah does and is: He saves.

I hope you have come to see that, even when you're facing the ugly in your past, realizing that your foundation is cracked or altogether wrong and needs to be taken all the way down to rubble, it's going to be all right. Let it all come down; you can see as in my story that you and God can face anything. God's perfect love gives you the ability to do what you thought you could never do.

The main thing I was freed from in my Exodus was the slavery of shame, achievement-based self-worth, and sin-filled regrets. It turns out the foundation of who I was, my very core identity, was based on "all about me." That is the wrong foundation. I guess this girl somehow got stuck in the terrible twos. Although I could love, share, and give and be known as a kind Christian woman at the age of forty, I was fully self-serving. If I didn't see a benefit directly to me or my family, I would not do it. Again, wrong foundation.

I guess that survivor mentality of coming from the third world and trying to assimilate and be American got the best of me. I learned in my own little world that I had to blend in yet find a way to stand out too, work the crowd to be liked, work hard to be promoted, and hustle my way to the top to be recognized as good. All that rubbish had to be ground down to rubble.

I was placed gently by a loving and restoring God on His firm foundation. My new identity was child of the one true *King*, nothing more, nothing less. There was no greater position to hold and nothing else needed to be done. I no longer had to strive to "be enough." God had taken care of everything. He put me on His firm foundation, and together we were on our way to the promised land—but first, there was a tour to take. This slave was out of Egypt, so to speak, but the slave mentality was not out of me.

"Odilie, welcome to your tour in the wilderness." Just like my biblical ancestors, I was brought into the wilderness with God's guidance and light leading. I heard Him speak into my heart: "I will give you the healing Word of truth. I will sing songs over you every day. In My living Word, I will tell you of inspiring people just like you, until you are healed all the way through!"

HIS SACRED HEART FOR YOURS

REFLECTIONS

A Glimpse at His Heart …

A Step into the Sacred Chambers of His Heart—His Holy Word

I remind myself, "You are my strong tower. Your word says, "In the middle of trouble, He shall hide me in His pavilion; in the secret place of His tabernacle, he shall Hide me; He shall set me high upon a rock" (Psalm 27:5 NKJV). I will think on these things; Whatever is true (Philippians 4:8 NIV).

In His holy name, you are safe. You, my dear, are free to choose to do right. The truth has set you free; One choice at a time. The rock of your salvation will keep you.

Jesus said: "I will show you what it's like when someone comes to me, listens to my teaching, and then follows it. It is like a person building a house who digs deep and lays the foundation on solid rock. When the floodwaters rise and break against that house, it stands firm because it is well built" (Luke 6:47–48 NLT).

Take a praise break!

"King of My Heart" by Kutless, published Jan. 30, 2017.
"Fighting for Me" by Riley Clemmons, published April 12, 2019.

A Guided Prayer for You

Father God, thank You. You are my redeemer, and with that, You protect me all of my days, even when I didn't know You and recognize You as my strong tower. Thank You that with this teaching and leading I will allow You into all of me, even the parts I'm ashamed of or fearful that they aren't good enough for You to be in. Lord, one drop of Your precious blood and mercy cleanses all of my dirty. You, Lord, carried all my sickness, sin, and shame so that I can walk upright in your Holy protection and guidance. Because, Lord, You are my refuge, evil can't touch this. The good work being done in me will cover any and all of my poor choices and even the vilest of sins. Help me, Lord, accept this amazing grace. You died so I could live free of anxiety, sickness, and depression. I will say of the Lord, that you are the guardian of my soul, spirit, mind, and body. You will see me through with grace, whether I see full deliverance or this is my cross to bear. I trust in You to see me through.

Write what you hear God wants you to know about you being hidden in Him, so that you can heal, become bold and strong in Him. What areas of your heart are you hiding from God?

Can you begin today to allow him in and make Him your secret bunker of protection? Where do you want to be bolder and stronger?

LOVE BROKE THROUGH

Your white space …

3

A TENDER HEART
FEELS OTHERS' PAIN

*God will move heaven and earth
to get you to know Him.*
*I believe I got a deep compassion for injustice
built into me at a very young age.*

My first memory was handing my mom my baby brother's blanket to clean up her bloody lip. Loud fighting words were exchanged, and then I watched my dad strike my mom. My mom escaped the drunk's pain and fury and came to give us comfort and safety. The three of us cleaned up her blood, and I remember hiding and cozying up in a closet. The closet was mirrored. Tears and blood were wiped up by my roughly three-year-old's hand. The two loves of her life, mother and father, were at a combination of war and love for years. It wasn't right to have heard the fights, seen the fights, cleaned up the fights, run from the fights, and gotten over the fights as if nothing had happened. Horrific situations happened and then were brushed over like nothing had happened. *Ya pasó* is a phrase in Spanish that meant, in my family, "it has passed, let it go." I heard it too much as a young girl. Since my grandmothers on both sides had suffered drunken men beatings, it just was a sad way of the world, one that we needed to get past with little or no talk of it.

Privately, under my covers I was always praying it wouldn't happen again. I can remember very little of my childhood. I think I blocked it all out to protect myself. But what I can remember is terrible fear; somehow, the covers of my bed felt safe. I could barely breathe because I'd cover my whole self and grab the cross on my rosary, and I knew I would be safe to make it through. That young, I know my soul was praying for God's *love* to break through my family's problems and hurts.

Seeing pain, strife, heartache, anger, and wounds like this at such a young age built me. It gave me a tender heart of compassion for gruesome situations and the ability to respond to emergencies and keep my thinking straight. Some good attributes, some bad, but I was built strong, resilient, a survivor—just like my parents and grandparents.

Still, my familial and formative foundation was cracked for several generations before mine. The bedrock of the foundation for my trust was faulty. It couldn't withstand the tremors and quakes of life without serious leveling in all areas of life and relationships. While I was still in the womb, the country my mom and dad came from suffered a devastation of epic proportions: the Christmas earthquake of 1972 in Managua, Nicaragua. Perhaps the shock of this earthquake was stuck in my parents and all who suffered for many years. For a few generations I saw people in my family just replaying and living out spiritually what had happened physically.

In other words, much happened before the earthquake, and much destruction happened after the tragedy too. For years there were aftershocks and ripple effects that affected much of the family's function, beliefs, and relationships.

Get ready for drama munching … These were the days of our lives. Maybe my family just watched too many Spanish soap operas and started living them out for fun. Oh, please pass the popcorn, this is about to get intense.

These story lines were not a soap opera. They directly and indirectly happened to me. My sensitivity for tragedy should have never been piqued at such a young age. Nonetheless, there is good and God throughout each of these headlines, so read on. My family and I survived.

Murder happened.

Adultery happened.

Domestic violence happened.

Abuse of each kind happened.

Devastation and death of infants, toddlers and adults in a natural disaster happened.

Language, cultural and discrimination barriers happened.

Poverty happened.

Neglect and abandonment happened.

Divorce happened.

Sudden and tragic death happened, multiple times.

Repeated miscarriages happened.

Abrupt unplanned moves happened.

Unforgiveness happened.

Blended family happened.

Homosexuality happened.

Being left pregnant happened.

Street violence injuries happened.

Arrests and judgment happened.

Severe financial ruin happened.

Sudden unexplained death happened.

Being shunned by the church happened.

Civil wars on my streets happened.

Debauchery and moral compromise happened.

Repeated and destructive cycle of sin happened.

Through it all, love broke through each and every time.

Much forever changed, but through it all faith remained. With Christ at the *center*, we now more than survive; we *thrive!* Let these living testimonies be the proof of love that God *is*.

God was, is, and always will be present and *Emmanuel is God with us in and through all*.

Where was He? Why would He permit such pain and tragedy? "How do you see the Lord God and love in any of this?" you say. It is my hope that I may teach you to see that pain has a significant and eternal purpose, and love is always ready to seek and save the broken, hurting, and lost. Through each story I share, real people I directly loved were directly affected by each of these pains, some of them many times over. I'm grateful that I have been born to a family of believers, so we have that major gift.

So why does it seem we have walked under some sort of curse? As the saying goes, "Why do bad things happen to good people?" How can all this tragedy happen in one family? Well, as you know, hindsight is 20/20. So read on, and you will see how these stories played out. Most of all I pray for our good God, the Almighty, to show you how to see how His love can and will break through any and everything in life.

To reveal and talk about such tragedy and familial wounds is to not show you the scar, but to *reveal the healer of it all*. Jesus showed up on each of those accounts with a redemption call and a restoration path. You don't see *love* or *redemption* in your story or this story yet? Hang on: it's coming; no doubt about it!

God made me a good student. I love to study, learn, practice, and ultimately master. I have been a student of life long enough to realize that you get good at what you practice most. Throughout various tests of life, I found you won't flunk out if you keep at the test. Yes, you may need to repeat the lesson or the test over and over, but each experience builds good things in us more than bad.

I've also learned to trust my training/instruction and not panic just before or during the test. I have learned that the Master usually remains silent but present during the whole test. I've learned that I was placed in my school and with my classmates so that we can learn from each other, support one another, and make one another better students and ultimately help each other graduate.

In this life school, real-life classes mean real people live lives out in this school of hard knocks. Real people have fallen into deep pain and had to get back up while deeply wounded. Each life-altering tragedy changed everyone in the family, and the ripple effects change forever. So as I grew up and moved through my various apprenticeships of life, I studied both human successes and the tragedies. I noticed there was a pattern of choices giving way to either redemption or demise. I've taken notes. I know that every family has stories like these, maybe not as bad, maybe worse.

THE FLESH VERSUS THE SPIRIT— PRIMAL OR CARNAL LEADING VERSUS SPIRIT-LED FOCUS AND LEADING

Something that comforts and empowers me is the realization that I'm not the first one in the whole timeline of human experience to live through this. Second, if you start to read the history books and think upon the Bible's examples of human triumphs and trials, you'll see that the human race has had the same set of challenges and temptations since the beginning of time. Families today will get through. If God shared those Bible stories to teach us about what kinds of relationships and accomplishments we could realize by knowing and trusting in Him, then I'd best read up and see how it can apply and relate to me.

Time and time again you'll see a common theme, that God makes a way when there is no way. He is faithful to help us through. I came to know for myself that what God did for one he would do for all. We all come from the same human bloodline.

We don't have to be star students to notice that we tend to make the same mistakes. Left to our own devices, we are led by primal instincts. We are in fact descendants of Adam and Eve. So we inherit a fallen or carnal nature which focuses on serving self first; it is the base of our fleshly nature. The mind and the eyes see, the body feels, and it goes after things instinctively. Read every story, and you will see that it truly is the same set of temptations. The enemy of our soul, Satan, doesn't come up with any new material. He used the same set of temptations on the first humans and even on the Son of God, fully God and fully human. Yet all sin is born of these same human temptations: the need to be seen and recognized—also called egoism or the pride of life; the lust of the eyes and flesh, or hedonism, the want of hunger and satisfaction; and materialism or the desire for power and wealth.

Yet as Jesus showed us how to handle all temptation, remember, the Word of God reveals that He was tempted on all accounts yet never sinned.[1] So we don't need to remain fallen and tempted. Jesus defeated death and sin for good. Not only do we have Jesus as the Messiah who paid for all sin on the cross, but He also taught us how to escape the devil's tactics of temptations against our fleshly nature. He showed us that a mature Christian can be led by the spirit and deny the flesh. We are released of the instinctual needs of the flesh and can balance what we do with spiritual maturity. As when Jesus was tempted in the desert, we are shown to talk back to the devil by reminding the devil of what God really said. We are taught to fight temptation with the written Word of God.

So again, as we accept the call of salvation in Christ Jesus, we immediately become a forgiven, delivered, or redeemed (fully paid-for, ransomed for Him) people. Through the salvation brought about by the cross, and by the automatic indwelling of the Holy Spirit,[2] we—whether Jew or non-Jew—are grafted into one set of His people.[3] All His people share the promised inheritance that includes the special rights, privileges, and promises that come with being a child of God. So just like the Bible's long-ago saved and favored people, we are set apart and will all be saved. God's still in the business of seeking and saving lost people.

He has a plan of greatness set aside just for us, once we are rescued and redeemed. For the Word says that it is the Lord's saving grace that works through us, His people, to accomplish His will and good purpose.[4] You and I are saved unto *good works!* Our salvation was planned long ago in God's plan for us to do amazing things in His name before the foundations of the earth. So if any part of me wants to do great and be great, I had better get with the greatest story ever told, the Bible; and get in talks with the greatest Author and Perfecter of all faith, our Lord and King.

Bottom-line truths that can totally be backed by the Word of God: If I feed my spirit, my spirit grows in godliness and infuses me with energy, wisdom, and adventure. If I feed my flesh, I grow out and down in energy only to end up damaging my long-term health. So now when I should find myself in my greatest sufferings, I do hold on and trust that God is working on something super-good! History and the present show that everything that our God does leads to a complete and even greater redemption.

Notice Jesus; He rose up out of a lengthy list of trials—rejection, humiliation, beating beyond recognition, a crucifixion, and a grave sealed up with an immovable stone—only to be resurrected! He was so transformed that He could walk through walls yet fully eat in the same body. I would say that resurrection was better than ever. I am made in His likeness, so in following Jesus, I will rise too! Can you imagine when we get to see personally what Jesus's transfigured body does? Did you know we will get a transformed eternal body so that we will be like His glorious body? Amazing![5]

Until that happens, how do we live in the current difficulties and even sometime seasons of intense pain? Don't lose heart, you can live through the worst times of your life with an internal peace. A spirit-led heart and mind and body become stayed or fixed in peace. They are unshakable and sure always. If you, like me, have lived through much trauma you know, or I can tell you, that there is still much good and love that occurs in the middle of all that. God protects in the midst of all these tragedies.

That is what the apostle Paul calls the peace that surpasses all understanding. In the tough times we still can love and move through good while living in a bad situation. How? The steady presence of a living God gives you His peace. It is His love built into us that gives hope, endurance, and a supernatural strength and leading. So if you currently find yourself in a season that's tougher than you, rely on God's supernatural ability to see you through. He always is protecting, loving, and guiding us whether or not we even believe in him. He just does. Observe this spiritual wonder. For every time I have heard a person describe going through a very taxing time and then getting to the other side of it, and then say the infamous words, "I just don't even know how I got through that," I say to myself, *God is how you made it through*. It's God who sustains us and allows us to have our very being. It is only because of God's keeping and supernatural aid that they or I have ever made it through. If you or someone you know finds themself in a bad spot, do not give up; the good is just around the corner. God always comes. Be brave enough to hold on till your better and brighter and lighter comes. Believe me, it is worth the wait. Hold on for one more day.

Don't say, "God doesn't care about my situation," or "I haven't seen good or *God* in so long that I wouldn't recognize it or *Him*." No, that is not your story. You, have *God* in your story. So if you see no good in the situation yet, just hang on. He never fails. Good will come out of any and all of it, if you give all of it over completely to God. Only He can make something beautiful out of a mess. If it's not good, it's not over.

But here is the difficult part of faith, the wait and the process. I wish that God's redemption for me was like the "bippity-boppity-boo boutique"—poof! All transformed into the complete royal beauty. But God is not our fairy God father; he wants us to have some sweat equity and skin in the game. So let's get in that game in play. A new star player (*you*) just got subbed in. The game just got better, and this is going to be a good one!

This game has quarters and different players and coaches who all have their part to play critical plays. But in the end the truth is that it's more than just a game. It's your everything; your purpose and happiness depend on it. So let us get to making great teammates with two of our best life's teachers: meet Mrs. Pain and Mr. Processes. Your diploma will be a major in healing, wholeness, identity, purpose, and a minor in becoming. But this school of healing can only be passed with the Holy Trinity as your headmaster and your teachers, Pain and Process.

So here I share some of my process to shorten your mistakes and soften your learning curve.

In much of God's healing I have realized that *super* good comes of tremendous loss.

It was these harsh and vivid experiences have built into me a tremendous sense of compassion. Yes, shock and awe and resiliency were built into me too. If you have suffered a devastating blow, I'm sorry because I know all the suffering and questions and anger and denial and sadness and disbelief that it comes with, but here is the light at the end of that dark tunnel. In the suffering, you can rest on a promise given to you and even played out in an example by a mighty God. That promise is that the present sufferings pale in comparison to the glory that will be revealed *in us*. Did you catch that? Glory set aside by a mighty God to be revealed in us!

A SPIRITUAL MINDSET DEVELOPS

So out of that extensive list of tragedies my family or I myself have suffered, I can hold out. I don't have to understand why it happened. I have learned it will all be better than okay. I have learned to trust the process of healing and redemption.

> I'm talking about that very thing that devastates you; it can warp-speed elevate you.

Why? I have lived it enough to know. I have learned that I can respond in emergency situations with trust and strength. When I say hang on to your faith because it is all you have, it is because for all my life I have seen the fruit of it turn surviving into thriving. In clinging on to God with all your might, you get carried safely out of the tumultuous environment and into an internal peace. The peace stays on the hope of a better day in which you will rise up greater than ever before.

Out of each of those vile and sin-filled or leveling sad tragedies previously listed, out came a victor of faith. A pillar of strength and a beaming beacon of light too emerged. The life track that my family was on may have been pain-filled, but the one thing my family had going for them was God.

I encourage you that if you are in a terrible circumstance, go get a Bible and hang on to God as if your life depends on it, because it does. I'm not talking about life-or-death physical life. For I have seen many people live as if they were a walking set of dry bones, lifeless or numb, closed off or completely removed emotionally. What you thought would almost take you out ends up giving you a tremendous amount of drive and purpose in life. I'm talking about that very thing that devastates you; it can warp-speed elevate you. I'm not exaggerating; I've seen it firsthand time and time again. Yes, I've seen it myself, and I'm also living this property out.

I didn't know this until I started being engrossed, immersed, and hungry to know more about the God who died for me. In that process, I stumbled upon the well-documented promise of God that He is a restorer and renewer of life abundant. He also brings justice to all. So if tragedy is handled properly by bringing it *all* to *God*, our Lord, He will help us rise up out of the ugly and difficult into people who are better and stronger and have a deeper level of appreciation for all of life.

For God said, if God is for us, who could be against us? Jesus came to save us. He knew my and my family's complex issues and sins and still was pulling for us to snap out of sin and step into our good purpose and power instead of repeated struggle. He saved us repeatedly from our self-destructive behaviors until we were well enough to get in step following Him. I often wondered why God keeps on saving me out of my stupid choices. It was so we could get free and live on purpose for God—all so I could get on the "right track" on my purpose. He made each of us on purpose and for a specific purpose. He will do anything to get me and you to live the blessed life we were always meant to live out, not that tired, old, tragic soap opera that has our life stuck on repeat.

I do not share all this to air out dirty laundry or embarrass my family, but I hope to present to you a story of faith, hope, love, and what coming out a winner for Christ can look like. I feel compelled to share this, because the love of God became so full in me that now I love more like Jesus does us. I have learned to love all people not just the ones who look and act like me. I now don't run from the difficult and messy or broken people anymore. I now want to share life and help them get free of what bogs them down. In my quest for living out God's purpose for me, I've seen the type to get better and the type to get bitter. Some people seem to stay stuck, maybe they don't want to make the small sacrifice it takes to make big transformations. They never allow themselves to do the difficult and be fully honest with God and themselves. In honest processes, no secrets remain. I brought *all* of the pain, loss, shock, and disappointment. I wanted to move up and on. It had to be done. It's important to face and process and work out each stage of healing and process with mostly God—and a godly counselor helps too! The alternative is you stay stuck in an event and never grow through it. In this stuck state, what was meant to be a stage of building becomes an almost state-of-being.

> *I was Stuck in a phase, what was meant to be a stage of buiding became a state of being. We aren't meant to be stuck in a state. Just like God, we are to be on the move. Like the word of God in it we are dynamic, active, living. Living in the word, we can be purposeful in every phase of life.*

As I took responsibility and reflected upon all that I had been through, in God's care and promise, I reminded myself that I could face any of this as a healthy, whole Christian adult. What hurt me before could not hurt me anymore. I was under God's spirit leading. I finally let myself face the difficult feelings I would not let myself feel or sit in before. I was afraid if I let myself express anger, I would not be able to be the happy fun-loving person I enjoyed being. I was afraid that, if I cried all that I needed to cry out, I would not be able to come back to calm, rational, and reassured. I was always taught to put the uncomfortable and inconvenient aside and repress what was coming up, like Elsa in *Frozen*. Conceal, don't feel; I knew that play well in the game.

Then God revealed to me that He would safely take me where I needed to go emotionally—go so that I could "let it go!" He promised that with His leading I would make peace with all the pains, and He would help me use them for good. All of that could only be looked at after I had sobered up. I was stuck on a hamster wheel of denial. In that triggered cyclical state of survival, denial, achievement, perfectionism, running away, and abuse, I would get nowhere over and over. I had to face my coping mechanism honestly and get off that hamster wheel. I had to see, really see where I landed.

Then God said, "Enough is enough." God gently asked me to assess where I ended up when I was driving my life. He then helped me go into the attic and the basement of traumas. In his merciful guidance, he safely cleaned them out with the breath and love of

Jesus. In His saving, amazing grace, I got off the dysfunctional train to nowhere, sobered up, and slowly but surely died to addictive and abusive patterns. With God, I saved my marriage and my kids' childhood. I healed; I was freed and was able to forgive; and I continue to do so daily. Reality is and shows me that my Bible lives. It tells me a word relevant to my life now—that I am to work out my salvation in fear and trembling.

I know you notice that the state of the world today absolutely makes us fear and tremble for our future. But in the hope of Jesus, we revere that it is God who daily saves us for His special purpose. God says that He has plans for hope and a good future.[6] Knowing and living that biblical truth makes me say to myself, *Savior, keep saving me!* So 365 days and 24/7, I put God in the middle of all I live in. Then He leads me into the work I am called to do.

We are each called to be co-creators. Again, He chooses us on purpose and for a purpose, that excites me daily. No one can live my life for me. So, on the daily, I practice a daily treasure hunt. In my hunt, I dig out of me and life all the amazing things God saved and chose me for. What I want you to get out this chapter is that *the same goes for you!* No matter your age or circumstances, you are chosen too!

A NEW LOVE COMES TO LIFE

God gave me the will and ability to show you, through my personal experience, that within the guardrails and in biblical guideposts and lights shining on God's precepts, we can find our own path in life. It's reported to be a narrow road that only a few find. But with God it becomes possible to find, follow, and fulfill our own amazing God-sized life. What that looks like in and through you is as unique as you. Love is so much, so full, and I go into a rich description of it later in this book. But for me, and in the healed and free Christians I see moving powerfully in God's love, a holy love is an unwounded and unfiltered openness.

Think of a beautiful puppy, kitty, or baby. It's available to engage with and does so with joy. Love is a choice, not just a feeling. I frequently challenge myself, as I want to heal and deconstruct "filters and wounds" I've previously put up to survive. With God's wholesome and holy love those filters and wounds are being deleted and replaced with a trusting and believing for the best of love, people and perceptions. Frequently as I feel guarded or mistrusting, I remind myself that when I operate in God's holy love, I come most alive.

So since I am on a mission to _LIVE_ in all capitals, I dare to love. This may seem naive and too trusting to many, but I trust in my Protector to guide me and give me spiritual discernment over all of my life's affairs. So as I dare to love, I act and think on my choices to love and to do what is most loving. Truly I allow myself to dig into that phrase. I think, _How would God love?_ Generously, lavishly, encouraging and building, authentic, respectful not pushy, and relentlessly unoffendable. That is my goal; that is how I want to love. I want to love like that. God's love invites and draws in embraces all. If I accept this type of love freely from God, it fills up so much as to overflow this love out onto others. It is God who breaks down my barriers of fear, rejection, and judgment.

So if I find myself not behaving lovingly—and believe me, with four kids and a super-packed schedule it happens more than I'd like to admit—I pause for the cause. I retreat to God's sacred heart so He can fill me back up with Him, only to go back out having asked myself what is the most loving thing I can do, and then I do it. And the key to do this over and over again is to be like Christ and expect no reaction, no return; remember, un-offendable. Then on the cool chance the person reciprocates this love, it is a beautiful thing!—a glimpse of what our God might feel when we love on Him and accept all of His love. Yes, I want to love like that!

So, as I help you deconstruct your barriers to love, let me humbly attempt to describe a godly type of love. I'll ask you to review my two favorite descriptors for love in the Bible. Love is described in the Bible—685 times in the NIV Bible—so I urge us to dig though the treasure trove of scripture regarding what love means for us. I'll begin with the most convicting love verse I know and love. If you haven't heard, *convicting* in my own words means prompting to change and drawing us more into godliness. It's a lovely call from the Holy Spirit that comes with His power to do something we were not able to do before. When the Holy Spirit shows you or me something that needs our attention, He always comes with the power to do so. So you were called to read this book on love, so with it will come the power from the Holy Spirit to love better!

So on we move, with the 1 Corinthians 13:4–8 (NIV). Its overall theme is that love assumes the best or believes most positively.

> Love is patient, love is kind, it does not envy, it does
> not boast, it is not proud. It does not dishonor others,
> it is not self-seeking, it is not easily angered, it keeps
> no record of wrong. Love does not delight in evil but
> rejoices with the truth. It always protects, always trusts,
> always hopes, always perseveres. Love never fails.

Wow, isn't that bar high! That was read at our wedding. I hoped for that type of love to live in my home with my amazing and ravishing husband. I never saw that type of love. My hope for me and my husband is that we would be blessed by God to break the three marriage curse we each had in our family line, several generations back. Back then, divorce wasn't as acceptable as it is today. So you could say that Brad and I were praying for divine favor with our marital union. I can thank God today as I celebrate twenty one years of an awesome and blessed marriage, that God gave us this type of love. I'm so thankful. It's not like our love or marriage is perfect, but we do put *God* in the center of our marriage. As we honor our vows or covenant, we can be more be loving and thoughtful of one another.

A new way the verse has come to life is in my relationships, especially with my kids. *"Love is patient and kind."* I was born into a family of screamers and hitters; we are Spanish, and that is how most of us were raised. It takes a whole lot of Jesus to not express what you lived. So again, no shame to what happened to me in my parents and their parents. I just say this again, that with the love of Christ, what has happened for many generations can be broken and then blessed. I am a work in progress and an example of the power of Christ's love. You can love differently than you were shown, at any age! No excuses.

There is much more to say about Christ's love, and with each chapter forward I'll circle back around to love and how it works with some of the biblical tools I'll share with you so that you can love and love better!

Love is so richly layered. I continue to comb over scriptures in an exhaustive study of love, very frequently. The continuing study grows and matures my capacity for love—to both receive it more freely from God, based on grace, not works, and give it more freely in that way too.

But for me, I hope that my ignition had created a combustion in your heart, or at least a spark to begin your own exploration of love. Let me open up your eyes and hearts to godly love, also called *agape love*, with those wonderful verses I reflect upon so often. I am raising four teens, you know; I need to remind myself what true love is *all* the time! Love is first of all pure, non-self-seeking, peaceable.

> A new command I give you, Love one another. As I have loved you, so you *must* love one another. (John 13:34 NIV, emphasis added)

> By this *everyone* will know that you are my disciples, if you love one another. (John 13:35 NIV, emphasis added)

> Be devoted in love. Honor one another above yourself (Romans 12:10 NIV)

If that doesn't start a spark, get the paddles of life. I'm not giving up on you!

HIS SACRED HEART FOR YOURS

REFLECTIONS

A Glimpse at His Heart …

A Step into the Sacred Chambers of His Heart—His Holy Word

I will think on these things; Whatever is noble … (Phil 4:8 NIV)

The noble do what is necessary for the greater good.

Blessed are the broken hearted …
Your victory becomes my victory.
"But thanks be to God! He gives us the victory through our Lord Jesus Christ." (1 Corinthians 15:57 NIV)

I waste no pain. I collect each and every tear of yours. Because of your pain—greater is your reward. In this life and eternally. Dive all in, into My deep love, and you will know Me deeper still. You will be compassionate for the things that break *My heart.* Love you so much!

—God

A praise break to inspire you: "See a Victory" by Elevation Worship; "Mosaic" by Ryan Stevenson, 2021.

A Guided Prayer for You

Father God, I've realized that You have planted in my heart and mind a purpose and desires that I could only realize with You. They are so great that I'm willing to give up what I comfortably know and step into Your will and plans for my life that are for both my good and Your glory. I know that the path is not clear for me to see right now. I have too much demolition rubble in my space. But, Lord, piece by piece, You will move what needs to be moved. In You, Lord, You redeem me, You restore me and re*new* me altogether. Father, all of You for all of me, from this day forward. Let's do this!

Your white space …

4

THE CLIMB-UP OUT OF LIFE'S RUBBLE

Only in Christianity do wisdom and love and light find you. All other religious practice is earned by the follower in seeking higher versions of self. In Christianity He takes us, broken and sin-filled, and loves us into sanctification.

Oh Lord my God I cried out to you, and you healed me. (Psalm 30:2 NIV)

My sweet mama's foundation is leveled, a sudden move happens, and her first baby is on the way! So much was happening, while in the womb, I'm telling you I remember! Hang on for earthshaking and world-toppling backstory ….

Awakened by the first strike of an earth tremor, in a baby-doll silk pajama, she scrambled around the violently shaking room. The house was trembling so badly that she couldn't walk to get dressed. She went outside as she was; with immediacy and necessity, she was in survival mode. Both my mom and dad left their newlywed home arm in arm. It would truly be years before that survival jolt shook off them.

Together, they scrambled the small-town streets to find safety until the violent earthquake had taken down their entire city and world as they knew it. In this time, Christmas of 1972, in the small yet affluent part of Managua, Nicaragua, entire hospitals, political palaces, schools, and thousands of homes were leveled. If the people of this lovely town were not killed by the sudden impact of walls and ceilings coming down over them, then they were killed slowly by injury and asphyxiation from being buried alive. To add to the devastation many were killed by fires, as two-thirds of the town went up in flames after the earthquake and the toll of deaths reached approximately three thousand people.

To watch your city and roads split in half and see your neighborhoods moving through rubble to find loved ones and belongings, I can't fathom. My mom and dad had to stay focused on their family's situation; they couldn't pull over to help the neighbors in their struggles. With pure focus they arrived at my dad's sister's house. The siblings of both my mother and father, all in their early twenties at this time, were all very close and involved on a daily basis with navigating newlywed life, budding careers, and baby-ville. My *tía* or aunt in Spanish was married and was a best friend to my mom and super close to my dad. She had two babies already at this time, one five-year-old heart-stealing boy with caramel-ribbon curls, and one Goldilocks infant girl.

As my mom and dad physically ran to each relative's residence to check on their safety, they ran their own little search and rescue operation. First, imagine having the courage to do that. I pray that you or I would have that selfless courage to show up in a mess of devastation and be of help and resource. A brave recognition to all my family that lived through this experience. Not one of my living family members can speak of this event without great pain, bravery, and courage. On their shoulders and by their example, my generation and the next has resiliency and survivorship built into us. Previous generations in my family, faults and all: your unity, love, faith, and bravery saw you through. This is a testimony that, though it be life-changing you can rise out of any deep tragedy.

So back to my parents' seek-and-save mission: my tía's house was first on the list as the closest. At this home you couldn't imagine the pain and shock. The five-year-old baby boy was crushed and dead. The infant baby girl, survived; when the wall fell on top of her crib, she was kept in a cave of safety until her loving mother could come pick her up with the reassurance that she would not perish. My dad helped my uncle, father, move pieces of rubble until they could get to the limp body of this short, innocent life. Imagine, my mom and aunt had known and loved and taught and played with this little life for five years already. Yet he was robbed of life and a future in an instant; now they could only say an abrupt goodbye to that love and hope.

They physically carried the two children to the next relative's house. There they bathed the sweet and still warm body of this toddler who had died.

In the next twenty-four hours, now Christmas Eve, the town was fighting fires still; medical tents and rubble were everywhere. Surviving people were walking around trying to piece back together what was left of their world. During those twenty-four hours, my mom and dad learned that another young five-year-old cousin had died, the Devastating.

My mom went to check on her mother, her world and love; her father was her world too, but he was in a neighboring city about an hour away, so she didn't see him in all of this tragedy and confusion. From what my mom tells me, he was still not really speaking to her, because only five months earlier she had eloped, and he was bitter about that. Anyhow, she recalls checking on her mom and her three youngest siblings. My grandmother was in such shock that she just tried to keep the children calm and didn't have an immediate need for my mom and dad. So on they went.

They checked on more family members. My dad's brother gave the shirt off his back to my mom, as she was still in a nightgown.

The young adults of the family kept moving amid the devastation, the smell of death and ash everywhere. Mom said they were like walking zombies, numb from all the pain and shock they needed to process. In that twenty-four-hour period they buried the dead and stayed close together in support.

Lo and behold, an American B52 relief plane landed to retrieve natural-born American citizens. My mom and dad and aunt and uncle and their infant baby left all they knew behind and were flown to the States for safety and relief assistance. They had dual citizenship, as my grandfather had some sort of business in California, and they were born in the States.

My mother could not even say goodbye to her parents, siblings, or even lifetime friends. That filled military plane processed everyone in Pensacola, Florida and then took people to relatives who could help them get back on their feet. Somehow, after that stop they were sent to Louisiana, where we tried to get on our feet as a traumatized young family.

I was in my mother's womb the whole time. The fact that she didn't lose me as a miscarriage is an act of God. They had more of God's favor working for them, because somehow, with less than twenty-five dollars in cash and a baby on the way, my mom and dad started a new life as Americans.

They say gestational experience and trauma makes a person resilient and strong yet very sensitive in compassion. That whole first few years of my life, I promise you, my heart and soul remember. I couldn't give you one detail of physicality, but my soul and heart know it well and remember it perfectly. As my barely speaking English mom sorted out and processed what had happened to her, she said that I was a great listener as a baby. She built into me a fierce alliance to her wellness and a tender compassion to survivorship. She describes that I supported her with a will to live and a strength to build a life in a new country.

That is where I believe I get my tenacious spirit. I hung on to that womb for life, clamped like a pit bull.

This was also the first account that *love broke through* for me and created beauty out of ashes, literally.

> *When your world is reduced to rubble, there is no other option than to begin again.*
> *In that level of devastation only the strong in you lives to make it through.*

A baby girl was born to two broken and traumatized and unsupported young adults.

So what does this passionate, dramatic story stir up in you or me? As we can see from this story and other earthly tragic occurrences, a very instinctual fight or flight will gets activated, and we humans use this energy coming from the deep reservoirs of godly strength that will carry us through so that we live.

For you and me, with what we are going through today, what can a story of survivorship raise up in us? It is very applicable to the world of today. Much of what we see and live through tries to shake us up like an earthquake on our own reckless scale instead of a Richter scale. I can tell you that if you hold this book in your hand, you have a good plan and purpose you must live for. This shaking of all you know is to shake out what is unnecessary for your purpose and to build into you very intrinsic and necessary qualities that can only take shape by what you have been through. You will have, and claim, and walk out of the rubble and into your own resiliency with your own redemption story. In God-led restoration you will walk in a daily amount of grace and hope.

So when you and I have all been shaken, it is crucially important that your head and thoughts stay in the same day your "behind" is in. Otherwise, I believe you have stepped out of that day's dose of "daily grace or daily bread." Just as in the Bible when God's people collected more than their daily bread, it spoiled and stank. So it happens when your thought life and problem-solving steps out of today and into the "what-if world." When that happens, you've out stepped out of your daily grace and mercy, which is promised by God to be provided for fresh daily.[1]

So here we are, our lives in a metaphorical rubble. How do we rebuild this new era piece by piece? You will get through this releveling of life. In the work ahead, God is sure to keep you in balance. God is a master builder; he never puts on more weight than our spiritual maturity can support. Yet I can remember plenty of times I have packed on and taken on a weight load of demand that was beyond my foundational capacity. True power and strength come in submission or yielding control by humility to a wise God leading you into what to take on and say yes to.

Speaking of buckling under the weight of something you weren't ready for, that's also how we learn to balance boldness and humility. That is why it feels <u>soooooo looooong</u> when we are in prayer for the answer to come. He is refining our hearts' desires to align with His more. He is developing our balance of rest and trust with faith and action. He is strengthening our spiritual core and strength so that when major blessings or major storms come, we won't buckle and be washed out of our home, only to be tossed to and fro by the waves of life, as the Word of God says.

Early in my marriage and the babyhood stage of motherhood, I was supremely blessed—four babies in four years blessed! The demands were beyond my resources and capacity and maturity to ask for help. To make things worse, my foundation was sinking sand and man-made; can we say achievement-driven perfectionist? I caved and crumpled, and it all came tumbling down before God showed I was living life "my way."

If you don't already know this, let my life reveal to you that a life built on your self-worth coming from and being equal to only your accomplishments has no solid foundation. The minute a weight load heavy enough to challenge your foundation comes along, say an injury, illness, or loss of job, your entire built-up life will crumble, and so will your self-worth. If you aren't (insert your title identity), then what is your worth? Who are you? Whose are you?

Believe me, these questions are on your life's test. You must know them back and forth, inside and out … or the "world" will tell you exactly who and whose you are. Think about all the labels the world has tried to put on you. Think about how hard it is to take that label off your mind. I'll tell you how hard—like erasing a tattoo hard (no, I don't have one, but a friend underwent a tattoo removal process—it's not pretty or fun). Hard like removing wallpaper, like removing discount store stickers off a gift hard. Do you know how much Goo Gone and hand sanitizer I have gone through to get that sticky adhesive off? The same goes for our psyche, our sense of identity. The label always goes on easily, but it takes way more effort to remove it. I'll touch more on this in the identity thief chapter, so stay tuned. For now, be discerning before you decide to put on a label and make it part of you.

Back to me crumpling, there it went for me. My life—the blessings and demands—became too much for me to bear and made my faulty foundation give way. So I was brought to the most basic level, the ground. If you have never suffered a leveling, thank God for that. Maybe your character didn't need as much refining as mine, but I'm sure that as you are building a noteworthy and meaningful life, you can relate to your life work all coming down at once! Either way, let us learn from this tender and real story.

If your kingdom comes toppling down, how will you respond? When unfamiliar circumstances or the unexpected come (hello, 2020?), especially in sudden change, how will you respond? What do you do to survive the chaos? Will you mind-numb? Escape in work? Cling to your comforts? Will you use your protective mechanisms, like isolation or some sort of addiction?

I think I spent a minute in each of those, until I had a meet-with-Jesus moment, and He honestly said to me, "This year's word for you for Me was *trust*. Are you going to trust Me, no matter what? Will you trust Me, or will you put your trust in you—your need to understand or create your own protection methods?" See, all those and many more methods of coping in crisis are self-focused. Survival methods and protective mechanisms do work; I can attest that they work. But they do lead to dysfunction in some sort of spirit and whole-soul wellness.

In studying sociology and psychology in college as well as reflective study in my own journey to health and wellness, that self-focused method of survival does lead to misery through dysfunctional communication and relationships for you and all those around you. I have lived and experienced this firsthand. When you are caught up in survival mode, it is common to feel as though you are the only one having this set of circumstances. "Nobody cares about me; I must look out for number one, me. I am just trying to survive." But, for every choice you make, there is always a suffering parent and or suffering family members who have to live in the wake of one's choice.

This made me sensitive to knowing that there is gravity to each of my choices and that when I put only my needs into the consideration of a choice, I'm behaving selfishly. Having come from a family that has lived through one world war, several civil wars, two dictatorships, natural disasters, marital strife, poverty, and losing everything two or three times, discrimination, and a comeback or two, let's just say, I've taken notes for as long as I could first watch and learn and second reflect and write.

So after my selfish nature was brought to my attention, I could then see how badly I had sinned against God. My self-centered decision making had hurt my family, friends, and community blatantly. Since then, I try to make decisions differently Now, I ask myself three questions before I make any choice. When you find yourself in circumstances that are beyond your control or that you didn't see coming, it is best to respond in one way.

1. Drop everything (meaning all your swirling thoughts), and go to your knees in prayer.

2. I remind myself I can trust God. When you exercise a developed or even undeveloped reliant trust in God, your trust in God grows. I have seen myself that God will move heaven and earth to get you to safety. So trust that. If you have developed over time well spent a mature faith, you can confidently rely on and trust that God will see you through and lead you to where He wants you. In the uncertain times like illness, sudden deaths, and sudden lack of capacity, one mature in faith clings to the promise of *God*. You keep hanging on to those promises until your days get brighter and better.

3. I keep on affirming that God is for me and you; He loves you and will never leave you! This is Christ-focused salvation and survival method. In this crisis survival method, you will more than survive—you will thrive!

My family and I have lived through each of these choices. I can tell you from personal and observational experience that clinging to God through faith as your time-and-time-again Savior will spare you of much suffering. Our self-centered survival tactics and protective mechanisms only lead to quirks and fake masks of success in our personality and our behavior.

Those fake lives we build will eventually all be shaken down. I built the image I wanted to be but didn't have the inherent internal worth to sustain it. I built the life I loved to say to the world and myself, "Look how well I turned out." I put on a front until God shook up my life and all that was false came crumbling down.

I didn't think I was building a fake life by running away from all the trauma I lived through and witnessed. I just knew in my God-given spirit that what I lived was not of God. It was generations of hurt, broken, and striving people raising hurting, broken, and striving people. I learned at the Ranch that until they are taught different and healed up, hurt people hurt people. So I didn't want that anymore. I had to heal back to the deepest, darkest wound known. But back in college, my first experience of life on my own, I knew enough that God wanted better for us as a family and me. So I built up huge defenses and covers to appear okay and normal to others. I literally buried all of it and never let it come out. It was too painful and never to be revisited again.

I laugh because if painful memories got swept under a rug, as the saying goes, then when all my rugs were used up, I piled them up in the closet. This pattern led to full mental basements and attics, all the way up to a whole mega-sized storage unit of locked-up pains and disappointments. I can tell you this approach does not work in dealing with disappointments of life. One day, your brain, the storage unit owner, will say to you, "I'm not storing all your stuff anymore." That landlord of your soul will say, "Enough is enough. I'm sick and cluttered," and then put all your ugly and dysfunction out on the lawn for all to see. So I highly recommend dealing with your pains before they become an all-consuming drama-munching episode of Dr. Phil.

See, the traumas we live through, if not processed all the way through with God's healing love, will cause us to develop these filters, wounds, and calluses that complexly distort and desensitize us from the beauty and joy of life. Yes, at first, they help us get through the brunt of the transition into a "new normal" but leave us jaded, bent, bitter, and (worse) cold-stone numb.

Allow me to work another illustration out for you on this. You "muscle up" and face this life changing event like a big kid" "I can get through this, and I will." Pure stiff-upper-lip grit; you get through. But then you are stuck with the emotional and psychological defenses that inhibit your living life freely and tenderly. Your emotional bandwidth is clipped in the lower and higher scales, and at any moment you find yourself short-tempered or irritable with no cause. Why? Because you armored up and never took the armor off.

You keep that armor on because it works. You become an extremely controlling person, and when anything unplanned and unfamiliar makes you nervous, you can retreat to your safe place in order to stay "secure" in your psyche and body. To put it to you personally, as a result of what I was exposed to and lived through as a young child, I had a list of "protective mechanisms" that helped me endure all my life's recurring earthquakes.

> I will tell you a place where we are all equal and leveled to the exact same, at the foot of the cross. The word of God says, we all have sinned and fallen short of God's glory.[2]

I can tell you until you heal your world's repeated trauma and reactionary cycle, you will relive it and re-create it, unintentionally.

The protective mechanisms for me were people-pleasing and approval-seeking, escapism, perfectionism, attention-seeking, numbing, faking a persona, or camouflage. I lived that way less and less successfully, surviving for forty years of my life. Then, at year forty-one, I underwent my own emotional completely leveling earthquake.

Out of that rubble, I decided to trade in my protective mechanism tools for God Almighty's transformational tools. I wanted a different outcome than what I had seen. So that called for "doing a new thing"! With Christ I would survive a new way. This time I wouldn't have to hang on for dear life to what I could control, the way I did in my mama's womb and thereafter.

This time I would thrive in my survival by letting go: not just a little but, completely. It was my "all chips in" moment. I was tired of controlling, and doing, and looking all perfect so that I would feel worthy and loved. I would go down to my own emotional and psychological ground zero and let go of all that I had built up to prove I was worthy and good. I would let God tell me who was left in this rubble. He would break through the ashes and find me. Does anybody else find that incredibly inspiring? To lose all of you, so that you can have all of what God intended for your life? That was me. I had no hope left, only God's in front of me.

So how can one healthfully make it out of a leveling moment? That is as individual as we all are. It's as different as the circumstances and obstacles in each person's life. But I will tell you a place where we are all leveled to the exact same, at the foot of the cross.

There, at the foot of the cross, each of us is a sinner fallen short of the glory of God. There, bare or naked and in Garden-of-Eden honesty, we can admit we are scared. We can admit we have been deceived and are ashamed.

Take a moment to think with me on this Garden of Eden "I'm covering my shame" moment. Think about sweet and fully provided-for Adam and Eve. They didn't cover their eyes, their hands, their heads. They covered what was different about them. I can remember myself covering where I am different. Can you? Think of most of us starting as early as elementary or middle school, covering so no one would notice where or what was different on us. We just wanted to blend in.

In complete honesty, I can admit I was in desperate need of a savior and that I waited too long carrying the burdens myself. Like that same little self-centered child, I wanted not only to cover what was different, but also to prove that *I can do this myself!* I'm not little; *I'm big!*

I then came to the point in my life when it was obvious I couldn't carry my burden (my cross). Like me, did you keep falling to the same thing over and over? That's okay; Jesus Himself remembers this shame and weakness. Remember He that knew no sin, shame, or guilt became it and wore it on the road to Calgary. Why? So that we wouldn't! When Jesus comes alongside you and me and says, "My sweet child, you weren't meant to carry that. Here, let Me take that for you. I died for this. I died for you. Let Me help you. Give Me all that burdens you, and I'll give you all of the power to keep going through Me"—there you will find freedom for the first time. I can't explain this, as it is so different for all. But a release of burden and a lightness of love is always in the story.

Are you wanting that release of the image, the duty, the burden of being you, always the provider and holding your whole world together, like I did?

Stick with this story, and God is faithful to bring an individual message for you. Even if you didn't battle childhood trauma or addiction, just being a human in today's world can be exhausting. I don't know one person who doesn't say, "I'm so tired."

There is rest for the weary, and as the story develops, I'll share with you all that God has shown me. Through my barely surviving to making it by a long shot, there are lessons to help shorten your learning curve. In my self-made accolades, my leveling, my redemption, my restorations, my revivals, and my faith ~~walk~~ race, there are lifesaving principles. If we are willing to look and listen and ask ourselves and others, God is faithful to send us answers and good help!

RECKLESS LOVE CRASHES IN TO MEET ME

Now back to realizing you *do need* saving. Picture this: You are in a building, and it's on fire, a raging, life-taking inferno. You see no way out; all exit points are completely inaccessible. Now imagine a big, strong firefighter who comes to help you. The firefighter lifts you up and gives you clean, breath-saving oxygen and a head and face shield to block the smoke damage. Given you were on the brink of being burned to death … tell me you wouldn't leap into the firefighter's arms in gratitude! That is what Jesus is to each of us, a complete savior and blocker of all the elements that harm us in this world. More importantly, he saves us from the eternal fires of *hell* in eternity.

So let's take a look into your and my Savior, Jesus Christ. You may think you aren't in a burning building, and your life seems pretty cool. You have done well on your own, and you do not need a Savior. May I challenge you with this thought? This life is just practice and preparation for the eternal one. You are going to live forever in paradise with your Maker, or you will burn in hell, yet live in regret, forever. That's grave news. Even worse, really kind and good people go to hell. Your life, eternal life, depends on what you decide to believe about one Person, His name is Jesus. The good news is that you do have a Savior, and if you confess with your mouth and believe in your heart that Jesus is Lord, you will live with Him in heaven.

Allow me to walk you through another level of challenge. He wants you and me not only to acknowledge Him but also to spend time getting to know Him. There is a famous Bible verse we do not want to hear applied to us or anyone we love. We do not want to be one of those really good people who receive really bad news in heaven. Imagine you at the pearly gates of entry only to hear Jesus say these fatal seven words: "Depart from me, I knew you not." Ouch. That should keep me sober, literally.

The bottom line is this: He died, so that you and I wouldn't. Every bit of your and my life and freedom and continuing into life eternal depends on the belief of each one of us. If one accepts what has been freely given—your Savior, Jesus—then He is your way to everything you have ever wanted. He becomes the way, more specifically, your way into Him being all you have ever wanted and to you being all you have ever wanted to be and more.

How do you receive this Jesus? Open up. Open your mind up to beyond what you can understand and see. Open your heart, the seat of your affections. Open your arms and spiritually embrace this gift. It's okay to have questions, reservations, and doubts. He just wants you to meet with Him. No person who meets Him stays dead or ill, let alone the same.

I like this plan, paradise in eternity and a life worth living on this side of eternity. Your Savior, Jesus, wants your freedom way more for you than you do.

Picture this, when God designed you, He marked you with, say, His unique thumbprint. I call it a *God print*. It is described in Ecclesiastes 3:11. He has placed eternity in each of us. The day we accept him as our Lord, that God print becomes visible to you and all those around you. Like that magic marker that reveals the hidden writing in a kid's tablet, the Holy Spirit reveals who made you and who you are made to be. Your heart, mind, soul, and spirit come to life in a way you have never known.

Immediately we are prepared to become more divine, like our Maker. By each of us coming to know more of God Himself, we come to know our own unique selves better too. All the gifts and traits God placed into our *God print* become discoverable. That God print is the full express image of our original Maker, *God*. Just as we carry the DNA of our biological parents, when we come to believe and accept that we belong to GOD, His divine DNA comes to life in us. Each of us, as we grow in faith, grows into the likeness of our spiritual DNA. We can see that we are patient and giving like never before; that is not of us but of *God*. More of our *God print* is coming to visibility to us and others by the power of the Holy Spirt.

Do you ever wonder why we are each so different if God only ever wants us to be like Him? I did. I sought the Word and Him for this answer, and I believe He gave me a great answer: *for your specific purpose*, you are made uniquely, complexly, beautifully you.

You may not know it, but you and I carry a place for the Spirit of the living God in us. As I told you it comes the moment we are born again, the moment we are believers in Christ. It remains unfulfilled until you choose to have that Holy Spirit make a place in your heart, soul, and spirit.

This God will pursue you and invite you all of your days, until you return to Him who created you.

You have a protector whether or not you want one. This protector will go to great lengths to get you exactly where you need to be and who you need to be with to serve your purpose in life.

This Spirit of the living God will see that you make it through all of your circumstances. He is a deliverer, and He is sure to carry and hold you through any terrible devastation and loss.

One day you will look back and know that the Spirit of the living God has always seen you through to get you to this point where you know him personally as never before.

This one and only God is way bigger than the devastation you face. If you are in this season now, lean into knowing your God more than the need to know what will happen when all this is over. That's only for Him to know. For now, you know who knows.

Love stoops to meet you where you are[1]

Just as God's people were supernaturally protected and provided for in the wilderness before they reached their promise land, so you and I are God's people now. He will send messages to lead us by day and night. Back in the desert it was clouds by day and fire by night. For it is written in Exodus 13:21, "By day the Lord went ahead of them in a pillar of cloud to guide them on their way and by night in a pillar of fire to give them light, so by day or night they could travel."

We Christians are on the move too. We are known as God's hands and feet, meaning we are called to do His work. What an honor, right? We are also a light in the darkness of today's word, because of His clear guiding presence and love, leading in us.

Love never fails.
(1 Corinthians 13:8 NIV)

There is a *real-life* survival tactic when your world has been shaken. You are left with only room to rise and invent what happens next. You will rise out of those ashes because you were chosen to survive. Because you survived, you should honor your Savior with a life well lived. So here is how you can begin again.

Your God will walk through every fire and lead you through the poor visibility times. Here is how. The Spirit of the living God plants a knowing of God and eternity in each human heart. If your world was shaken like mine, God is bigger than the world that just crumbled before your eyes.

1. Breathe, just breathe.
2. Walk out your prayers and grief. Run if you can—one foot in front of the other, no looking back.
3. Drop the need to know why; just hit Delete before you think of it.
4. Assert your courage. The Lord gives supernatural courage while we are in the deep waters or the wilderness.
5. Trust that you are exactly where you need to be, you have exactly what you are supposed to have, and just the right people are around you. If it were not so, hold on; more change is coming. There needs to be a specific condition for our purpose to play out. Trust that God has a good reason in it all. We may never understand, but we have faith because we trust it's all part of the plan for our good.
6. No matter what you just suffered or have seen, any leveling events—e.g., sudden death, sudden loss of job, sudden illness, sudden tragic marital change; that accusation: Yes, it's not fair; no, you didn't deserve it—God will use that horrible thing to build you in a way He couldn't without it. Your God still loves you and me, and He will see you through!

7. Tell yourself, I will survive. He died so I could live (Jesus). We will live to honor what was lost and the God who loves us. We will be victors in and with Christ.

   We will not be defined by what happened.

   This is not the end of you or your story.

   You will grow in wisdom, strength, perseverance, character, and love for Christ and people. All because this has happened to you.

8. Your pain becomes for your purpose—if, *if, IF* you use the pain and devastation, face it, and move through it. This is a soul and spirit formative event. In your pain will be beauty, and purpose, and glory, if you allow it to serve you.

   Watch out for the shortcut. Resist what I did at first, burying it all under the rubble and never looking back.

9. Remember, you can't be free from what you won't face. Fear is a chance to *F*ace *E*verything *A*nd *R*ise. *Face* your biggest fears, dead in the eye. Put God's love into that fear, and it has to leave.

10. Lean into the sovereignty of *God* All-Powerful, who gives life and takes it away. There is a beautiful verse in the Bible that will comfort you very much in this shaken time, two of them, in fact. One is that He is near to the brokenhearted.[1] Said another, secular way, the vinedresser is never closer to the vine than when he is pruning it.

    Then know this promise as yours. He brings beauty out of ashes, the oil of gladness for mourning, the garment of praise to a heavy heart (depression can't stand a chance with God in the middle of it). But in order to move into the beauty-from-the-ashes part; you must be brave enough to step forward into the process and transition to life, a new one.

    Whether or not you wanted this is a moot point. You and I are here, so what happens is completely up to us. We can't control what happened to us, but we can control how we respond. You and I survived, because we were meant to live out a purpose. Lean into that discovery! Make these truths yours. Along with God the Father, Jesus the Savior, and the Holy Spirit, His power and guidance will come alive in you. He is for you, and He has *got* you!

11. This too shall pass. Keep doing the next right thing. Seek God for comfort, worship, and guidance. If you leave Him out, it's just harder. His grace softens the blows of true reworking in the spirit. His grace also puts a cover of mercy over the nastiness of the situation you will have to walk through.

12. If you have a difficult day, certainly that will happen, just clear the schedule as best as you can. If you can't sit in the trust that your *God* will empower you to get through, stay the course of His goodness just for today! Then get some sleep. Rest in heavenly peace. Weeping may endure for a night, but joy comes in the morning! That is a Bible promise for you! His mercies are new and catered just for each and every day![4]

13. Be real! Be real about what you know and do not know. The Lord says, I cannot bless who you pretend to be. Jesus will meet you exactly where you are. Not where you pretend to be with everyone else. He is big enough to handle all your bad attitudes and questions, even doubts as to the kind of God He is. Just because you have doubts or questions doesn't mean that you can't be fully in love with Jesus.

14. We can't see ourselves or our God wrong and expect to live right. When we are thinking all wrong, our lives show it. So take all your walls, wounds, hiding places and spaces straight up to the throne of grace, and Jesus is sure to give you back what is true, noble, right, and just. Give up all that you have known or not known about yourself and God. Let Him tell you who He is, and while He is at it, I'm sure He will share who He made you to be.

HIS SACRED HEART FOR YOURS

REFLECTIONS

A Glimpse at His Heart ...

A Step into the Sacred Chambers of His Heart—His Holy Word

Come to me, all who are heavy laden, and I will give you rest. (Matthew 11:28 ESV)

I will think on these things; Whatever is right
It is right that Your grace, O Lord, holds me now.
In all my questions You are always the answer.

Imagine God speaking this directly to you: "On this side of eternity, disappointment is inevitable; misery is optional. I know of all that has hurt you. No pain goes wasted. I'll use it all to build you. I collect each and every tear of yours. Because of your pain, greater is your reward. In this life and eternally, you will know Me more deeply still. Because you have felt a deep pain, you can imagine and are now compassionate for the things that break *My heart*. Your heart and My heart now beat as one."

Take a praise break to inspire you!

Come to know your God through His names. Be moved. He is an *awesome God!*

YouTube video: "He Is" (The Names of God) by Eric Ludy, 2014.

"Love Broke Through" by Toby Mac, 2015.

A Guided Prayer for You

Lord, I'm ready to move. I'm fixed on You as my savior. My hope is in You. I want to lay hold of Your good plans for my life. Even if the move is not how I expected to get there, I will trust that You will get me to where I need to be. I am adaptable. The vision for my life remains; the plans may change, but I'm so thankful that Your blessings and purpose for me will not expire. You will keep speaking until I understand. I may not see the whole set of stairs, but You always night-light the first step. It's important, God, that I seek You so that I may know You. In knowing You, I will know what to do and rest in Your peace. Peace of mind is priceless. Thank You, God; You are clearing and renewing my mind.

Your white space ...

5

THIS FIGHT IS FIXED—
THE REDEMPTION

So I was delivered immediately from addiction; that was my redemption. But the restorative process comes along in a layered type of healing. When the redemption turns to restoration or restoring me to my healed and whole self, that came more like a marathon, slow, steady, and enduring. In this chapter I will reveal the fight I fought to accept that God really did want me, well and whole, completely restored.

Beside the moves and the frequent fights, suddenly Papa would leave. Likewise, Mama would often threaten to leave. By her mid-twenties she learned how to drive, so we would leave with her on an "I'm out of here" drive. Where we would go, I don't remember. We probably would just drive around until it was safe to go back into the house, when either the bout of rage had settled or my dad would pass out due to drunkenness. It is truly embarrassing to say this of one's father and family life. But I bring this out to inspire those who find themselves in this sad state of brokenness. You will find a way; *God always makes a way!*[1]

What I do know is that every single family line has the problem of sin. With that come pain and brokenhearted people. Maybe you lived a clean-cut life of God's favor and goodness, but even in that situation almost everyone knows the pain of a wandering loved one—one who can't get their act together for whatever reason. You can at least relate to that friend or relative for whom you want salvation so badly. All of us who walk out the good fight of faith with our Lord know how much we wish, pray, and hope that that certain family member or friend would choose life. We want a good life for them, in faith and following Jesus. We know that the mess they live and sometimes drag us into would be so much better if they would give up their way of doing things and choose the Way. That was my prayer for so long for my dad. I would break all his cigarettes and pour out all his booze in the toilet, all while crying out to God, *Save my dad!* What he was doing was hurting each of us and messing up our cute family!

Funny, when I started drinking alcoholically, my kids and husband did the same thing to me, cigarettes and all. Ouch, I can attest that whatever dysfunction you haven't healed from, you will repeat. I say these embarrassing stories to bring you strength and courage that there is a way out of the dysfunction—totally out, not escape it and pretend it's not there. I know that millions of people hide their family pains because we were taught to hush and not speak of our family's "dirty laundry." The Lord knows every family has it. The Word of God tells me not one is righteous, no, not one.

In my years of working through the dirty laundry and getting it cleaned and/or donated. I can say that God performs miracles! That this college "party animal" finally settled down and gave her life to meaningful things like my first Bible study with church friends! That was a miracle!

Totally not random fact: my first one was hosted by a woman who had lived with an alcoholic husband, and he and their marriage were saved and freed, including their children too—just the hope I needed! Another totally not random fact: I got there because her blessed daughter invited me to her faith-based baby play group called "Beyond Laundry." In those totally not random names, places, and people, I healed. I healed and saw what real faith can do. I healed at that point to the level that I could *see*. Sometimes you can't see how deep the basement of pain goes. But God is a gentleman, and He will wait till you have the right tools and support system before you go digging in the caverns and swamps of pain and dysfunction. You have no idea what you buried and where. But just as in my medical training, I learned when working with an earwax impaction, you start working from the known to the unknown until you get to your landmarks and all is clear and removed.

In those prayer groups, God made a way for me to make Him my go-to Counsel. As I prayed personally for the distant married couple, for jobs, for the apathetic child, for the medical miracle needed, I saw a miracle-working God right in my circle of young moms. Together, we prayed circles around the situations, and God faithfully moved on our behalf.

Outside that circle, I have prayed for the spouse who believes that "that one thing" is under control and not tearing their family apart. I have prayed for the person to be able to move out of overeating, which keeps them in a cycle of shame and self-loathing, but they just don't know how to do differently. Each of them wanted something different—wanted out of the hard situation so badly—but somehow year after year not much had changed. Some of them were even "in the right place," that is, the church, the Bible study, or a self-help group. But they had not come to a place of complete disclosure with themselves and their God. I have come to find that that's why twelve-step programs all begin with full surrender.

Sin and evil want a place to hide. So I pulled back the rugs and opened all the closets, I called it all out of those dark places in my own family. Why? Because sweet surrender is not as sweet as amazing grace. I live free of shame and embarrassment now. I share these difficult stories and pain-filled situations so that you'll have the courage to face your situation. There is a better way to fight this fight of sin, condemnation (guilt), and shame. I found a new way to fight. This is why I share the depravity of the situation so you can see that a mighty God can pull you out of the most disgusting of places.

Firsthand, I have seen what sweet surrender can do. To be completely turned over to God is sweet surrender. The end of me and my knowing how is the beginning of God's miracle-working power. All who have turned their will and way over to God have healed their families and even literally raised people from the dead! I've prayed for it all firsthand. All these people who are fully sold out to Christ have come out of sin, shame, guilt, and fear and now live free in success on every level. A song that was quite popular in the Christian music scene says, "Unstoppable God, let your glory go on and on. Impossible things in your name shall be done." I'll reference it later, so you can take your very own praise break.

So how come I started to fight a different way? Pleading, wishing, hoping, and begging were not working. Jesus selected me for this fight. I loved Him, I was praying, but I still was losing my family and career and relationships right before my eyes. Jesus needed me to pray like a victor, not a victim. That's why I didn't back out of the fight. I know, as David did when he went in to fight Goliath, that I was sent in to win! So you and I, just like David, can know that when we get sent into a fight, it's to come out winning. If a battle is lost, do not fret; it's not over until God says it's over. Keep showing up. Get with your Lord and Savior, and find your *why* power. When I found my why power, it overcame my will power. You see the difference? Where your willpower gives out, your why power takes over.

So I ask you again: What is your why power? Mine was the gift of my amazing husband and four healthy, great, beautiful, talented, smart, God-loving, funny children! I had too much to lose. God gave me the privilege of raising them, I knew the pains of abuse, addiction, lies, and poverty, a product of a divorced home and stepparents and blended family issues. Lord Jesus, help me spare my children from this cup! I had to win so that the current generation had a fighting chance to thrive and know love, so that the generations to come would be saved and live in blessing instead of more generational curses and sin.

I clung to the verse "Do not be discouraged; Do not be dismayed for the Lord, your God, goes with you."[2] I clung to "All things are possible with God."[3] I had them stamped on leather bracelets and wore them and said them several times a day. I stand here to tell you that your situation is not the worst of all and beyond all hope. Although it is natural to believe that when you're in the midst of a fight against a giant, do not believe the lie that your situation is beyond hope and beyond forgiveness. I can tell you it's not! God can do anything! Use God's hope and God's faith. The Word of God says at our weakest and emptiest, He is our strength.

Let me continue the story of what I had to heal from. What I saw of conflict resolution comprised verbal and physical lashing out, breaking things, throwing things, and reminders of atrocious unforgiven laundry lists of mistakes. It was wrapped up with the last word, a list of curse words, a slammed door, and a promise to leave. Sometimes we did. Someone would always walk out.

The following day looked like this, most of the time. Remorse would set in, and my papa would beg for forgiveness and swear he would never do anything to harm us again. My mom would swallow the pain and keep him to save the family. That unpredictability cycle along with frequent fights felt like a Spanish soap opera. My fear of a sudden "bad day coming soon" was always there. My mental escapes were constant. I would mentally dissociate so that I could stay in the hope of a brighter day. I would also pray my rosary at night. I do believe every "Our Father" and "Hail Mary" helped keep me in faith that God was going to help us out.

For a brief time, we three kids and my parents moved back to their native country, Nicaragua. There were wars in the home; there were even worse ones in the streets. At home things got worse.

There was an official civil war in the streets; our young men family members were forced to leave us to serve as enlisted soldiers. Many people suffered. Scarcity, upheaval, and tensions were there on edge, both in and out of my home. I remember that once we leaned our mattresses and held them up to the family room windows to dampen the shots fired and protect us from the crossfire in the streets. That was incredibly frightening. All this, they say, makes one nervous and anxious and controlling in life. I resorted to my siblings and cousins as my joy; our faith in God was our hope of better days ahead.

Meanwhile, my papa was caught up in the wars of a man in addiction, pain, and trauma he never dealt with, so he resorted to what looked to me like escapism. He would constantly and yet unintentionally hurt the family and disrespect his wife.

You can't imagine what it's like, seeing the woman you love and admire beaten. My mom would hide the black eyes and fat lips behind dark glasses and closed doors. I later found out this was a generational recurrence. Other woman in my family on both sides had dealt with this, among other painful repeating skeletons. In my spiritual prayer work, I came to find out that until a family member breaks the spiritual dark forces, and the chains they try to keep us under, a family is almost doomed to repeat the same mistakes. They are called familial spirits, and their one purpose is to keep us families bound and living the same generational lies and sins. Though prayer and wise counsel, I broke every chain and faced every demon. I was not going to do as I was shown. Put on a public happy face and privately deal with things.

When I went to rehabilitation, we did an "issues" family tree. Both my husband and I had tons of skeletons in our closets. Addictions, depression, anger issues, anxiety, buried pains, failed marriages, these were just a few of the demons my ancestors fought. The ones I observed fighting most closely the demon I was then fighting, alcoholism, were my dad and grandfather. I can say that my grandfather, with faith and family, defeated his giants. My dad did not.

In all of that, I never remember being verbal about processing such painful life circumstances. I remember just being held all like little chicks under a mom's arms, with her and my grandma repeatedly saying, "Ya pasó," which means "it's passed." Like saying, "You can calm down now; it's over. We don't need to talk about that; just forget it." I can't remember ever talking about any of our feelings or soothing ourselves any other way than denial, distraction, and escapism.

So I learned to play the cover-up and masquerade game. I was good at pretending everything was great. "Yes, there's nothing to see here except that we have a pretty, loving, supportive, and gathering family. We will just not talk about the bad days or the problems that recur. We have a good family name to stand on, so at least we have that going for us."

In the small, poor country of Nicaragua, my mother's side was full of respected politicians, authors, even a president of the country, a few doctors, and young men studying at "the unofficial Harvard of Central America." Those were just the men; the women of this period were told to just to be gorgeous and support and serve the men's needs and egos. My aunt and mom were not allowed to have any educational needs met after about the twelfth grade, because that was when they would marry a respectable man and start their careers as homemakers. This was an improvement; the previous generation only got educated to about the middle school years.

Yet what I did see was women rising against cultural repression and getting educated professionally on their own. I loved the empowerment and drive they showed, which helped me overcome the financial and academic rigors and obstacles of my university training. I learned from a young age that if you worked long enough and hard enough and did not quit, you would make it.

I also learned some street and relational wisdom—for instance, you don't need to "wear" or bring attention to your hardships. Always help the less fortunate. Just because you come from hard times doesn't mean you are less than anyone else. With faith and hard work, you will overcome. And finally, Put on a happy face in bad times; no sense in being a complaining pessimist. I still practice those great resiliency and survival skills in everyday life.

However, in my quest to do things differently from what I had seen, it just wasn't enough to be better off than the previous example. I was after what my Jesus teaches, true wholeness and healing. I wanted to thrive in life, not just survive. So I set out to discover what God says about living above life's hard circumstances and what it is to actually live in His kingdom, in the present life. In my faith study I didn't even know that there was a set of promised care that God gives his people when they live in obedience to his will and ways. I came to know Truth, and the Truth set me free to live differently— not just to replace one addiction with another, but to really heal and be delivered from it. I came to know that in His kingdom, He reigns and rules on a different set of principles in resiliency.

I learned what was meant by "pressing in," "going to the throne boldly," and "leaning in on my faith." When my body and mind were too weak to stand, I could lean on the solid "rock of ages." God's kingdom and care are immovable and steady, even in the worst of earthly circumstances. With each passing day, God was and continues to be faithful and good to me. He would lead me into the wisdom and people that I needed to "stay the course" He wanted me on.

In Him, I learned how to practice my new faith-based growth tools and way of living. With my new God's kingdom skill set, I traded in the street hustle skills and was now living out and realizing great dreams and promises. This created in me a hunger to know more of what kingdom principles and promises are and were. Through one of my Bible studies I heard there were eight *thousand* of them for me to discover.

I was googling sobriety tools when I first went sober, so my spirit knew that God's promises were something I wanted to hold a lot of stock in.

With those tools I could withstand the refining fires that the Bible speaks of. I can't say I have earthly living thing all figured out, but I'm growing and receiving more grace and godly wisdom and boldness and courage. I am growing, and growing is an indication of abundant life.

So I press on that same course. I'm in training, and I'm freer and better off than I ever was and on my way to being better than I have ever been!

I'm learning more of those things that happen when you live and operate in kingdom truths, such unspeakable joy, peace that surpasses understanding, provision of needs met beyond explanation, complete healings, anointed ability to do what I normally could not do, holy boldness, and blessed assurance.

But to live in the promised land, one must remove that slave mentality. As the Bible describes, once the slaves were freed of bondage in Egypt, it took some of them a lifetime to remove the bondage mentality from their physically freed self.

So I did not want a lifetime of feeling mentally bound and lied to. I still struggled with accepting love from God, I felt deeply unworthy, and my self-talk was downright abusive to myself. As I walked through deprograming this toxic mindset, it was hard work, I must admit. Some people have lies fall off of them immediately, and some of mine did, but I honestly consumed biblical teaching and prayer with scripture and worship to be "renewed in my mind." I knew it was possible because my Bible told me so. So I would keep seeking God until my emotions and toxic thoughts were overcome by the washing of the Word, and the blood-bought healing and wellness came at last.

After years of silencing my negative self-chatter with alcohol and self-worth based on accomplishments and status, I had my work cut out for me. My floods of thoughts and emotions were so overpowering that I truly questioned my mental health, wondering at times if I was bipolar. With the help of counselors and pastors and open communication with my doctors and fervent prayer, and a lot of running, I was delivered of that terrible mental battle. All of those lies must bow to the name of Jesus. I just kept praying and praising my way through every day. That poverty mindset I had and many other distorted core beliefs that created distrust and fights in my early marriage all shrank back and fell off me, just as the Word of God promises.

Even the more deeply entrenched thought patterns were rewired, for instance, how at a youthful age I heard wounded sayings passed off as truth. One was "You can't trust men, and don't depend on them." When I became a wife, marital advice came from a wounded mindset. I was warned of the "runaround" dangers in a marriage: "Don't turn your man down when he expresses a need. If you keep your 'dog' (husband) well fed and stroked, he won't run around on you or leave."

I can tell you, as a young woman who didn't witness a loving and trusting marriage until much later in life, that that's not a healthy place to start a relationship from. O Lord of lords, did I need You or what. Please deprogram-destroy these faulty foundations! Also, Lord, because I seek and honor You, please help me pass along more godly marriage advice to my four children.

My mom married young and tried to give second and third and fourth chances and work the marriage out, but addiction won, and divorce happened. With that memory seared into strong neural pathways, I swore to myself that I would wait to marry until I was older. Then, educated and older, I might hope not to have these immature man pains.

The fears and insecurities were deep. Without my even thinking or meaning to, they came out in my dating and marriage too.

You can't imagine how painful it is to write these words about yourself and your family. So why would I? Because we are human. Science has long documented that we learn best by modeling and peer influence. We were made to thrive and operate best in community. We are wired to love, learn, and grow together. It made me feel better to know that I was not the first person in history to live through such growing pains, and I won't be the last. So if I found out how to overcome common human struggles and limiting mindsets with God, how could I not share? I was radically overcome by a genuine transforming love; it felt as if every cell in me had changed. When that kind of love overcomes, you become love itself. So love can't help but to be naturally what it is; it shares lovingly because it cares. I now jump at the chance to tell all who listen about the hope that can help all my human brothers and sisters.

Why? Because love saves. When I was commissioned by the saving grace of God I accepted His love and then became His love, then could give out His love. Like a good mirror, I just reflect what I see. I see a good and loving God, and in turn I can be good and loving to others. Anything less feels burdensome. I have been in the common human condition of going through the motions and doing what everyone else seems to be doing. I know how inauthentic that is. I know too what it is like to long for and ache for who knows what.

All that left when I made Jesus my Way of love and life. His love comes and His hope fills all burdens with purpose. It's like a hard workout; you feel amazing afterward. All the pain is worth it when you see the positive results.

The pain I lived does not need to be passed on. In fact, that is what saved me. As I held each newborn of mine in my arms, I would be in awe of love. I said, "Wow this is how God loves me—incredible!" So, it was the love for my children that awakened me, to how great God's love is for us. I longed to be better for them.

As I was learning in church and my time with seeking God, I saw that with Him, I had a new identity and an important future. My familial mistakes would not be repeated. So instead of passing on a broken and flawed way of life, I would pass on a story of redemption, healing, and restoration.

Moreover, the Word of God says I am healed fully by the blood of the Lamb, Jesus, and the words of my testimony. So, the pain is never in vain! To be human is to fight battles and to struggle. As a teen and young adult, I thought I was the only one struggling. I thought for sure no one could know how I felt—so broken, empty, and dissatisfied for no reason at all. *No can know I'm so clueless.*

The enemy of our soul's purpose and salvation wants us to remain discouraged and unaware of who we really are or what we really possess. Instead, the enemy wants us chasing the next thrill, achievement, or shiny thing. People then come to realize that all the possessions and wealth in the world can't buy what really matters most: time, genuine love, peace, or unspeakable joy.

So to win at this game of life, *God* must come first. Once we learn of what God did for us, just because He loves and wants to be with us, we learn more of Him and more about who we really are. It starts simply: He made us for His own and our own enjoyment. He gives of Himself as triune three-part God, so that we never feel like we need to live life apart from Him. God made us in His image and shared all that He has with us freely and generously. So we can relate; think about the person you love most—it could be like a child or the pet you adore—and how you would give your all to do for them.

But back to our relationship with God, how we messed it up by doubting God's complete care and goodness. We say to ourselves … did God really say? Then, thinking we can "do life better ourselves," we go our own way and do our own thing, only to find out that we've caused unnecessary trouble for us and the ones we love most. So God fixed it all in *love*. He sacrificed His own Son to heal our broken and empty parts. He made a way for us to know Jesus. To know Jesus is to know the Father, for the Word of God says that He is the exact representation of the Father God, creator of all and in all. Then, Jesus died to pay for all our sin and disease—all so that, in Him, we could live fully and have eternal life.

So back to me learning about how much God loved me through my kids, I was willing to die to my selfish and broken ways so that I could have a better relationship and legacy with them. Isn't that what God did through Jesus, for us? Uncanny, I tell you. I died to my broken and self-medicating and overcompensating self. In that experience of a sweet surrender of dying to my self-seeking nature and my self-glorifying ways, I could now share in the resurrection power of Christ himself in me. I would then come to "real life," and the struggles that had once paralyzed me or taken me out were no more.

In my new nature and Christ-powered self I could "do right and be good" with no effort, just love! This was all so awesome for me. Liberating. Exciting. Anyone who knew of me before knows that I've always been enthusiastic. Well, God leveled up my enthusiasm, by making me all about doing all that I do through the lens of loving God through people. I finally took my place as His vessel. He pours all his *love* and healing power in me; I pour it all out to the people in my life, and He fills me back up! All this happens by way of the Holy Spirit, who is God present and alive in each of us who accept Jesus as our Lord and say so. Prayer is the Holy Spirit's activator of God's things and purpose in our lives. So I learned to pray every way I could.

So, this is *my big why* ... because I have come to the revelation of all this. All of it is too good to be true, but it is true! And it is possible for any of us!!

I love being the Lord's ambassador and vessel of His good. I know that He is growing me to be even bolder and a larger vessel of His greatness. I can't wait to see what more He has for me, and that is what keeps me at His feet, per se, telling him He is awesome and that I'm ready for whatever He wants of me. I know that apart from Him, I am no earthly good and that the best and lasting parts of me are with Him. With Him, I not only make a big heavenly impact here on earth, but it outlives me in the now and forevermore. Bless the Lord, O my soul, that makes me want to worship His holy name!

In the Lord's leading, I become wise in *Him*. I'm not clueless anymore, so long as I create the time and priority to seek God first in all. Pray first and *often!* Let's be clear: I'm not struggle-free, because this is difficult to practice. But so long as I keep at it, I am assured He is with me, and I'm improving.

STEPPING INTO MY FINISHED WORK!

I love learning all the ways the scriptures tell me that pains in all forms have been healed by our Lord's sacrifice. He may not deliver us from pain, but He is faithful to step through it with us and let the pain be a positive one for our spiritual growth. He took the brunt of our pains as He was lashed all 39 times. The word of God promises that by His stripes we *were* healed. Did you catch that … the word was written in the *past tense*—meaning already done and overcome. What you and I are currently fighting for, it's a done deal. *It is finished;* that is what Jesus said on the cross, for each of us about all of our life's needs and battles.

When I believe it, I can receive it, it comes to pass on earth as it already is in heaven! As I share this made-for-TV drama, it loses power over me. The pain and sting that I used to feel when I told of it, or even thought of all the dysfunction, is removed. If I cry now, it's because I cry about God's goodness to me. *My tears are now resurrection tears.* My tears are also prayers of my faithfulness to Him. My tears serve as prayers of protection over the blessings and treasures God has entrusted to me, my children and all the friends and family I love so much. Now that I'm a member of *God's* big church ministry, I meet and fall in love with more people all the time! Thank You, God, for growing my heart, so I could love more!

So in this finished work of Christ, as I share my story, I get to partake in God's glory, by setting more captives free! To bring things full circle, I realized that in secrecy the burdens and shame grow. Every single family has brokenness and generational sin. I can say that only in bringing our pains and sins to Jesus are we set free of committing the same errors we saw. Every parent wants a better life for their children, and as an adult, I now understand the sacrifices my parents made to give me a better life.

On the other side of the coin, all kids want their parents to be present and loving, to care about what matters to them, and to be someone they are proud to introduce. With God's healing love, I can honestly say that now our family honors, admires, respects, and grows in the love and faith that can only come from God. From one generation to the next, from a place of humility and healing in Christ we can now ask difficult questions to one another, instead of having the blanket Hush policy we used to practice. The pains in our family history are now the amazing redemption story of our restorative God.

> I tore down my faulty foundation. Made
> lessons out of my early childhood quakes;
> and this was my fight out of my rubble!

I can say I caught myself making some generational mistakes of parental physical or emotional absenteeism. In all honesty, for me it was not born out of that intent, but more out of survival. I know most parents "check out" because they are busy just trying to survive. Sadly, many kids live in the reality that they have a place to stay, food on the table, and chores to do, and that is all the parent is able to provide. This is usually because they face their own survival battles and are parenting not from a place of wholeness but one of brokenness. We parent from a strong sense of duty and responsibility, in a place of burden instead of blessing: Like it's my job to feed and care for and provide for all these mouths. Let's just make it to this next school year. I had developed that paycheck-to-paycheck mentality. It was all I saw and knew. There was little room for play, just duty. I can't ever remember playing or any positive memory with either parent, other than just being hugged and loved on for reassurance.

Back to how this affected my raising my kids: what a wounded person does is overcompensate. So I played with my kids a ton and had a very hard time disciplining them. This approach needed some repair too, I was a mess, and I didn't know how to parent without yelling or hitting. I bottled it all inside and let it all come out in my late-night binges of wine, after I got the kids to bed at first, then into "homework time," and then into anytime. I would clean, jam out to music, and drink my frustrations away. Sadly, I found them again as I sobered up. So I'd drink more often. How would this vicious cycle come to an end?

When I was a child, faith formation was big in our lives. The first time I can remember faith was in the first grade in Nicaragua. I went to a Catholic school, and there I learned my prayers to rehearse, and I loved of the safe environment (no fights broke out there). I felt alive in the nurturing and supportive church community. I can remember being liked and loving school. I learned about God, Jesus, and Mary, our holy mother. I found comfort in heaven being on my side and keeping a watch over us. I got hold of my first rosary, and I clung to that rosary as if it were God Himself. I can remember hiding in closets and under my sheets, just me and my rosary. I would pray my way to safety. I could feel the peace of Jesus coming over me and getting me through the latest insurrection in the home.

Emotionally and psychologically I can remember being a survivor again. Some of those same "earthquakes' that my family survived would seem to forever haunt us. Our earth never seemed to stop quaking in turmoil. At an early age I discovered my dad had severe emotional wounds, He came from a divorced and blended family, a rich and well-to-do one. He witnessed domestic violence so much that it resulted in watching his own dad get shot and killed by his stepson. He was around the age of eight. A bit like the Spanish soap operas, only in our life it was real. The men were good-looking diplomats, the women "of good blood or genes"; this was important in my grandparents' and parents' time. So in this real-life Spanish soap opera we had the beautifully dressed women, passionate, manipulating, and sometimes angry. The men, "run-arounds" or womanizers, all drank heavily and then would beat on their woman to take out their frustrations, pains, and disappointments in life.

Who knew the desperate housewives of Nicaragua ever existed in the late 1950s? But they did. So my dad and his three biological siblings and three half-siblings all witnessed the death of his dad as a result of domestic violence. Here is the point: family wounds lead to more family wounds until they all meet and are reconciled to Christ.

I must have been around eight when I heard of this tragedy, and I felt sorry for my dad and realized he'd had a rough childhood. To add to the awful tragedy, about six to twelve months prior to marrying my mother, he was involved and was the driver of a motorcycle accident that took the life of his brother, who was sixteen at the time. To live with the guilt of accidentally taking his baby brother's life was a very hard pain for my dad to live with. However, when he met my gorgeous mom, a.k.a. Mrs. Nicaragua in the real Ms. Universe pageant, that sped up the healing. He had hope in my mom, and she was really good for him. My mom said that she loved him; he was a good and loving man, and she felt that she could heal him with love and a good life from his tragic emotional wounds and traumas. So I think my mom was trying to have me understand why my dad was the way he was.

I escaped all this madness in play with my brother and sister. We were all only two years apart in age, and they were God's gift to me. If not for them, I wouldn't have survived our family hardships with any joy at all. Yes, with them we played in the basement and outside. We were so good at playing pretend, we would design makeshift houses and in them build the families we wished we had. We would play loving parents and babies; we would play lawyers and teachers. So cute; we would play out our wrongs and right the world in our imaginations.

Relationally with my parents, as I said before, I have only a few fond memories. They involved singing and listening to music all together. Music and dancing and hugs when there were no fights— that was our family's laughter, joy, and healer.

I do recall feeling really uncomfortable in my seemingly frequent geographical moves. As the new girl in the class, each time I battled feeling like the outsider. I battled not seeming to be proficient in the correct language we were learning in. If I was strong in Spanish,

I was supposed to be in English, and vice versa. I had to work through what seems like a lifetime of being the new person, or the "transplant." So, thank God, I got really good at making friends and finding commonalities with different types of people.

I can remember feeling shame because I had to repeat a grade. I was deemed not to know enough English to get into the grade I was supposed to be in. So I'd embellish the truth or twist it, or just make it up. It's sad, but I would tell my classmates lies in my broken English, to make up the life I wanted so desperately to have. In my lies, I shopped at the best places, not Goodwill; we would eat pizza at Pizza Hut, not Spam in a pan; we would go to the pool on the weekends, not stuck at home with no money to go out.

In school and at home I learned to rise to the top of the do-gooder list. There was favor and nice attention there. I became very obedient. I was afraid of any authority figure. I was afraid to disappoint them or to cause a fight or be in trouble.

Ultimately, I had become distanced and calloused with the dreams of normal family life. We were poor and on social assistance, Dad was always working, on three jobs for many years. Mom was watching us and studying to be a hairstylist. My mom was such a great housekeeper, she was always cleaning and cooking, I think it that was her therapy. When we moved as a family from Colorado to Florida, I had a feeling my parents wouldn't be together much longer.

On a funny note, I later noticed as an adult that if I was upset or stressed out, I would clean, so I get that from my mom. I must live in the peace of Christ all the time now, because my housework seems to be always behind and a mess. Somebody stress me out, would you? I want a clean and tidy house! Not really; my nerves can't handle any more than they have to. Let us each just keep the peace and put away what we each use. Everything has a home, great moms say!

Anyway, I seemed to have created my own little world of disassociation; psychologists call it imaginary lives, emotional detachment, escapism. All are survival techniques to safely navigate turmoiled upbringing. We moved back to the United States, under my grandparents' advice, to save my dad from self-destruction. We moved to where my dad had his siblings. We moved to Florida; as psychologists say, people try to use a marriage, a baby, a move, or a job to cover up something or to save someone.

This was an uphill climb for all of us, and my mom gave us some level ground when she terminated her marriage with my dad to save us, she said. Of course I didn't see it that way. My dad spiraled down, and it would be seven more years of heartbreaking addiction-related story after addiction-related excuse before he died at the early age of forty-five. "Drinking-related illness" is what I was told. I disassociated with this pain for ten years before I dealt with it.

You see, too much pain I delivered in one paragraph ... that's why I put it all away, and I hid in college to find myself. Sadly, my faith was far from me. I think I was mad at God for having everything fail on me. He was there—I knew He was—but I was in so much pain I didn't want to talk to Him, because He had let it happen. I'm sorry now that I did that. All the time I behaved like a rebellious and careless teen to God.

The fights never seemed to leave me or my mindset.

I fought always feeling like an immigrant (although I was a natural-born citizen).

I fought being the transplant or new girl all the time.

I fought coming from poor beginnings and not having enough to pay for college at the University of Florida.

I was ashamed and I would do any good or admirable thing to prove I was a somebody, not a nobody.

I fought rejection for camouflaging in the wrong color of chameleon in my surrounding. There was no way I would be the real me ... they would not hang out with me, and I liked being liked. Why? Because I liked them. I've always been a lover of people.

I fought not having the right family to come from, blended, divorced, left, even gay.

I fought the perception that all the people I loved would leave ... so I fought to please people so they wouldn't. There is no authenticity in that. I would just accept whatever love they were willing to give, and I would do anything to be a good enough person so they wouldn't leave me.

I fought not enough finances. I worked three jobs and seventeen-hour days at the age of nineteen and never quit, to make tuition, car payments, and rent.

I fought to find love. I didn't want to be a spinster, so I sold myself short to guys, who mistreated me.

I fought to finish school in the right amount of time. There is no time for discovery when you have a career at which to start earning money.

I fought the perception that I would never depend on a man. Mom had told me I would be trapped in the relationship if I didn't make my own living.

I fought my religion and prayed God would keep me in control. Obviously, He let all those awful things happen to me. So God became the far-off God. I was banking on creating me, a self-made American dream.

I fought fears of repeating my family's failed marriage mistakes, now the love of my life had a similar background. So we fought to break the patterns and begin life together.

I fought my biological clock. I had to have three kids before thirty-five, because after that, genetic disorders and special needs were more prevalent. By the grace of God, I had four in time.

I fought to prove my worth. Achievement became my everything at home and in social circles, career, the corporate ladder, and my fight to keep fit and trim and hot for my husband.

I fought to keep my crutch, my addiction. I justified that I worked hard and accomplished a lot, so I could play harder.

I fought to become a practicing Christian again. After my first year of dating my now husband, I began to read the Bible again and "used" my faith to ease the pains of growing up into an adult. At this point God was still there only for emergencies in my mind and heart. I went to church occasionally. I justified this by being a good person who didn't steal, cheat, or lie. Being a good person and believing in God was enough for me at this time. For that I paid with many mistakes, and I'm sorry, Lord.

YOU'RE TOO HOLY FOR ME

When will this fight end? Aren't you done reading about it? Try living this bloody mind-scambling fight! Exhausting!

Well, as God had given me more grace and planted a bigger love for him in me, I sought Him more. I joined Bible studies and made Christian friends.

But there I go fighting again. I fought the belief that my Christian friends were too holy for me; we would only worship and study about God together. There is no way we could enjoy an all-encompassing authentic friendship, no way.

I fought being a double-minded and two-faced Christian. One foot in the kingdom and one foot in the very self-pleasing world. I practiced the philosophy that four days of the week my body was the Lord's temple; the other three it was my playground.

I can't tell you how hard I fight still, to admit what a far-from-saintly soul I was. All these awful things I did to me, my family, my friends, and most regrettably, my God!

Thank You, God, for pulling me out of this horrible way to live.

I fought being superwoman to my family. They would never know my struggles. I would figure it all out. *I've done this before; I'll do it again.*

I fought to get to the top of career. I opened up a private practice with four babies. Why? Looking back financially, we needed the help to pay off our doctoral study loans, and I wanted to be valued by my husband so badly that I thought he would love me more. He grew up admiring his working moms, so I became one too. He would admire that I made good money and was a successful doctor practicing audiology next to him. That came at a price he and I would later pay.

I fought to find more validation and worth by competing in races, volunteering on philanthropic boards—all so that I could somehow feel good enough. I had a blessed life, so I had to prove my worthiness to my husband, family, and community. I was also trying to please and do good for God. If I could earn His favor, He would help me not to lose my mind while raising my four babies. He would help me keep the family He had given me, and my husband would not leave me.

I fought God. He was speaking to me and warning me and telling me what to fix. But I wanted to do it my way. My relationship with God was distant, primarily because I had put so many elements of my life above a relationship with Him. I was in sin, so I didn't feel adored or known by Him. I was too busy going after people's adoration and recognition.

I fought trying to do the right thing by getting a hold on my drinking and compensating my inner battles with busyness. Yet in human effort alone, we are sure to go back to what we know. I kept falling into the same sin-filled trap over and over.

> There isn't one broken or desperate situation You can't fully renew, including my broken heart when my kids wrote the "Mom, please stop drinking wine" letter. I still have it.

I fought self-loathing. I didn't like doing wrong or not being good enough. I was a perfectionist on some levels through and through. So if I fell short of my own too-high expectations, I would drown in self-pity. Then I would go do more good stuff to feel better and bleed out from exhaustion, until I lost the fight.

In the end, all the "fight or flight" in me had become depleted. Thirteen rounds and the last fight, but there was nothing left in me to be proud of. I had diluted it all out with drinking to cover everything up. I had become exactly what I swore I would never become. I became just like what I saw when I was a little kid. Most every adult fears becoming the worst they saw in their parents. No disrespect to my whole family or parents; believe me, they did a great deal right. It's only that the human psyche tends to grab the trauma and drama and lack and only remember that.

What I wouldn't give to have more of those good memories rise up in me. I know they are there; I just can't remember more than a handful. Mom, I'm sorry if I can't remember all the good you did; you did so much to make our family survive and thrive as fresh Americans. I know you were loving and present in amazing ways, or I wouldn't be who I am today. So thank you for carrying your load and ours until we were big enough to become who we each came to be. Hopefully, seeing the fruit of our lives now helps you feel accomplished and appreciated as the type of parent you were and are now. Mom, thanks for fighting for me when I couldn't fight for myself. It was you and my siblings who fought for me to come out of the denial and depression I hit. I was so depressed and mad at myself. With your help I was able to learn to forgive and make peace with myself again. Thank you for coming alongside me and being a great example of humility, faith, and survivorship.

THE TKO

But before all that healing happened, I ran far from all that was buzzing in my mind and heart. I'd go through all the motions—be at this event, host this gathering, work, volunteer—only to find my soul cluttered, confused and numb. I would end up back to exactly what I was running from, self-hatred by now.

I screamed and fought to get respect from children; knowing I was being foolish by "getting silly"; that is mommy talk for "Whoa, my drink has made me lose straight thinking and talk." So I'll excuse myself by calling myself silly instead of "a drunk." Ouch, how is that for that memory?

But, Lord, thank You for living amends. Thank You that You helped me quit while the kids were still young, and my marriage still had love to restore.

There isn't one broken or desperate situation You can't fully renew, including my broken heart when my kids wrote the "Mom, please stop drinking wine" letter. I still have it. It reminds me of what God saved me from. I'll never go back, so long as I stay abiding in Him. He who redeemed me will get me onto becoming.

But before victory happened … I still fought. What can I say? Old habits die hard. I fought to do rehab my way. Even when therapy was on my terms, a medically led detox with outpatient group meetings, I would cycle out.

The cycle went like so. Do good, achieve. Work hard to prove to self and others that I was good. Fail on some level of a six-ball juggle. Numb self to forget the "I hate myself" feelings. Pick up another ball to juggle; maybe that one will make me like myself. Drop the balls again. Drink again. Do good again, to erase shame and guilt. Compare. Fall short. Drink again.

Never-ending. Depleting. Self-sabotaging.

This cycle had to stop.

Lord, I want off this merry-go-round fight

1. It's not merry anymore.
2. I'm throwing up a lot. I'm sick. My mind wanted to drink because of anxiety. My body screamed, "No more." Sounds pretty miserable huh?
3. By God's grace alone, He let me "tap out," as they say in the MMA world. I was a bloody sinful mess and He saved me anyway. Yes, I needed saving. I finally said yes to His way—The Way.

Keep reading to see how I discovered *the Way, the Truth, and the Life!* Keep reading, and you will see how God showed up and made me a *real* woman of faith. *No more masquerades.* He loved me fiercely and saved all who mattered to me.

In the hard work of process, I faced my character flaws, protective mechanisms, and distorted core beliefs (this is a term I came up with to describe the lie that I was believing to be so true because I'd lived it so long. Like my biggest one: affection and love are earned). Let me at 'em ... God said, I'll take each of those false lies down with one Bible verse; one biblical word and it's out like a light!

So I got out of the boxing ring, where I was losing, and tapped out. I gave God my boxing gloves, and my enemy was TKO. Nothing can stand against *Jesus!* Jesus saves!

Sad stories, right? Well, Jesus is serious about your and my deliverance! His name is over all! Do you have a big bully in your life beating you up? Tap out, and give the fight up to *God.* He never loses a battle!

This is how *real love* met my identity. *This is* how *love broke through* this losing cycle of sin, pain, and defeat. *He* built into me that as a redeemed child of God, I am forever *His,* empowered to live righteously, not because I am perfect but because I am perfectly loved! He built into me true identity—*His.*

If love broke through my years of reliving self-made earthquakes and personal mind battles of insecurity, He certainly can break you out of yours, whatever they may be. And if you don't have a cycle to defeat, really reflect to make sure nothing is there. If there truly isn't, thank your Lord, and know that you can serve as a voice of healing to all the people who may have suffered less than ideal situations and still fight. I'm so grateful Jesus affirmed in my spirit that He had genuinely called me out of my own hell and that He had a good future for me to step into, but that I needed to accept His lavish love completely, before all that I could become would take root and grow. I accepted this message was truly for me and I wasn't going to pass up such a good God-honoring and fulfilling life. After that my prayers of faith changed and became more effective. God said to me, "You are forgiven and restored, completely renewed in mind, heart, and soul. Now talk to Me and others as though you know it and believe it, with confidence and authority! *Know what I tell you and live it. Be ready at all times to share why you have the hope and authority you do.*" So now I do live more boldly, and I'm getting even better all the time! *To God be the glory!*

HIS SACRED HEART FOR YOURS

REFLECTIONS

Imagine – A Step into the Sacred Chambers of His Heart

I will think on these things; Whatever is pure

What lie are you believing that is causing you to lose the fight? One by one replace the lies with what is pure and peaceable and most loving. Speak them aloud; it's like a washing with the Word. He makes us pure.

> Just as Christ also loved the church and gave Himself up for her, so that He might sanctify her, having cleansed her by the washing of water with the word. (Ephesians 5:25–26 NASB)

Take a praise break!
Song: "Unstoppable God" by Elevation Worship; released Nov. 2014.
"Help Is on the Way," Toby Mac, 2020.

A Guided Prayer for You

Lord, I ask You to activate in me communication with You. You, Lord, are a loving God and interested in all of my affairs, interests, and desires. God, if I can't find words of my own to communicate and relate to You, I just humbly close my eyes and open up my heart to You now. I may have no words, and that is way more than okay. You, O Lord, get thrilled when I just glance toward You in thought and heart intention. Begin there with me, God. Thank You that You are a gentle and patient God. You don't force Your ways on me but gently guide me into more meaningful ways to communicate and understand what You want to share with me. I am thankful that I am free of older beliefs that I would anger or offend You, by not praying right. Lord, thank You that You have called me by name. I know the battles I faced or worry about are not my own. You will fight for me and always win. If You win, Lord, I win, because Your Word says that to live is Christ and to die is gain.

LOVE BROKE THROUGH

Your white space …

6

THE GREATEST SUBSTANCE SWAP OF ALL

*I Am Redeemed
How God's Renewal Helped
Me Swap My Substance*

Here are just a few questions and self-talk when faced with end-of-yourself moments about doing differently.

Okay: I can do this! I faced my new reality. Like it or not, I'm in sobriety in recovery—I'm dying. I'm in AA.

So I'm a perfectionist and a do-gooder by nature … this is not okay! I just got called into the principal's office! Yes for real! Oh my goodness,

Lord, what have I done? I tell myself it's gonna be okay! No, no, it's not okay ….

Okay: It's okay that I'm not okay. It's okay that I don't know how, right?

It's happening! Now I'm making the biggest substance swap ever; from the comfort of misusing *booze* to using "faith"!

Okay, the Bible calls faith a substance. Think about it. This substance won't trip me up. Yes, faith is a substance that builds.[1]

Faith … I have none in me right now! Faith in You, God. I know You are able, but will You help me? I'm still struggling, so how do I get more of You, God?

So then faith comes by hearing, and hearing by the word of God![2]

New plan: okay, so I will intentionally and feverishly seek to hear the Word of God. My YouTube search begins to hear good online pastors. I hungered to hear a sermon teaching—multiple, in fact, on the daily.

Therapist at rehab says I need new tools in my toolbox. Really? What does that even mean?

Okay, Google, what's a toolbox?

I can specifically remember when I was struggling with the thoughts of quitting drinking again. Drinking is just so everyday and common, advertised heavily and sensationalized. As a super-social person who likes to be a part of the fun, it was hard for me to change the way I viewed drinking and socializing.

Maybe you have never had a problem with an excessive indulgence. But that thing that you face or have to learn to live with (or without) is the same thing that I face. What is that thing? A role in life you don't want to play, but have to? I don't know what your thing is. It could be embracing widowhood or the loss of a child; it could be infertility, trouble with finances, or repeated relationship failures. What if you struggle with homosexuality or sex addiction, or if your self-esteem is so poor that you let yourself be walked all over? It could be excessive worrying or recurring depression or other mental health instabilities. It could be as common or simple as OCD.

Whatever the thing is, your thing and my thing have the same problem source, answer, and solution. First off, "the thing" we face has a purpose. That purpose is to call us out of the lie we are believing. The lie that makes us revisit that thing over again. Second, the purpose is to free you from that cyclical trip—to replace the lie with the Truth, the Word of God. Once I replaced the lie—excuse me, the *lies*—with truth and grace, with Jesus Himself, the One who is known as grace and truth[3] in scripture. Then I was on my way—on *The Way*. He is the way of escape from all our patterns that bind us. Jesus said it Himself, and we are to follow Him. So long as I stay close to Him, He keeps me free of my own entanglements.

I can go all the way back to the language written in the Old Testament and see God's will for me. It was clear for all of humanity all along. As written in Genesis, humans were always intended to walk and talk freely with God. That was a really neat moment for me as a believer, I came to believe and receive that the whole and entire Bible has promises and guidance specifically for me—for everyone who comes to believe. What a gift! That really was clear to me before in my faith walk and previous faith-seeking practices.

> *I surrendered the need to see the goal made. I switched my mindset to living the goal instead of making the goal.*

So when God's grace gave me repentance (the will to confess my sins), I reconciled myself to God. To reconcile is to make the relationship right. I took my shortcomings and inability, my sin-ignoring heart, and exchanged it all for the blood of Jesus. The greatest swap of all—that is what the gospel promises. Jesus paid it all for me to claim His blood as my salvation and right standing with God. Because this Catholic girl finally quit trying to do right, I finally just *stood* right with God, completely forgiven and able freely to come to God for His love, help, and full acceptance as I was, by just being. God loved me. He came to me at my worst and said, "I paid for all this to be *gone, remembered no more. Come, follow Me, and I will give you rest.*"[3]

This lover of Jesus could finally live in the saving grace and power of the gospel message. I now enjoy walking and talking charismatically with God *about everything.* I am not alone.

I could bring every detail of my mess to God. So much renewal was needed. I had three businesses to run, four kids to nurture and raise, a marriage to repair, and a two-story household to run. All while facing every buried trauma and giving God my totally broken self. The gravity of doing it cold stone sober scared me. There was nothing to soften the blow or take the edge off. I just had never lived this level of "real"—not ever. Vulnerability, transparency, asking for help, admitting I was wrong and didn't know how or what to do next. That was just nuts, to me. Why would someone want to live like that? I was working all that out, learning. I was in process. So meeting that complete insufficiency was painful for me. I've always taken pride in doing things myself and making it an achievement.

You would say I was achievement-driven. So to have a goal that was not readily attainable for me was foreign. Well, as my girlfriends from college and my family all reminded me, "Odilie, you can do anything you put our mind to. Put your mind to it, and just do it." So there I went to "do it" as they say, one moment at a time. As they taught me in rehab, "just for today."

I surrendered the need to see the goal made. I switched my mindset to living the goal instead of making the goal. This helped me a lot because I have always and still continue to be missional or goal-driven.

As I walk and talk with God, He gives me (and you) the grace and truth to victoriously overcome that "thing" that truly is no longer our issue. Once we focus on God more than "the thing," we get closer to God. He reveals to us His strength at work through us, because the thing that used to have power over me and you now has no power over us at all! Amen to His glorious power at work in us.

Just when the story or the gospel message couldn't get any better, it does! God then gives us full access to use His "resurrection power"[3] to reveal in us something so good and so glorious that only God could take the credit for it. This is all because you and I had the courage to hand over to Him the thing that got out of control in our hands. In His very capable, mighty hands, He is liable to make more out of your hopes and dreams than you could ever have imagined.[4] Why? Because He wants good in our lives more than we want it for ourselves. He wants freedom for us way more than we want it for ourselves.

Think about it. Just like when you are cheering on your child or spouse or a relative that you really love, you want them to win. More: you want them to win big-time. No one wants a Big Win for us more than *God*. He is the God of more than enough. He is above all this worldly stuff. In fact, given the opportunity to really lead us, He will give us more than we could ask or think or imagine for ourselves.[4]

So I'll tell you the same thing my dear friend told me when I was struggling to give up the second set of habitual "crutches" in my life—you know, when the thing I gave up became another thing I picked up, "just while I adjust to quitting this thing, I'll use this other thing as a Band-Aid or training wheels," per se. All because I didn't have the right tools. Said another way, in the bicycle analogy, it's the struggle to balance the weight of what I was carrying and still ride squarely and on my own. Either that or I was secretly rebelling and exercising another thing to show that I still had some control over what I was or wasn't going to do. For me, I think I was in a deep depression over not drinking; believe me, pathetic, I know. I realize that probably your reason for having a hard time accepting whatever you have to accept is way more significant. Perhaps a legit mourning comes with a lifetime permanent injury, or an unchanging diagnosis, or a death, or any other thing you can't change. All those reasons are so much more valid to mourn loss over; this I know. But what if the thought of not toasting at my daughter's marriage or wedding dress shopping day makes me cry? So what that as I was receiving IV vitamin infusion therapy during a medically led alcohol detox, someone brought up the Sonoma and Napa valleys, and I bawled crying. I was really looking forward to celebrating an anniversary with my husband there.

God knows it all. He knows you may miss the thought of playing kickball or four-square with your cerebral palsy son or daughter. Either way all those hopes of "one day" matter to our God. So I don't have to feel stupid or guilty because I'm mourning something that wasn't supposed to be for me. God knows all our hopes and dreams, even the ones we don't even know we have in us yet. He cares that I am giving up something I wanted for myself. As you and I let it go and accept what He prefers for us, our growth, He rewards us with better.

BROCCOLI VS. ICE CREAM:
Learning to Like What Is Good for You

It could be that you love potato chips or Breyer's ice cream, and you now must choose kale chips and broccoli, all for your betterment. He knows that giving up Breyer's for broccoli is quite the adjustment. He knows one is so immediately rewarding and tasty and the other not too much. He knows no matter how futile or pitiful our reason for mourning is; he knows the sacrifice it takes. He knows how much you'll need Him to not do that thing you love and miss doing.

Ultimately, He knows that coming into acceptance with something that happened to you that you would not choose means a lot. He knows that your very attempt to come into agreement with what He wants for you, which you don't want, requires so much faith work, belief, and prayer. That is the transformation and closeness He is after. Transforming and preparing your soul and spirit are way more important than our mortal inclinations.

I've realized that once I've overcome that fight-or-flight for closeness with God instead, miracles happen. Once I saw the magnificent work God did in me to redeem me and change me, I wouldn't want to undo what it took to get me there. That thing that hurt so bad was the very thing that gave me the sweetest reward. I no longer wish I could change the thing that changed my heart so much. God brought me a great and real strength and belief, through that thing I was so mad about. I ultimately grew into a surrender of the need to know how it will turn out. I released the need to understand why. I let go of the need to see it "make sense." As I remembered that God is good all the time, I trusted that what He brought me through would eventually make sense either here on this earth or in eternity. I also accepted the promise that He does reward us for our pain and suffering in eternity. The Word promises I will be rewarded for all the trouble and hurt I had to endure.

The apostle Paul says to count our trials joy! Really, that is nuts. I'm not there yet, but I do cling to that promise that having given up what entangled me, for a closeness with God; will be unmeasurably worth it! Every time "I want" that former fleshly way, I say to myself, I choose Your way, God. Right now giving up Breyer's for broccoli is terrible, but I know that it will be way worth it soon. With all my sacrifices, I may never get a physical six-pack stomach in this world, but I will get that spiritual six-pack for eternity in paradise. In common language, we do our part, and God does His. You do your best, and let God do the rest! What He asks us to give up is always for our best.

There is a verse that describes a premise for the promise I speak of: that the glory of your improved temple or house will be greater than the former.[5] You see that you and I are God's living temple! Let us treat it honorably!

If I keep pressing into God's strength in my weakness, i.e., deny the flesh (the premise), it will all play out with a promise. I like to think of the promise as a prize. Hey, the Lord wired me for playing to win!

So now my game-of-Life strategy is to be the channel or vessel that the Lord uses. How? A completely yielded heart to do whatever He asks of me. It's never more than I can handle. Believe me, I know it feels like it, but He is greater than anything we will ever face.

So how did I become so yielded to God's will and not mine? I lie down flat and cry out to God; I still do. I lay all of me down physically, spiritually, emotionally, psychologically. I lay down my pride, my control, my way, my agendas, my hopes and dreams, my responsibilities, my "know-how," my circle of influence—all of it—and I give it all over to God. Believe me, until I moved my whole imagined self-seeking self completely out of the way, I couldn't be my best self. Before then, I stunted my own personal growth, fulfillment, and happiness in life.

When I turned over my will, life became joyful and worth living even in the hardness and disappointments that life comes with. You see, it is our will that sets us apart from the rest of creation, as do our language or words.

Your Words Create Your World. You are living what you are saying.

So miracles will happen in life when I turn over my voice and will for God's leading. Believe me, He wants our individuality and the unique way we are. He wants us to create, just alongside Him. We have a choice to know and love Him; and when we give Him our will and our words, both yielded over to the Creator of the universe, good stuff happens. More than magic happens; miracles happen. How? I have come into agreement with what God wants for me. So in that I've just activated God's good and perfect will for my life. I've also activated my faith by God's resurrection power! How is that for a substance? I can't say that I love faith in the building part, but I do love it when I see what it built. I embrace the mystery that faith operates in unexplainable ways. It requires believing in what one can't see. So instead of being frustrated in the wait of believing, I trust that faith is building what I can't wait to see happen. No matter if the wait is long so long as I say the Word of God over the situation and stay in expectant hope, a good plan will come to be!

The other funny thing about faith is that it is like muscle: the more I use it, the stronger I get. The more I use faith, the further and higher it takes me. Faith takes us to His higher ways. Faith is the building block to my leveling up to a better life.

Sometimes, I just want to stay put. But then God gives me a glimpse or a vision of what we could be. So I go to work. He moves me to move; that's my faith at work. As the apostle James says, faith without works is dead.

So I keep my eyes on the prize or vision God puts in my heart and soul and I move, faithfully. In my short experience with faith, I have experienced my own parting of the seas. I have been flooded by a powerful loving affection from God. He has proven to me that His love is as fierce as a tidal wave coming over me. After I saw and experienced this amazing grace and love, I will never stop exploring how He loves me. Like a great hunting expedition or treasure hunt,

He always keeps me interested and going on what I might catch. I love that I can find new ways to adore God and speak to Him and heightened ways for me hear His leading. All that happens in flow, not force. I never knew that God is so inviting, He wants all to make it into His way of living life in abundance. That is why He wants us to surrender our attitude that we know better than He does. In that sweet surrender we receive more than enough for our never-enough.

MY NEXT STAGE – BOTHERED BY LIFE

Bothered is where I was next in the process. Let's just say I'm a slow spiritual learner. Here might be a good time for a story. So if you haven't aced your test the first time, this is for you. If you have aced your test the first time, don't get cocky; a harder test will come. Stay humble and kind; that's where the real power lies.

There I was in sobriety with friends I adored and admired, except that they could and still do drink. It was my first gathering out in public where there would be drinking in front of me. Free pouring all around. I was wanting to maintain the relationships, so I had to use my faith and believe God would empower me to say no and be able to enjoy myself while I was at it. From going to AA meetings I was told to have a wingman or sober buddy, and if that wasn't possible or enough, to call someone in sobriety. Call me an AA reject, but I just refuse to live my life like that. I'm not going to run to the phone every time I feel uncomfortable or over my head in life. I knew that the reason I was called to be sober was so that I and my family could be delivered. I also knew that I had the highest accountability partner possible, *God*. So down to my knees at a party I went (I was in a removed area). I prayed for God to strengthen me. Just what came of my heartfelt, earnestly seeking prayer, with a note of believing hope that He could and would help me? He did.

In the beginning of all this socializing, I was fearful of being overcome by my former rebellion, the kind I had seen in myself in college. I would do so well for so long, only then to say, "It's time for a recess; I deserve a hall pass. I'm doing whatever I want." I didn't want that to come out of me. So I prayed.

But as my therapist in this first year of sobriety said, "You are not going to fall into a pool of wine or vodka. So just walk away from that temptation, and you'll stay on course, one moment at a time." I had no problem resisting the temptation. What bothered me most, was that *I still wanted to drink*. I still wanted that release, that escape; I wanted to be that giddy and playful girl I was under the influence. I prayed for that to leave me. I prayed, "The Lord is my Shepherd I shall not want" (Psalm 23:1 ESV). I was so mad at myself for wanting something that was such a negative influence. I hated wanting something that had hurt me so often.

If I'm honest, it probably had something to do with wanting my dad's love and attention. He would hurt me so badly, but I still wanted him. Despite all his dark sides, I wanted his adoration and acceptance, reassurance and guidance. I'm sure a psychologist would say I created a pattern, addicted to hurtful rejecting love. There it was, the root of it all: cycles of dysfunction that I had spun in for years. I needed God's healing and complete love to break the cycle and heal the brokenness. When you let God's love in, it hits deep, more on that later.

So much bothered me about sobriety. I was bothered that I was different and would be treated differently at parties or gatherings. I was bothered that I couldn't do that thing. I was bothered by the fear that other people in sobriety would speak all these fear-based stories to me about relapse. I did even know what that was either. I came to find out that it was falling back into your old ways, caving and using that substance you used to use to comfort you. I was bothered by the indefinite nature of "You don't drink forever." I was bothered by the fact that if you were sober for five years and then drank, you would have to take the Day 1 chip at the AA meetings.

I was bothered that a family member that was close to me went sober and, in my eyes, quit living. He only stayed in his house, never went to gatherings in the family, because there was always alcohol of all varieties. He became social only in very small doses. He would visit with the children for a little bit, long enough to impart his love and wisdom and then go to his room and listen to classical music in a rocking chair. I thought to myself, if I had what he had, then I could not do that. I loved being in a crowd with people. How would I socialize comfortably with people drinking?

It bothered me that my dad relapsed from his sober stints way too often. I was bothered by the fact that my dad ultimately suffered a traumatic brain injury in a park from a drunken brawl with another drunk. It bothered me that he was never the same. It bothered me that he was admitted to a psychiatric hospital to help rehabilitate him. Gotta love that, my dad is in the "nut house," addicted, hurt on every level, and I'm in denial or completely not recognizing this. I couldn't, really; I think I would have broken, literally and mentally. I had to stay on course, trying to make a life for myself in college.

It bothered me that rehab at the hospital didn't work; he lost his mind and developed alcohol-induced dementia. It bothered me that he died of consequences to those choices. His body couldn't take the abuse anymore. I couldn't take the heartache of loving him so much anymore. I could now desensitize the shock at his increasingly lower rock-bottoms. I became emotionally removed from him. I would have to face that later.

I'll tell you what didn't bother me: I had written my dad off. He had lied to me and hurt me deeply too many times. Though he was near death and ailing in health, I didn't go visit him. That bothers me still today; how could have I done that? Answer: a calloused, closed-off, stony heart. If you can't reach my heart, you won't hurt it.

Now I was an adult, fighting the same demon that had him, the generational sin of addiction and abuse. It bothered me that I had become what I hated. It bothered me that I felt no one had shown me how to do differently, to cope differently, to love differently. It bothered me that, I didn't have a sober model, someone I could admire who was in sobriety. I needed a success story. I never found that in the AA halls or meetings. I didn't want what they had. What I saw was pain, failed relationships, daily lament and regret, and struggle.

I left the AA halls after a year. It was the best decision for my sobriety and mental and spiritual health and growth. I had a year under my belt of sobriety; stats were peaking in my favor now.

AND SO I RAN

Upon my second approach to sobriety, I chose a sober coach, the Holy Spirit. He was the willpower I didn't have and the best coach I could ever have. In surrender, I could finally hear the leading of the Holy Spirit living in me. I was going to walk with Jesus daily into whatever life looked like in sobriety.

So this is a "sobriety my way" story. It's funny that I ran for therapy. The first marathon I did, I trained running from what I was. In that training period I was fighting to stay sober. I was running from the version of myself I hated and all that I was afraid of. The first full marathon race I ran was space-themed; it was named *Challenger*, and that it was for me. I finished it, but I failed the challenge of not drinking the celebratory beer at the end of the race. I went back to drinking after a six-month clean period. Just like the *Challenger* shuttle blew apart, my sobriety did for me too. I said to myself, *I'll do it my way*. I was in defiant denial, a bad combo. For three months I avoided sobering up. I remained "comfortably numb." I drank myself into depression, a catatonic type. I didn't care who knew I was struggling; I wanted to be and get better but I didn't know how.

I felt lost, truly like something had died. Ridiculous, I know, but totally true. Alcohol was no longer in my bloodstream, but it still claimed too much of my headspace. I had not renewed my thinking. I was trying; I was going to Bible study to help me renew my thinking. I confided in my long-term friend and all the girls of the group that I needed prayer, that I wanted to fall in love with sobriety, that I didn't like sober life yet, I wanted to like it but couldn't.

I was riding the bike of sobriety but not enjoying the ride, and I was using training wheels that were limiting my enjoyment. With those prayers and trusted Godly counsel, my fears, as silly as they were, were banished through God's word of life spoken over me. It was like a soothing balm of calm to my scared and weary heart. So I will share with you that encouragement that was shared with me. Take this to heart.

"You don't need to fall in love with your sober life (a.k.a. life without that thing); you need to fall in love with Jesus!"

So, set aside the fact that your thing is way different than my thing. With proper and custom-made tools for coping with the hardships of life and with a healthy support system, we can thrive and rise to healthy living. In order for me to get out of denial, I had to know the full effect and breadth of what I was facing. I wanted to learn what addiction was and how to beat it. So I asked for help in finding a faith-based addiction rehabilitation program.

I had tried it my way, and I didn't want to fail again. This time I was listening to God. After all, the Word of Life says His way is the only way. I was fighting a pattern that kept repeating in my life and had plagued previous generations. I was going to, with God, boldly face me and my generational sins. I had to do this, so that my children, myself, and my marriage had a chance to have a good life.

So after thirty days of rehab away, I came back to run some more. This time I was running to become who I wanted to become. Instead of being afraid and running from what I was, I was running into who I'd become as a living expression of God's redeeming love.

In my mind I ran like Forrest Gump, like Rocky and Apollo on the beach, like a champion and overcomer. As a Christian I don't believe in luck or coincidence. I know it's a blessing and/or divine appointment. That being said, guess the name of the next marathon I signed up for?

Discovery.

That I did.

I discovered how to feel feelings, stress and doubt and worry, without drinking them away. So could I invite you to discover with me the good that God wants out of us. He already has it packed in us; in faith's discovery we can get through this new process and find or discover that treasure inside of us. So let us as grown and loved adults *FACE* Everything and Rise, not fear everything and run.

I've heard a lot of variants of this acronym, but the important thing is that with Jesus holding us safely, we now face anything we have ever feared. His perfect love casts out all fear.[5] I'll give you a hint: Fears, more often than not, are allowed into our lives to bring us closer to God. This thing will also teach us things about us we didn't know.

In addition, it will also reveal something about God's character we would have otherwise not discovered. For me it was "not alone or forgotten." I had heard the Bible story of the three Hebrew boys, Shadrach, Meshach, and Abednego, who were asked to compromise their faith obedience to God, by bowing down to another false God of their age.[6] They refused, and King Nebuchadnezzar was irate and threw them bound into a fiery furnace with it turned up ten times hotter than usual. They went in; then as the people watched, they saw a fourth person with them. The three made it out alive, and what bound them was burnt off. There were four in the fire unbound; the other one in the fire was seen by the king as the very Angel of God. When they came out, they were reported not even to smell like smoke. The whole kingdom and the king were saved and now only worshipped the one true God of the three Hebrew boys.

Now that was a story that gave me hope. I want to live each of the promises of God, in their thousands. As believers, we are given the same promises as God's special people, both Old and New Testament promises.

So how would this age-old story apply to you and me today? I know that all of us feel the heat of life's pressures and demands. Though it seems that cultural, political, health, and climate threats have become ten times hotter, we will make it out alive and favored, not even smelling like smoke.

Side note: For me, I didn't want to smell like alcohol or cigarettes; those were my binding chains, and recovery was my refining fire. What is yours? Lack mentality, control, obsessive, mental despair, fear-based living and thinking? Don't you want to come out alive and free from what bound you? I did. And Jesus will not let you go through any furnace or trial alone. As we honor God as our first and only love with all we do and say, as the Hebrew boys did, He is sure to save and favor us too.

I felt incredibly weak and not able. But again, I affirmed what was possible through *God's* strength and power.[7] In my weakest, He makes me stronger than ever. At the end of me is the beginning of His miracle through me. No matter what, I was daily affirming what God's holy Word said, not what my feelings or facts showed. Through the Bible-based affirmations I custom wrote out, I learned that God wanted *me* personally to know and receive His abundant grace. How the Word of God actually renews our mind!

The top reason I ever drank in sadness was because I couldn't do it right. Do what right? Anything, in my mind. I wanted perfect outcomes, so ultimately, I could never achieve what I wanted to be and do. I was not enough, yet I didn't let up. God would rewire my head, and now I can be present with what exceeds my desire to have it perfect. I kept affirming that I was being healed of those lies. I would come to believe that I must first accept love to fully love; being a child of God was stand-alone enough. In my complete insufficiency He was supremely sufficient. I learned what it meant to lean in on God. I learned what a relationship with Him was like. I learned that He died for me to succeed at this. He would be with me and get me through.

I stopped over time, feeling singled out in my trial. Instead, I reminded myself I was called and chosen to a different and better path. I was meant to stand out and stand up for a better way to raise a family. I felt in good company; God picked His most legendary and highest preforming people in the Bible to have major obstacles to overcome. I studied these history makers' ways and lessons to apply to my obstacles. All these biblical examples literally came to life. I could finally see that in tremendous loss and affliction, these ordinary people worked for God despite what they had suffered. It wasn't easy, but it was worth it.

So if God has allowed a major life change into our circumstances, then we can know that God has a good plan in store to more than get us through it.

FALLING IN LOVE—
A LOVE I NEVER KNEW

Thank You for loving me just as I am. That was the realization that made me love God so greatly. He wanted the best for me, and I was on a relentless pursuit to discover why He wanted me to know Him so. Since before I was fashioned in my mother's womb, God planted gifts and good plans for me to live out. I wanted that. I would make the next part of my life about fiercely pursuing knowing God and His ways richly. In that and from that overflow, I would know the will and plans of God for my life. They had to be good because the enemy tries to steal and sabotage what is valuable and a force for good.

If, like me, you have had some severe attacks that stole, killed, or destroyed something in your life, that was the enemy. God only gives life abundant. He creates; the enemy perverts or twists and copies. It is the enemy that is the father of lies and accuser of the brethren. All this is written out for you get a hold of who is the author of the story lines in your head. It's written in John 10:10 and this verse came alive to me and was finally the revelation of my life. I started to evaluate everything I was thinking, saying, and doing through that verse. Then I could know whose kingdom I was serving, the King of heaven and earth, the author of life abundant, or the Lord of this world, the force for evil—Satan.

I knew that God had called me to walking and talking and creating with Him more closely, with no entanglements that stole, killed, or destroyed my relationships and purpose in this world. My thing was to be fully present, sober. I went to work on how to master it. It had mastered me long enough. So I drew on that powerful verse of God's Word to get me through hard days, the down days, and the why-me days. I would get down on my knees and say, "God, I know You want this for me more than I want it myself. I trust that what You have for me is better than caving to my temptations. Get me through this because Your Word says that I will. You always provide a way out of temptation. Your word says to rely on and confidently trust in You, God."

If I fix my focus on God, not my problem, my God reigns, and my problem shrinks. I affirmed daily that greater is He within me than what is of the world (whatever I was struggling with).[8] I would say out loud, "I believe Your Word and its power to help me. In my weakest moment, You, God, are nearest and most available to me. You are described as immediate and speedy help. I do believe that if I call on You and invite You into the battle of each choice I make, I win." Then, the temptation would pass, and I moved on in thanksgiving.

But the "missing" was frequently there. I kept praying, "God, take the desire away. When will I not feel jealousy for those who do life and are able to 'unwind' with drinks? How come they get to? What did I do so differently that got me here?" I just kept praying and saying, "I'm sorry, God, that I feel this way. I will choose to believe Your Word over my feelings." I learned to affirm frequently that courage is greater than > comfort and faith is greater over > fear and He is greater than > I. *My greatest challenge became to keep trusting God to get me out of my head's fiery trials.* Could I really believe what God said in the Bible about us believers? Could I really believe that His message was truly about and directed at me? Like a holy salve, the Word could be applied specifically to hurting hearts, not just the more holy people.

I did believe in God's promises and His miracle-making ways. I just kept reading my easy reading Bible so that I'd come to believe in my heart and know in my mind and be sure in my spirit that *God wanted me well!*

I would come out free and dancing about the furnace like those Hebrew boys, if I chose to obey God and not bow down to the false God of quick escape and comfort. I knew that because Jesus died to have me live free and abundantly, if I stayed faithful to the process, life would get better and sweeter than my life before.[9]

Little by little my daily struggles turned into daily gains. His transformative power in my life was at work. I affirmed that if God truly did die for me to live free of shame and guilt, then I would relentlessly get to know God until I was given this gift of freedom from my harshest critic, *me.*

I know God did not die a brutal and extravagantly punishing death if it was not for our complete healing and forgiveness of sin. It was not my mission to white-knuckle my way through raising kids and sobriety; no way. He loves us better than our parents love us or we love our kids. He is the *good Father.* In His strength, I persevered. I was living life to the full in His grace! I learned to celebrate my smallest and largest gains with tremendous praise and thanks! Little is big in *God's* kingdom! I kept inviting God into each and every bit of me and my life's choices. He kept making sure I'd win.

The remarkable thing about making it through temptation is that self-discipline grows. It's like a muscle; the more I used it, the stronger it got. I knew that God chose us for each of our battles so that with him we could win. Purpose-stealing giants of fear, doubt, and despair will fall to faith used and hurled at any giant we face. God planted in my heart the truth that we were born to win, in and with Him. I was born to more than survive, I was born to thrive. "Born to *win*; thrive, not just survive"—those phrases rose up in my spirit. I wouldn't let up until I saw my life become more like a thriving and less just surviving. The Bible describes God as the Master Gardener who prunes and cuts back what needs to go. I loved that I confirmed that vision when I read that the gardener is never closer to his vine than when he is clipping. I pictured I was being clipped and held all the same until my life looked like a beautiful and colorful garden of life.

The bottom line to helping me and you thrive at life and succeed at overcoming "that thing" is to say to self, "Listen, you with the bad temper or negative viewpoint, you clearly won't be the winner here. Jesus is victor overall. I claim His victory over my life and torment of doubt, you must *go!* I serve the God of peace, so you, taunting with reminders of my past mistakes or what I'm not good at, you must leave, in the name of Jesus." This has never failed me and helps me thrive living in God's glory. When I give credit where credit is due, He wins every time. When we see Jesus as personally claiming victory over what attacks us, we realize it's not about our strength, but His infallible strength in us. Grace, what powerful thing.

HIS SACRED HEART FOR YOURS

END OF CHAPTER REFLECTIONS

A Glimpse at His Heart ...

A Step into the Sacred Chambers of His Heart—His Holy Word

I will think on these things; Whatever is lovely

This is a new day. Love has not given up on you. You are His beloved and are already lovely. Lovely is easy on the eyes and soul; pleasant. "Come to me all of you who are weary and burdened, and I will give you rest ... learn from me ... I am gentle and humble in heart ... (in me) you will find rest for your souls" (Matthew 11:28–29 NASB)

Take a praise break because you are His! You were meant for so much more than where you have gone on your own. Now that you have given God the pen to help you write your story, the story is just now getting good!

This is just the beginning.

The best is yet to come.

Song:
"Known" by Tauren Wells.
"You are Loved" by Stars Grow Dim.
For a special love letter to you, see Appendix A in the Extras section.

A Guided Prayer for You

Lord God and King, I now give You the pen to my story. I now realize that You loved me so much that You wrote me into the whole timeline of eternity as a critical character of a purpose You need only me to fulfill. You are so serious about my individuality and my name that You wrote my name in Your hand too. Lord, that is so special. I am so thankful and joy-filled that You love me so. You know me so well and want me to play a role for You and Your purpose. Lead me into knowing what You are like, and help me be more and more like You. I thank You that as I learn of You and Your ways, You will reveal more to me. You are a promise maker and a keeper of them. Help me unfold the promises of Your glorious ways on my story. Lord, once You share the script with me, help me not forget my lines! I love You, Abba Father!

Your white space …

7

YOU'LL CONTINUE TO GO THROUGH IT UNTIL YOU BREAK THROUGH IT!

*How Not to Plateau or
Go around the Same Mountain
Over and Over Again*

BELIEVE AND RECEIVE

I hope that you get this faster than I did. First things first: God loves you before you do one thing right. He died for us while we were unbelieving and sinning terribly against Him. So right off, come to know and receive that you can never in your own right be good enough to receive all that God has for me and you.

Are you ready for it? *God sees and knows all.*

He knows you better than you. He knows your sitting and lying down. *He knows your thoughts, your intentions, your inclinations.* There is nowhere you can go apart from God, *whether you admit he is your God or not.*

Before I came to believe that God had asked me to give up certain habits and fleshly character traits, I didn't want to go where God was calling. It could have been that my nine-year-old daughter wrote me a letter asking me to stop drinking wine. But then I realized I that did not reflect a Christian woman. I was living a double life. I didn't want to change, but I did want to "know God personally," as a further-along Christian might describe. I was hungry to know Him but felt nothing yet. So I clung to verses that gave me a vision for a better way of being. I had always wanted to be godlier, and this was my opportunity to seek and study and know more of God.

If I was called to a sober life to bring God glory and be my best self, then I would. Once I came to the end of me, I held on to the Savior who was holding me.

I heard in my spirit, the verse the apostle Paul wrote, "To live a life worthy of the calling you have received. Be completely humble and gentle; be patient, bearing with one another in love."[1]

That verse made my soul spring in motivation. It also began to literally renew my perspective, to change my mind. As the secular world says, change the way you look at things, and things will change. But with the true and transformative Word of God, I gave that happy mantra some Holy Ghost power. I transformed my mind and as a result saw the same situations differently. Though I really didn't want this change, I wanted what it could give me more. I desperately wanted to have a relationship with God. Moreover, I desperately wanted to save my kids and marriage from the pain and wake of my addiction. I knew that God could and would give me His power to overcome my cyclical and sinful, immature ways of coping with stress.

I wanted to come fully into myself. I knew I was living beneath my spiritual means. I felt that call, that God had made me to be *His* more. Since I had a habit of numbing my pain before, what would life be like living on all five senses?

I'm telling you, my soul always felt too much; my mind thought too much. So as I drank, I would numb away what I was feeling and thinking.

How did I get so sensitive? I think that was built into me as a very young baby. My mom said that she was ripped away from her life as a daughter of privilege and means into a life as a pregnant foreigner with no means. At only nineteen years old, she suddenly was a new wife to a husband who worked to provide and had a dark side. He would drink excessively and was way more than harsh with her. When I was born, she said I became her love and best friend. She said she would speak to me as if I was a fresh journal; she would write into my soul her pains and loves. She said that I was great at consoling her crying and that she loved holding me.

I value that memory she speaks of. I'm sure I was the most adorable baby and toddler counselor, I can see my cute brown-eyed baby-self smiling, cooing, and taking her mind off of her very difficult life adjustments. I'm sure that I said with my eyes and soul, "Mama, I love you. You are so beautiful to look at, you are so fun to be with. I love it when you come get me in my crib, it's my biggest joy. I love it when you speak to me. You are the best *mama!*" I recently reenacted this with her, and we just laughed and cried and thanked God we had each other, even if we sometimes get under each other's skin. None of that matters; it's petty stuff, and love matters most.

Anyhow, my mom had no support in this big move. Remember in the 1970s there were no web chats, or even phone communication between countries; phone calls even within the United States were costly.

Money fights were common, sometimes over the phone bill because at times it came to three hundred dollars, which back in the seventies would be a ridiculous amount.

So to defuse the situations, I was Mom's comforter and entertainer. She apologizes now for leaning on me too much and brainwashing me against letting a man dominate me, but I'm sure I loved it! With all that one-on-one attention, I loved her so very much; she was the only person I wanted to be with. Babies are sensitive souls; they are fresh from heaven sent, so they disarm and comfort like the best of them.

As I grew, I didn't know how to handle this gift of sensitivity. I think I became too sensitive. Then as a teen and even young adult I had a really tough time shaking off the upsetting nature of whatever was happening in life. People liked me and they would share disturbing or hard things. I became a great listener and people would love that I was compassionate. They could see I genuinely cared and that I would try to comfort them. So all that was great, but it stayed with me. When I was of age, drinking helped me unload it. It was a normal way of dealing with stress in my family to drink after hard days.

Then to worsen my nature, I loved approval. I knew that being an overachiever and perfectionist got me the recognition I craved. All of these were good attributes that, when used and unloaded properly, make one a great person to be around. But those same attributes become terrible character flaws when a person has had a traumatic upbringing with little to no leading on how to adult and manage stress and handle decision-making and finances.

It didn't help of course that my high school years were plagued by more family struggles. I had five men leave me and my family. My precious grandfather died; I was super close with him. My uncle, my godmother's husband, was suddenly taken in a fatal plane crash. Then there was my stepdad, not my current one; he rocked our world in a short ten-year period. What happened with him is really a whole book in itself, but to be brief, I felt betrayal, major trust issues, and heartbreak from him. I fought tooth and nail not to let him into my heart; as a fifteen-year-old, I thought he was too young, carefree, and clueless.

In my heart he stole my mom, my relationship with Mom. Truly all did change when he came into her life. So I didn't want to give respect to a guy who had robbed me of Mom's attention and stolen the chance of my mom and dad getting back together. That is a silly childhood dream; most children of divorce wish it too, but then I got over it. Or so I thought. Once my stepdad proved himself faithful to our family, Mom and we three kids bonded and lived our teen and young adult life all together for ten years. We even got two precious new siblings out of the mix.

Then came the heartbreak. He broke my mom's heart and left her pregnant with their second child. The clincher: he was leaving Mom because he decided to become involved with another man. Even though he was a product of deep hurt and abuse in many ways, I despised him for so long after all this drama and turmoil and heartbreak he caused.

So I compensated in many unhealthy ways. We older kids all tried to support my mom through this emotional loss, the ruin again of her family. In our Latin religious family this was a major no-no. But there was no saving the marriage, he was repressing being homosexual and admitted he wanted to practice the gay lifestyle. To make it all worse, he tried to hide it from us; he was embarrassed. He promised me that I wasn't losing a dad, that he would always be our dad. He lied. He lied about so much. All that worsened my trust issues.

For me it awakened the same hate and trust issues I had towards my biological dad. The memories that formed early on that were so conflicting. My tendency to love the one that hurts and ignores me most seemed to double or probably more in strength. I'll blame that on teenage hormones, a very distant relationship with God, Daddy wounds on top of Daddy wounds, ugh disclaimer; not my current

Stepfather, He is wonderful. Anyhow, it was all so dysfunctional and pain-filled and embarrassing to me.

I hid it all from all my mom; she was in way worse pain. I hid it from friends and buried the pain and focused on other things. I was always good at dissociation and escapism. I wanted first love so badly, I accepted whatever love was given to me. I was promiscuous; all that young love was dysfunctional, obsessive, addictive, and full of betrayal too. Oh, there went some more self-esteem and trust. I believed I was damaged goods and unworthy of respectable committed love.

Then my real dad died, just as I was trying to build a life for myself at college. I was a mess inside. I never even went to see my dad before he died. He had hurt me too deeply, betrayed my trust too many times, and lied all the time. I moved on, or so I thought, I wrote him off too.

It was easy to hide my pain in a college lifestyle of promiscuity and drunkenness on the weekends and major achievement drive and excelling in academia during the week. I was in full focus of becoming "something valuable": a doctor. When I wasn't taking more than a full load of classes, I was working double shifts, partying, and throwing myself at men. Terrible, and totally what you should not do when you are processing such pain and dysfunction. But as I learned from my two dads, hurt and broken people will hurt people and break more things.

The gravity of dysfunction has no bottom. It goes all the way to the core of the earth, till death. *But!* There is hope, the Lord our Savior defies gravity and dysfunction. He is Messiah, the Savior of all the world. Now I know of that Savior, but back then, God was a far-off uninvolved entity I would meet in heaven. Back then, I didn't know anything about a Savior who helps me live daily life well. I would meet my Savior in a born-again type of way, later.

The Savior I now know, Jesus, can heal anything. I hadn't known God like that yet. He was just the amazing God in the sky I'd ask for blessings and protection from. I was a Christmas and Easter Catholic and a really bad one at that. I pretty much only spoke to God when I had to hit the "Oh no, I blew it" button. I lost my closeness with Him, but He never for one moment lost track of me. He was always protecting me from myself and nudging me along on the path and direction that would lead me back to Him.

Now a young professional, a doctor of audiology. Look at me now, Mom; I made something of myself!

The party lifestyle and binge drinking that I learned in college was hard for me to break from as I become a young professional as a doctor of audiology. If I'm honest, I hid my deep sense of worthlessness and insecurity in my earned title. The title gave me a sense of noble value. I loved serving as a specialist of hearing and balance. Monday through Friday I was a diligent medical professional. I diagnosed and treated from sweet one-day-babies to amazing veterans with no residual hearing left. I taught them how to hear the first time with cochlear implants and hearing aids and rehabilitated them into living with hearing loss or auditory processing disorders.

Living as a newlywed with no family or friends in a new city was exciting but also hard. On the weekends I thought I was some Hollywood, professional partier. Somehow, I stayed a high-functioning alcoholic. I was still hiding a lot of me from myself, other people, and mostly God. All this led me down a slippery slope. Fast forward thirteen years, and when I wasn't a super-cute wife and mom and striving medical practice owner, I was escaping in wine.

I excused it with "I work hard, I deserve to relax." Truth sat in the wine inside the sippy cups at afternoon soccer. I abused alcohol. I had a drinking problem. *I had developed into the alcoholic I swore I would never be.*

I was sad inside for no reason. I was fighting my husband because I thought he was trying to control me and belittle me when he told me to stop or control my drinking. My cute family life became dysfunctional too; my kids, who were only eight and four, were telling me not to drink. How did this all happen? I thought I had outrun my dysfunction. Nope. There it was.

So when I faced all this, I had to believe only God could save me and my family. Only God could get this Latin party girl to quit drinking. At this point I was singing my high school anthems to myself: "You Gotta Have Faith" by George Michael and "Living on a Prayer" by Bon Jovi. What can I say? I hadn't too much Christian music in my soul's repertoire yet. That, and I'm a product of at the pop culture in the nineties.

So I was ready for real healing and more: a real *God*. I was ready to believe that my Lord and Savior had truly come to redeem me and my way of living and thinking and feeling and choosing. I had heard about grace. I was ready to receive it to become a better and stronger person. I didn't want to fail at trying to do right anymore. I wanted my behavior to reflect more of the good change happening on the inside of me. I was thrilled to receive this free gift of grace. I wanted to succeed. I wanted to heal too. *Amazing grace*—you mean I could have well-being and healing, all without earning it? This was so foreign to me. How had I "known Christ as my Savior" since I was eight and still didn't know that grace existed in this way?

I had to unlearn some bad religious beliefs, with serious study in the Word of God, the Bible. I paired hunger for the Word of God with hard-core psycho-evaluations, pain-filled therapies, and Bible studies; I reflected, journaled, worked out, and went to three different physical churches a lot! I did know that grace was mine to have freely, but I also knew enough about Bible story after Bible story that those who received healing had to do their part to receive the miracle. There was the thirty-eight-year-old crippled man in Luke. Jesus said to him, "Get up, pick up your mat, and walk." So I, too, would carry my mat and walk. I would "work, work, work" for my healing (they say this at the end of AA meetings). You see what I see: still couldn't do the grace thing too well.

LEARNING MANDARIN

I asked my therapist, "Why is this so hard?" I've never been so challenged in life. I could always do pretty well at things. Why was this so hard for me?

She said, "Odilie, 'it's as if you are learning Mandarin Chinese. It's completely foreign to you. You have had no exposure to it, and it's complex." That helped me be patient with myself.

I had an issue with being angry and hard on myself frequently. I would have full conversations with myself. I would say to myself, "Let's get real honest here. Who do you think you are fooling?" Then when I thought I got to the deepest level of source, I'd go deeper still.

I would ask God to help me do the work. I couldn't go back to my previous coping mechanisms of numbing, escaping, denying, distracting myself, self-hatred, overcompensating, closet hiding my feelings, or any other barrage of defense techniques. This had to be dealt with so that I could live free and become more capable of managing emotions and stress.

If I could relate my emotional or communication quotient to a type of dinosaur, when handling life surprises and stressors, I was a T-rex: a very large, angry beast filled with power struggles and inner turmoil, with tiny arms. Who can raise kids and live successfully with such traits?

With a smile on the outside, and a large crashing disposition on the inside, receiving grace was too far for me to reach with my tiny T-rex arms. I had to receive this grace.

The most valuable thing I continue to practice is that when I want to beat myself up, I remind myself that I am already fully known and loved by God long before I ever become saintlier. He fills my basic needs for belonging and authenticity and genuineness. Through honest and genuine praise and worship I believe, I was cleaned from the inside out. I now let myself receive good gifts and love from God and people.

I accepted and received that grace can't be earned. This grace is not only for all saints but for all sinners. I learned that grace wasn't just for addicts and adult children of alcoholics; it was for every well-formed healthy person too. On any human's best day, we are still not good enough, not one of us. That helped me. I overcame the religious belief that I had to do my penance and live out my amends forever for all the bad I had done. Wrong! False. Once I accept the death and resurrection of Jesus for my sin, past present and future, I can receive the gift of redemption. All my wrong is paid in full and forgotten. I know, that is exorbitant talk. But that it is the true story of the saving gospel message. In Christ by grace through faith, I am the righteousness (that means the goodness) of Jesus Himself, the only human never to have sinned.

So let me ask you these questions: Do you have any T-rex traits? Does a piece of you have a hard time believing you are lovely enough to be loved by a merciful and good God? Do you have itty-bitty T-rex reach about any of these: genuine friendships? confrontation? people pleasing?

We all need to expand our reach or capacity with respect to our flaws. But more importantly, I realized that without Christ, I derail. It would take me two seconds to go back to what I knew and did for a good bit of my life, what was familiar, but also limiting to my growth and my outreach to others as an image bearer of Christ. But with Christ, all bets are off. I become unstoppable; a sure winner. In Him I have a bright future, and His Word is incorruptible. It bears fruit and gives life, no matter what pains this life brings.

YET ANOTHER ANIMAL IN ME

Christ is known as both the lion and the lamb. I believe, since we are created in His image, we have a little bit of both those spirit animals in us. We all tend to lean into one tendency—either too much lamb and not enough lion, or too much lion and not enough lamb. This is where seeking and inviting Christ into our very core being helps us discover where we need refinement. Outside of our natural manner, which character trait do we need to develop by way of our surrender and leaning into His supernatural way?

My vulnerable humility, the lamb, was not a part I let out. That dependent, almost blind creature that would literally eat himself off a cliff was what I needed to be more of to heal? Are you kidding me? I was all lion, *roar!* But the end of myself, and its puffed-up pride, begins the real work of grace. Weaknesses, I realized, released God's greatest strength over me. It was written over two thousand years ago; why would it take me so long to learn to rely on God? The Word of God says that where we are weakest, *He is our power to overcome.*

One animal's way of being would be a soul-destroying way. All lamb, and you are a people-pleasing follower; all lion, and you are a predator ready to devour anything weaker or smaller than you. But surrendered to Christ, we can illustrate the supernatural situation described in the Bible: a Lion and lamb lying close together. Lion-like authority and lamb-like tenderness.

God chose me for this.

In all that I was going though, I kept reminding myself: whatever you face, He knew this would be for your good and growth. If you start asking Jesus-believing people what their story is, and really listen, over and over you will see a redemption. I have seen it in abrupt deaths, sudden divorces, terminal illness, and even wayward family members. Have you ever sat next to someone in church and seen them praise God for being so good, when that person had been left via text after twenty years of marriage? What about when their child has a terminal cancer, or their spouse is on a ventilator or has suffered a severe stroke? I have. It rocked my faith. I cried for them, I prayed to God to strengthen and cure their affliction. It strengthened my faith to see a passion for Christ in the midst of trial.

I prayed for protection from such pain and devastation. I wondered if my faith would remain under such trial. I know the closer I stay to Jesus, the more likely I am to remain in the cover of His strength, no matter what the trial. His name is my strength in life's storms. Never have I seen it fail: when a believer and lover of Christ keeps believing through the terrible times, God gives them double for their trouble. In each case God has been faithful to give a better scenario in their comeback story. How? Because God is a promise keeper, and His Word says that what the enemy tries to use to destroy us, God turns around and uses for our good. *If that doesn't convince you that you can and will overcome, then read on.* I will reveal what helped me not go back to my natural way of being.

I had been studying the names of God. I wanted to know more about the God who knew me in my innermost being. In the first book of the Bible God tells Moses His name is I Am. I wanted to read this and understand this for myself. Who calls Himself *I AM*? Don't you think that strange? I did.

In a self-guided study of the names of God throughout all translations, I learned that with the great I Am, I could experience Him to be whatever I needed Him to be. He was and is and always shall be what I need and what I am not enough of., He is Savior, defender, strength, provider, counselor, leader, and friend. He is all I'll ever need. Once I saw His strength would come help me every time, I said to myself, "I can't, but I can, through the great I Am." I wrote that on the back of my first marathon race shirt. I still say that to myself when I'm way beyond me, out of my league. I believe that that's where God wants each of us, going beyond natural capabilities. *I want to live a life beyond me and into eternity.*

More and more I trusted God with all that I wasn't and also all I wanted to be. How and why? I couldn't afford to go back. I had too much to lose. As they say in NASA (*Apollo 13*), "Failure is not an option." That kept me from going back. Where your eyes look to, your body goes; that kept me moving forward.

God's command to everyone says, "Love; love one another as you love yourself." That gave me a plan. *I hated myself. I couldn't forgive myself.* I couldn't even look at pictures of the past couple of years when I was really stupid and sick. I didn't know how I would forgive myself, but I knew who would help me. If the Lord *died to forgive me*, who was I to deny God's authority of forgiveness? I had no choice but to get with Jesus and forgive.

My plan … I would come to know God like never before. I would seek Him with all my heart and learn of those eight thousand-plus promises. I just started with the simplest ones I knew: Knock and the door shall be opened;[2] and those who seek the Lord with all their heart will find Him.[3] Just one of those promises was sure to lift off my own self-loathing. I did believe that with the living and transformative Word of God I would eventually heal and love myself again. If for some reason you don't believe it, dare try it. Do you know how many Christians came to believe by trying to disprove God's claims?

I had seen enough Christians go deep into the Word and lifestyle God provides, and I wanted that gift too. I would work with God to create the "blessed life" He died to provide for me. All I had to do was seek God, worship Him first and only, and trust that, though my progress was slow, I was healing and growing into who I've always wanted to be, loved and known. I knew if I kept at learning to seek the Lord first and to give him first place in my life, all else would follow. God said, "Seek Me first, and all else shall be added unto you."[4] Eventually I would live in God's providence and blessings. Yes, I knew there would be trials and sacrifices too, but the blessings far outweighed the cost of carrying my cross. I have always been tenacious; this time it would be about the things of God—His truth, not my buffet-style truth. You know, I believe in that, but I don't believe in this. I can do this, but I won't do that. This time it was His way all the way! I would. I would let nothing steer me off that track. I wanted to know God's type of love for me and to live in it.

Life without God's blessings is miserable. In fact, the Bible describes two paths in life, blessings or curses. Which one do I want to be on? The Word of God describes a choice between the narrow gate and the wide road. It's hard to live in the Christian narrow path sometimes, but then I get favor so massive and blessings so bright, joy so indescribable, that it makes it all worth it. I lived in misery and curses long enough to know that, though His way is narrow, it is way better! I pray, child of God, you get this quicker than I did!

Every time I doubted my call, my ability to go where He called and do what He asked me to do, I reminded myself: *God died for me to be able to conquer this!* Same goes for you. If you find yourself living the Christian life in the easy chair, I promise you, you are shortchanging yourself. There is another gear to your spiritual growth that you haven't discovered.

He doesn't need us; He wants us. He wants us all to be loved on richly by Him. I don't mean that in the money sense but in a depth of awareness. When we receive His love, we become His love and hence reflect Him and give out His love. All that reveals the blessed life to other people. This calls more people to the faith, which brings us closer to the return of Christ.

In that second and glorious coming of Christ, evil will be bound. Death, illness, and unjust pain will be obsolete. It sickens us to see evil take things and people from us for now, but God is the greatest over all. Soon enough, He will return what was unjustly taken from us. It is written that the gates of hell and its evil work will not prevail. When I internalize and stand on that promise, I feel as if I just knocked out Satan with Thor's hammer. In the best-of-all-time good versus evil fight, we win!

So if God died to conquer all the sting of sin and death and to give me and you an abundant life, then let us persist in the narrow road he gave us to ~~walk~~ run. Time is short; let us get our getting! God never takes away what He doesn't plan on giving back even better than what was lost. Believe me I know how hard this is to live out. Usually, your reward is not given until well after you are proven dedicated and faithful, which means tests of faith and time. Lots of it; sometimes we must wait for that reunion or reward with a loved one we lost until the other side of eternity. What comforts me most is what's a hundred years (or however many blessed days I live) when I have all of eternity to be with Christ, the blessed Trinity, the entire family, and all the angels and saints, including my gone-on-to-heaven loved ones.

Just like a toddler in wait on Christmas Eve, I know it feels like forever of a wait, either because you are so excited for what is to come or because it hurts that much to live right now. The key is that "right now" feelings pass; faith is eternal. Jesus gives the strength in the waiting. If it is hurting too much or you are caught up in feelings too often, give up the feelings as the dictator of your day. Feelings are great representatives and terrible governors. Let the Lord your God preside as the primary and highest elected officer of your entire being, and you'll learn to keep your feelings in check.

Now take it from this Latina hothead and drama queen, who stuffed my feelings before, I learned to give them over to God and His help in managing them. In my family, I've lost four father figures, a grandma, a grandpa, a sister, and a brother-in-law, along with several sweet babies and toddlers, multiple close friends, and mentors to sudden senseless deaths. Not only did I walk through the grief myself, but I watched and supported my family members as they survived their devastating losses. Jesus restores. We won't understand senseless loss, but He is faithful to give us healing to hold on and the hope of a sweet reunion, if we let it happen. We give the willing heart, and He gives the restorative work from devastating pains and losses.

I have lost a great deal in my life. So much so that I feared more pains of life. Would it happen again? Would tragedy hit even closer or harder next time? That's a terrible way to live, and I didn't have to live like that anymore! It's so hard to trust this, but do. If you do the challenging work of discovering the blessing alongside the loss, the sting of the loss will be removed by God's lavish love. God gives comfort. Walk in it, live in it. Take it, it is yours. Biblical grieving is only short-term, then Jesus's power is to be exercised. This means you have to put forth effort, with God. Jesus is to be taken up as our comforter and healer. Anger, that is sadness's big brother, anyway,

Questions and doubts He can take and handle them all. He is God over all.

Know that the communion of saints cheers us on. Until we meet again. Until then, keep taking all losses to Jesus, He is always giving us blessing and comfort until we are all together again.

DON'T RUN AWAY

The truth hurts sometimes. You can run, but you can't hide. Processing all this mentally, spiritually, and psychologically was a lot. Running helped me process what I couldn't say. Not because I was ashamed to say it; God had lifted the shame off me. But more because my English and Spanish languages could not put into words what I faced. So running became one of my spiritual love languages. In those repeated steps my spirit lifted up prayers. Though I had no idea what I was praying for, *God knew* exactly. All that running meant this goal-chaser signed up for another marathon. The third one I got smarter. I rallied my entire family, we partnered up and ran a relay marathon.

I have found that God uses life and our interests to drive us into the truths He wants us to come to know

Though the road you and I are called to run is the narrow road, he doesn't want us to go it alone. He wants us to do it in community and with support. It truly makes the journey lighter and more enjoyable. So I called our team my big Latin family. We ran our best race. It was an epic journey and a sweet finish. My grandmother was even able to be there, and that was pretty amazing because she lives in Nicaragua. She cheered each one of us through. God showed me that in networks of support we go farther! I even put that on our family shirts together: we go farther. And that we did, united and sharing the burden, we ran our best race. In community and family, we became obstacle slayers, by sharing what God spoke to us through the experience. For me, I learned how to draw from God's deep inner strength, perseverance, and hope of what was to come. This race was called Atlantis. And that it was for me; an exploration of a deep space of my soul. I allowed encounters with spiritual depths of His love for me.

Let me explain, in case you are like me. I took "God loves all his children" as a blanket statement, meaning God loves and cares for me in the masses of his people. But it's not like that; His love for us is not vague or general like the love for the world. His love is deeply individual. At about this time I was finally believing and accepting that truth. God knew me intimately and personally, not just as part of a large church body.

So, as I said before, I don't think there any of those race names was by coincidence. Step by step, I ran in my lane toward each of the spiritual advancements that somehow reflected the names and appointed times of those same races. Let us take note that whatever God has called us to, planned or unplanned, don't avoid it or store it for later review. Go through it, all while looking to and trusting God. He does have a specific message to show us, a particular strength to deposit that only that specific experience can give. It is for our good, or He wouldn't have allowed it.

So make the most of it, and run it—*not to impress, but to encounter.* An encounter is an experience. Although we can't explain it well, after a true encounter, you know that you know that you were very present with God. There in that experience, allow Him to teach and show you some element of God that you didn't know before.

For me, I let God speak to my spirit with each mile of life. If I didn't understand, I didn't get frustrated. I ran into wonder and curiosity instead of my previous way of running away from hurt and dissatisfaction.

Whether you brought this season on yourself or not is a moot point. God wastes nothing, including our mistakes. He even uses our blatant sin for our good and His purpose. I speak from experience.

If the Holy Spirit brings attention to a sin, then it is because He is ready to empower us to conquer it. I was blessed to find out that conviction is the Holy Spirit calling us to change with His power. He is not shaming us.

The devil, on the other hand, points at our sin and continually reminds us of it. It is known in the Bible as condemnation or guilt and/or shame. However, its presence on us can be incredibly heavy. The Holy Spirit, however, invites the will to change, and He empowers us to move closer, not run away. The devil also points things out to make us feel cast out. He then accuses us so that we're continually looking back to what happened and stay stuck forever in his rut of lies and self-regret and shame. One father, the father of lies, reminds us that we will never be enough. The other Father, the Father of truth, reminds us of what limitless could look like through *Him*. It is the triune or three-part power of *one holy God* that empowers me to become who He made me specially to be. See the difference? Who is your father? You get to decide.

So back to discovery. Can you allow yourself to step alongside me and my growth in overcoming that "thing"? Even just the distraction of doing too many good things can block us from our specific purpose and fulfillment. Can you see yourself growing up in a new awareness, a laser-like focus to be about the refinement of your character, relationships, and habits? Will you step into discovering with me? If you so choose, you'll step into your wonderful. The caveat is that you have to be okay with surprise and process.

You will? Great! I'm honored and excited for you too. I'll share more of how and what I discovered so that you can get to your own discoveries. Please know that as I have walked through this whole season of restoration and the documenting of it, I have been praying for you, the reader of this, your heart and your willingness. I hope you know you *are* prepared to do this, whether you feel like it or not. Stay dedicated to the process of honest discovery, and invest the time with the things of God. God has packed an express part of Him in each of us. He has packed a special purpose and plan in each of us.

In the wonder of loving God, we get to know the God within us. Therein lies the plight for patient discovery. *What has God packed in me? What in you?* It is all individual and as unique as each of us.

Just to remind you gently, it takes making God a priority and choosing time with Him over other activities. Cut out noise, and give God your free time. Believe He will show up for you, and press past the thought that "This is stupid of me ... I feel nothing, I see nothing ...." Press past that thought, and wait in hope, not doubt. Stay consistent, and redirect your heart, mind, and soul when attention wanders. Stick to consistently spending time with God. He will show up and show off for just you. Ask, and you shall receive.

God revealed in me ... *nah.* I was too bad and too unworthy. There is grace for that nonsense. Yes, grace was hard for me to accept, but is anything too hard for God? No! I'm still in the continuing discovery and adventure of what He has in store for me. The word of God says it's a new *thing*, a new way![5] I couldn't wait to have it play out. What was the new thing?

HIS SACRED HEART FOR YOURS
END OF CHAPTER REFLECTIONS

A Glimpse at His Heart …

A Step into the Sacred Chambers of His Heart—His Holy Word

I will think on these things; Whatever is admirable; To be admirable is described as deserving respect or approval. That's what grace can do, for me and you!

They will have no fear of bad news; Their hearts are steadfast, trusting in the Lord. (Psalm 112:7 NIV)

Take a praise break. You have just received a new and empowered Heart. Awaken to what unconditional godly love is. Song: Believe for it; Cece Winans 2021
Call it Grace
Unspoken Released Nov. 20, 2015

A Guided Prayer for You

Almighty God and Father, Your grace is so powerful. I thank You for unmerited favor, grace. I now realize that You loved me fully and completely before I ever did one thing right. You even loved me when I was so rotten to You. Thank You that once I confessed my sin, You forgave it fully. I ask You to keep me growing from grace into more grace. In Your grace, I become able. May I be more able to love You and be loved by You. I point to Your love as at the salve to all wounds.

Never let me stray from loving You.

Your white space ...

8

IDENTITY

Do New! It Is the Way. Fun Fact.
Christianity as a Movement Was Known
as 'The Way' in Its Infancy. 1

Okay, God—You Made Me New! How Do I Do New?

On this discovery into the depths of His love for me, I saw that God was for me in all things. When I saw that truth, I could defeat not only the habitual thing I turned to, but also the character flaws and perceptions that led to the habitual bad habit. One of them for me was "the hustle." I finally stopped the hustle and the bustle to prove my worth or make my mark in the world.

In a family that comes from the third world, you figure out how to do this hustle at an early age. I finally defeated the giants of "What's in this for me?"—a skill that comes with the hustle of survival mode. Anyone who knows the hustle knows how it feels and that it doesn't feel good. It always comes from intention to get more out the negotiation. You fight for favor, and you fight so that you come out on top. You are always defending yourself, as if what you represent is better and deserves more. It's an exhausting approach to life. So when I gave up my ego, I got out of the survival-of-the-fittest, -prettiest, -smartest, and -strongest race. With God's love, I appreciated people and the labor they put into what they provide. In seeing their value and effort, I didn't feel the need to hustle them anymore. Instead, I learned to love to pay them fair value.

Three of God's promises liberated me.

One, God is always with and for me. The Word of God says be still and I'll fight for you. (Exodus 14:14)

Two, God's favor, also known as His grace, His unmerited favor, comes naturally when I am living a God-first-honoring life. When I'm in the will of God for my life, He defends and protects me and provides His abundant favor. I found this freeing. I have a *big* dad who loves me. He wants me to treat people kindly, give generously, and treat favorably.

Three, another mental shift came. I stopped seeing my fellow humans as fierce competitors. Instead, I saw my brothers and sisters in humanity as my allies to my purpose and gifts. As the Word of God says, just as iron sharpens iron, so does one man sharpen another.[2] When my neighbor prospers, I prosper.

Lastly, it's just stuff. Stuff is just ash. When you decide to go "all in" for God, you learn to invest in what matters, eternally.

I learned through God's perfect love that the things of this world are just temporary. Suddenly, my eyes opened for what is unseen, the eternal gifts and riches. I never knew that time and kindness had so much value. In all my hours of praising and studying God's Word, He created in me an awareness of what really matters to Him. What matters most is his; his people's salvation for spirit and soul, and the Word of God. If you fall in love with God, you can't help but love what He loves: people. Once I loved and respected people and their crafts and talents, then I naturally stopped manipulating to get ahead in any context of relationship.

My old ways were shed. No more "fake it till I make it." With God, I now "faith it till I make it." I also am confident enough in who God made me to be myself that I don't have to fake anything. In real connection with people, I learned *it's okay to be lovingly authentic.* It's okay to struggle, to hurt, and to share.

I also learned that not all thoughts and opinions need sharing. *God wants us to go to Him for everything first.* When love broke through for me, I learned that a way to stay blessed and healthy is to run all that I think and say through the Word of God, truth. Truth is the Word of God and holds the presence of God himself.[3] So it's as if God becomes my health counselor and guides me to what is healthy for me to say and think on, both for myself and for my healthy relationship. I guess since I was used to holding everything in as a child, it felt utterly freeing to be comfortably transparent with the right people.

It was powerful to come to know that *perfectionism intimidates,* and *vulnerability and compassion invite connection.* This is great! Instead of being the chameleon I was, growing up, God gave me the courage to be my unique self, just the way He made me. Ever since, I love people. I love authentic connection with people, not fake conversations. We are each more alike than not. We all fight overscheduling; life is way too short to spend time making fake small talk. Nix the small talk when you meet and greet; take risks and share a compliment or a quick story. Engage with people. That bit of kindness makes people feel seen and accepted.

Remember this: when you meet people, don't think, *Oh wow, I look terrible. I can't say hi to anyone.* In a first encounter with a stranger, what people remember most is how you made them feel. Could you impart a piece of kindness and acceptance for eternity's sake? It matters; wave, smile. Even if you get the grump-pot who scowls at you, you just smiled at God, and He noticed your risk and kindness!

With God's healing and courage to be myself, I could be authentic with people. I could finally reveal my tender heart. That being said, can I be *real* and tell you it has taken lots of Jesus and correction for me not to say bad words about this situation. I grew up in a home where Spanish curse words were said frequently. When I learned them in English, I said those, too. Of course, not around my elders, or parents, but my peers. Oh, Lord, I have a billion "idle word tickets." The Word of God is clear: "I will say no idle or curse word or foul language."[4] If you cuss like a sailor in your head or in private, be of good courage. I used to be. For me, I now know it was all underlying anger and sadness and frustration. Now, I know how to channel that energy somewhere positive. You can overcome. I have and do 99 percent of the time!

I went from a sick love to being lovesick …

As you can see, it felt like an eternity before I could believe God cherished me, I couldn't love myself because I hated my shortcomings, my faults. That being said, though I gave love to others and shared love, it was conditional; it did depend on how they treated me. That is a sick love. When God gave me a new heart and a fresh born-again spirit, I became "lit" with zeal and fervor for anything in relation to God. I experienced unconditional love for myself, by first receiving it from God fully.

I'm embarrassed to say, but it took me quite a while. You can tell by what I've shared in the journey that breaking up with the distorted core beliefs or lies I truly believed about myself and others took a long time. Even if it takes my entire lifetime, I wouldn't trade anything for experiencing this level of love, unconditional self-acceptance, fulfillment, and purpose.

God is love, and when He awakens His love for you in your heart more purely and fully, it makes you lovesick—in a good way. Like in the Bible book Song of Solomon, it's a longing for that next meeting with a holy and good God. His second coming becomes something you truly look forward to. Your next encounter becomes a mystery you look forward to. How will He move you this time? What bit of revelation will He give about Himself or His ways or maybe a sense of His undeniable presence? It has done so much good for me, In His sacred presence I become 1. Priceless, 2. charged with passion, and 3. a source of energy for getting about the Father's business.

When I settled into this live and new heart and spirit, it was as if I could see and hear the voice of God for the first time. The leading and voice are not audible in the physical but audible in the spirit. The Holy Spirit could finally work in me. I had gotten rid of and confessed my sins and received full forgiveness for them. God is so holy that first I had to go through this exchange, pleading the cross as a continual payment for my sin. Sin blocks prayers, but in an active love and confession and acceptance of grace, I can have relationship with a Holy *God*.

So in all that trading of my former ways for new ways, God gave me a visual metaphor. I could see in my mind's eye, the vision of me climbing and hustling my way to the top of a statistical dog pile to make it. According to statistics, I was doomed for gloom, and I was told that by some authority figures early on that I was a nobody going nowhere but dysfunction junction. So I immediately used that as fuel to overachieving at everything. I fought my way to the top by excelling, in burnout ways.

Thank God, for in His healing love, He strengthened me to want what He wants—for not one to be lost. Jesus Himself said that He came to seek and save the lost. So in the new vision He gave me, I don't step all over my brothers and sisters in the dog pile to climb my way to the top. I now get my footing first on the solid rock, Jesus. I stand there; all else is sinking sand, the Word says!

Now I pull my brothers and sisters up alongside me, even up and over me! How? I encourage, I give, I shoulder and strengthen their struggle in compassion, and then I love on them. By loving and giving ridiculously as I can, I help others up and out of struggle and bondage. Then together we reach God's purpose and goals for each of us at the top. Accepting God's commission of speaking of the Gospel good news in all I do, if I have to I use words. Accepting this challenge pacified a little more of my lovesickness and instead gave me those butterflies to love on people like never before.

WHO I REALLY AM NOW, AUTHENTIC!

Child of the most high God, coheir with Christ, laborer of His good works and great things that God promised would come to be in John 14:12.

When I received that truth—that I could not lose my identity of saved, no matter how badly I might behave—I was freed. This wasn't an excuse to misbehave, but a desire to share, with all who were willing to listen, the power and freedom that come from knowing Christ.

With my new heart and time well spent in communion with God. I came to learn that the Word of God even says that while on earth, I can live currently in the blessings of heavenly places. That truth blows my mind. I have not even begun to dig into or sit in the understanding of this truth, but I keep pressing in and waiting for more discovery in that mystery. Because as Jesus is seated on His throne in heavenly places; He is in a position of rest and authority. He reigns. Because our God reigns as Victor; we can rest as believers in that promise, an assurance we have while here on earth. We aren't fighting for victory but instead are fighting from victory. That sounds heavenly!

In order to get more wisdom in living this truth out, I must spend rich time in God's presence, praising Him and reading His Word. In the time well spent with Him, there are treasures forevermore to discover. Don't let your mind deceive you; reading the Bible is not a waste of time. It is the best use of time, and in fact it is the only use of your time that will outlive us. The Word of God promises that time in worship and seeking God in His Word has present and eternal rewards. You want to be closer to God? Read His Word or even just the book of Proverbs or Psalms back to Him. The Word of God assures us that *He inhabits* the praises of His people.

I have a disclaimer. I'm no biblical theologian or professionally licensed counselor. What I share I share as a peer, a fellow and formerly struggling human. The struggle was so real in my life that it became unmanageable. Now the struggle of being a human still exists, but the light and blessings of heaven are so alive in me that a heavenly peace and perspective now stabilize anything chaotic, unpredictable, or unmanageable. My new identity is led by the Spirit of a living and holy God. With that perspective and sure sense of identity I've learned to reconcile my past, present, and future to the complete love of Christ. The Word of God says that love covers a multitude of sins. Those would include mine, so guilt has no place in my life anymore.

Later I will share how the past, present, and future made sense and inspiration for me instead of striving. But for the sake of the story I'm sharing, I'll have you read some more of what fractures were healed in my foundations.

As a goal-setter and -finisher, I thrived in the sense of accomplishment of a great work ethic. My style as the taskmaster and lover of my forever to-do lists needed a restoration too! So let me share some steps and tips that helped me tremendously. Again, the whole reason I wrote this book was that I was so distraught wanting to realize transformation in my life but not knowing how. How it happens is the Word of God. It is an instruction manual for life here on earth now. It is not a history book. It is the Word made flesh in Jesus Himself.

I know how hard it is to get this, but do! In this life, only souls and the Word of God are eternal. So any time spent worshipping God deep down in your spirit, and then loving on souls from that overflow and reading the Word of God, is a forever investment. Talk about the power of compounding interest! *Divinity makes you rich, in and outside of time. Godliness redefines what we know as rich in this world and make us truly rich!*

VERSION UPDATE – 2.20

It is no longer I who live But Christ who lives in me.
(Galatians 2:20 NIV)

My identity. My Becoming. Me, Only Way Better.

In light of today's trend to change or loosely define your identity, it is vitally important that we understand who we are and whose we are—and then that we impart and foster that sureness to our children. All children we should have the privilege to share life with need that sureness. The world is ever-changing, but God is absolutely sure. So as we parents know firmly who we are in Christ and in our God-given identity and sex for that matter, we will impart what to question and what not to question.

God is not the author of confusion or questioning. So we know that identity crisis or gender questioning is not of Him. God and His whole being, character, and ways are absolute. He is irrefutable and eternal, He is truth itself. Jesus was known as the best teacher of biblical truths because He did it with so much authority and understandability. So it is my hope that, with my story of hope and love and my prayers for you and some tips, you too will be empowered by a greater sense of your spiritual and complete identity. When you know exactly who you are, you can let go of rules with respect to how you should be. There you can be free to be fully you. With a God-given resolve we can confidently walk through any questioning on what roles we are called to play, as His ambassadors.

IT IS MISSION-CRITICAL

It is critical to your mission that you get your own identity firm. Your own future and purpose depend on it. Not only yours but those whom only you are called to lead and influence are depending on you to get this. So get it deep down in your spirit to be sure about you.

I'll share how this happened for me. Then get inspired, reflect, and commit to accept your true identity. When a question arises, like "I don't even know who I am anymore," and it will, talk back and answer yourself with what God said to you about you. Then walk in the authority He gave to just be you, first. Then do His bidding, healing the sick, feeding the hungry, and casting out forces of darkness that come against people you know and love. This may all sound lofty, but God did ask each and every one of His followers to do this. Don't overthink this; it's much easier to do than you think.

In today's times, this is what casting out forces of darkness looks like. You see your friend, and he or she is down in discouragement. You visit, call, text, DM, send a clean joke to them, look up to the heavens and say, "Lord, You know my friend is down; send a blessing of extra joy their way. Let them know You are there." And "Enemy, you can't have my friend. I'm a praying child of God, and I say, darkness and despair, get off my friend; leave." And looky there, you just bound up evil and sent good to go to work for your friend. In all that faith and belief, you just spoke out; you changed the atmosphere around you and your friend. You healed the poor in spirit, you fed your friend's hunger for hope. See, it's not an exorcism we are called to do, just kindness and prayer. Your love made your whole community and beyond lighter and brighter.

WHEN YOU KNOW, YOU BELONG!

All my life I would have said, "Yes, I am a child of God." But it wasn't until I became and acted like one that I truly became an authoritative, confident, ready-to-die-for-my-Lord child of God. When I finally accepted that unmerited love and grace that accompany salvation, the gift of the Holy Spirit, and the sure identity that I was indeed a child of God, I began to pray bold prayers.

It honors God to pray bold, big prayers. It shows Him you know he is a mighty *God* who can do anything. In that sure identity of child of God, who is heard by an almighty God, comes sureness. You trust that you know He is with you and for you. So if I don't get a prayer answered, I don't get mad at God. I accept His knowing better. I can't see what He sees, I can't understand what He knows. I must let God be God and trust in His plan. The sureness that I get as His child comes with a surety of *who He is*, ever worthy of my adoring, He is always faithful, He is good for all time, He is never forsaking and always with me.

So li'l ol' me, I am just *His*, just being that, I am already enough. This may seem super elementary, but there is a big difference between a label you wear, "child of God," versus the being you become in the sonship of your almighty God. In sonship, God just invited you as fully vested partner to the family business, His kingdom. We become coheirs in Christ. We are Royals! When I took the label off and became, the Holy Spirt ignited my core identity and changed all of me. If you don't have this, I so want this for you. In Christ, you know how to handle life in the real world with real problems, but you just sit in godly assurance instead of mind-winding fret.

The Holy Spirit establishes, anoints, and seals you as His. I took that all the way to the depths of my heart. Since then, I've lived more. Though I was living before, by the world's standards, I've come to realize that apart from Christ, I have no life at all worth speaking of. It is described in Ephesians 3.2 where your body dies, and your spirit comes to life.

It's like this: in the past I gave way to any whim I wanted, much of it super sinful. I was so religious that I thought I wasn't a sinner. Boy, did the Holy Spirit open my eyes. I was shown how in the past I unknowingly fought against God. To be apart from God's will for my life was evil. But then verse 5 explains that God's love was so great that He made us alive in Christ. With more time, prayer, and seeking, I saw that my life previously was dead and dry in depth, my bones empty and powerless. The words don't give the new life justice; I'm telling you, *alive in Christ* is *so* different and solid. In that authoritative being, you start to understand and see the difference between when you are in the will of God and His Spirit's leading and when you are not. A Spirit-led life will let you know more readily when you have slipped or have veered off into your own life tangent. You will become more sensitive and know when you are not "in the will of God" and when you have done evil in His sight too, sin.

Speaking of His will, what is His will for us? That we know and practice and teach what He said to us.

Here are some critical positioning truths from God's Word.

- *Whose we are:* His (Isaiah 43:1).
- *What He has given us:* our own specific purpose and role (2 Timothy 1:9).
- *Where He wants us to go:* with Him to holiness (Ephesians 1:4). To walk step by step, to hear and know His voice, to be in *real* relationship, to partake in creation with Him, as in the Garden of Eden (Genesis 3:8).
- *When we are to act:* now (Zephaniah 2:2). The Lord is near (Philippians 4:5).
- *How we are to act:* in faith (2 Corinthians 8:7), in holy boldness (Ephesians 3:12), and with God-given authority (Titus 2:15; Luke 9:1). We are to live as those who know the Truth.
- *Who we are to be with:* like-minded believers of Christ.
- *How we communicate:* constant praise, prayer, and thanksgiving.
- *What to wear:* the blood-bought righteousness of Christ.
- *How we affirm who we are:* we worship in every way with our whole being.
- *How we get there:* We grow in Christ with our church community. We are strengthened and accomplish the will of God, *in* community. We will never accomplish our greatest good alone. We aren't to be in the fringes of the church,

online only or on our own terms. We learn and grow best in the thick and thin of *belonging* and taking part with the whole church.

- *What will I say? Don't worry.* For at the right time the Holy Spirit will teach you what to say (Luke 12:12; reading the Word of God helps you know what God says about everything).
- *Why? Why do we do what we do? Because we exist to know God and make Him known—to be loved by Him and to love Him* (1 Corinthians 8:6; John 17:3).

Remind yourself of your *why*. It is called your *why power*. Why power outlasts your will power, all day long!

We do everything better together, so fellowship means to visit and to be friendly and familiar with people after the same thing. In loving unity God reveals more to us. He tells us of a good future for us, even when we are rejected or persecuted for having faith in Him. He sharpens our hearing and directs us. In community He pours out healing and hope for everything that concerns us. As we sit in that hope and belonging, we can know who we are becoming. We are changing, advancing; we are becoming altogether new. As we practice and walk out our faith, we can *know* we are in the will of God for our lives. How? In the center of God's will for our lives there is a supernatural protection and provision as well as a supernatural ability for all we need to do.

We are called *adored, named, loved, enough,* and *provided for.* When you know this down in your core and can say it, you know God has transformed you into *new!* Your 2.20 version just dropped, and it is working with no glitches! If you can't say this, *yet,* make yourself say so. Say this over yourself while you look in a mirror. You will know your identity in Christ is restored and healed when you can actually do this exercise. God says all of heaven celebrates in a roar of joy when a sinner—ahem, that's all of us—takes on the *identity child of God.* 5

I now remind myself frequently that I am who God says I am, I can do what He says I can do, and I have what the Bible says I have.

> In becoming, the first stage was *acceptance*. The most powerful thing I did was accept the call from my Lord. In Him, I would find my true being and identity.

You can see why I took the time to remind you of your Identity as son or daughter. What helped me come to know and proclaim my sonship was the *Bible*. There I did a Bible study on the armor of God. Since then, January 2016, I put it on daily. It was there in community, and led by a good Bible teacher, that I learned the Lord gave us tools right from the Bible. In fact, the Bible is known to most people as just a history book. But there is more to it. What more? To find out, read it, and do so with a good biblical commentary. Child of God, I truly pray you receive the freely available and relevant wisdom, guidance, salvation, and protection the Bible offers. To all who believe it is the living and active word, God's presence is in those pages with you.

I was a believer all my life, but I still had no idea it could be an instruction manual for life. I heard an acronym one time at church, and it really helped me see the Holy Bible as a lifeline. I think it's cool to share. BIBLE; BIBLICAL INSTRUCTIONS BEFORE LEAVING EARTH. I wish I had understood what the Bible gives at a younger age. When you pick up the habit of spending time in the *Word of God, you are actually picking up the presence of God Himself!*

Oh, that brings up a loaded word, *presence.* Loaded with *power, that is!* Here is my very infantile babble-like description of what the presence of God will do. It breaks through the regrets of the past.[8] It gives us heaven's perspectives on earthly problems. By his presence and grace, we are saved.[9] The presence of the living God brings relevance and joy to my present. The presence of God shows me the promise to my very bright future.[10] So I'm sure that as I study more and spend more rich time in the presence of the Lord, more will be revealed. That is exactly what biblical study is: constantly the story and depth of understanding builds on itself.

Let me hammer this home. It is in getting ahold of who we are now that we can most effectively *be*. We must choose not to let too much of our yesterdays and tomorrows take up our today. In the power of now, we can confidently praise God for giving us His wisdom and leading at just the right time. In His present leading, I can trust that He redirects me like a good GPS. So if my mind is saying, "Did you hear that comment about you? They called you an XYZ; they said that they felt sorry that you had that XYZ issue"— the Holy Spirit, ready to comfort and help me, arrives on the scene and tells me, *"You don't wear that label anymore.* You were delivered of that XYZ, and you *now walk in a freedom,* strength, and closeness to Me that only came to you because XYZ happened."

Instead of spiraling down in a pity party, I praised my way up to the heavenly perspective on all suffering. My awesome God-powered GPS showed me a better perspective to have in the now. The divine redirect always leads to higher and better with respect to where I am here and now. The Holy Spirit reminds me not to rehearse or nurse on what I can't do anything about. Outsiders to what happened to you will never understand that *you are not the label* or the event that happened to you. Child of God, *don't wear that as your identity—* XYZ victim. Instead, you are a child of God who overcame XYZ. That is what God says about us, and so should we. Even if you *didn't* overcome XYZ condition, you have it; *it does not have you!* There is the overcoming, no matter what the outcome was.

In all leveling life events that are hard to face, process, and get past, such as widowhood, a divorce, the loss of our health, a wayward child, a loss of life … *however that loud pain strikes us, it is the very greatest opportunity for us to hear God's voice most loudly.*

I personally refused to embrace any of the painful events I suffered to be included in my identity. We don't have to be a "whatever label" and remain a "whatever label."

Just like me, you CAN choose to move past the event. Of course you are altered, forever changed. But if God is involved, you'll be better than you ever were because of the very hardships you went through. Now I live differently. I use the Bible as the lifeline it is. I humbly gave up what I thought was good in my own strength and took on the great and awesome strength of Almighty God.

The enemies of darkness are after my soul and purpose; I won't surrender to them. They are after yours, too. There is a daily threat against each of us on the purpose, calling, and will of God in our lives. But don't despair; God made provisions, strategies, and defenses ready for us to use against our enemies.

> In becoming child of *God*, the hardest phase was *believing* that the message was for me. I had to believe I could be forgiven. In God's love I could now believe my inherent worth. He revealed to me just how much He esteems me, and that gave me the grace to love and forgive myself.

One is that I put on the armor of God daily. Look it up; it is described in Ephesians 6:10–18. I truly feel the difference of when I claim it out loud and put it on versus when I forget to.[4] As I put on my belt of truth, I remember that it is Christ's Word that keeps me on my path and strengthens me to the core. We all know that a strong core is a strong person. The breastplate of righteousness guards my heart because what I believe and say overflows from my heart as the issues of life.[6] The gospel of peace and preparation steadies me along with the warrior's shoes. Did you know that a warrior's shoes have spikes? With those shoes on, I can stand firm even on gravelly, sandy, or steep ground. The helmet of salvation protects my mind and what I'm believing and thinking. With it, I know who I am and whose I am. Then comes the shield of faith; it deflects the fiery darts of this world, which are meant to distract me or even take me off my purpose. The sword of the Spirit is the Word of God. It is mighty and able to not only disarm my enemy but also help cut away my own ungodly desires. The final piece of action on the offensive is to pray in the Spirit at all times. This is fervent prayer, meaning I don't stop talking and listening to God.

I came to believe and live in the powerful truth that He loved me enough to do all he did, for just me. My self-esteem was dismally poor before; I would never have been able to receive this before God gave me the grace to. When I esteemed God above all else, I didn't need self-esteem anymore. I now accepted and believed my inherent worth. He revealed to me just how much He esteems me, and that gave me the grace to love and forgive myself.

In this, I could finally accept instead of deflect anything good that God or people said about me. I know I'm not alone. Male and female, once you have lived in the world and have suffered insufficiency and rejection, you may have a hard time receiving a compliment. You know, the minute someone says a nice thing, you immediately deflect it and say, "Wow, they are definitely not talking about me. *They have no idea what I'm like*, and I'm not that good." With God's saving grace and healing, I have accepted the liberty to believe and receive good things, and that includes compliments.

This journey can be yours, and I celebrate with you if you have a life set ablaze by God's light and love. So for me the adventure of falling in love with Jesus gave me mission and vision for life anew. He empowered me with His promises and truths. These are His gifts to all His children. He wants all of us to be set free from bondage, so we can live in His amazing grace and unfailing love.

God set the record straight in my heart. His *love broke through* my bruised and battered raw heart. Maybe yours is calloused or cold. It is no matter; The Lord Jesus is the heart surgeon. He will get His rich saving and healing blood to all the parts of your heart that need wellness and function. You will get a new heart when you come to accept the gospel message and believe it to be true and applicable to you.[7]

The Bible or the Word of God renewed my mind so much that the desires I had for my previous life and habits are rarely present. I'm so thankful for that, *I love that I came to want what God wanted for me.*

I'm going to ask you to take a moment to look over and think about a picture I created to describe the battle for our heart, our affections, and our time. The chart also shows the fruit or the product that comes from our choices. As you all know, time spent with anything creates something; it's called the product or the fruit of it. It can be for good and your health in all aspects or for evil or result in the slow or immediate death of things.

For me as I looked over the product of all I was spending time with, it helped me know what to spend time with and what to cut out.

Let me preface the picture with some simple reasons why God loves us so much, and we are *His!*

1. We were made by God for His delight. We were made to love Him and be loved by Him. (Think how we want to become a parent when we see how so cute children are and how much fun it is to watch and be with them) (Zephaniah 3:17).

2. There are two forces that are jealous for your affection and attentions, evil (Satan) and good (God) (John 10:10; Exodus 34:14).

3. You are an eternal being living a temporary existence in humanity. This humanity experience is made to prepare us for eternity. We have a free will about what we do while here on earth, but it does have a result or a product. Everything

we do and say on earth has a result in eternity. Where we spend eternity is a direct result of what we think about God's Son, Jesus (John 3:16; 10:27).

4. We each have been given a special God-powered role that we can tap into or leave undiscovered. It takes risk and faith to find it (1 Corinthians 6:14).

Now carefully See this rendering for the battleground for your heart ...

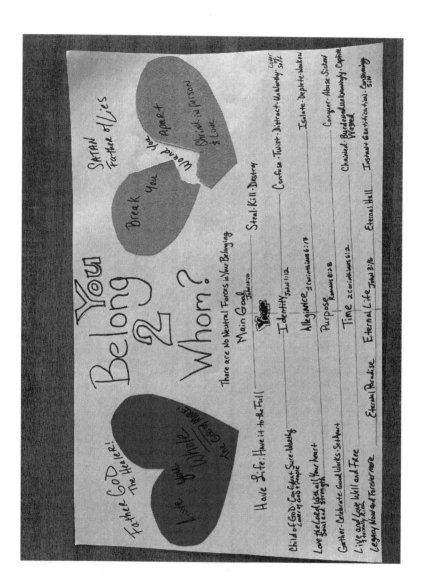

Image 1: Who I Belong To

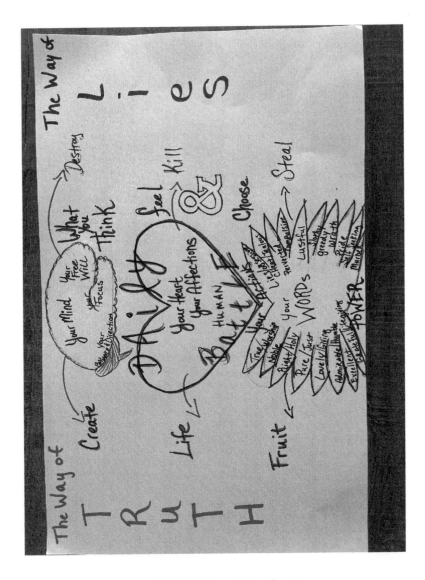

Image 2: Daily Battle for the Heart

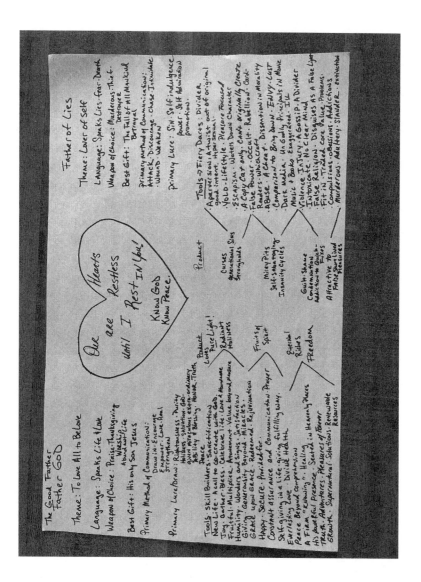

Image 3: Rest or Restless

For me, it was important to reflect on and point to what might cause me to have a hard day and what might create a good day. All I allow in my inputs has everything to do with the output of my life. I now choose even more wisely.

I hope that it inspires you to recognize the "fiery darts" on your day to thwart you, distract you, or discourage you off your specific life's purpose. In the same vein, I hope you prioritize creating more activities rooted and grounded in Christ, so that in and with Him you can give and reflect authentic love for God, self, and others individually.

All people want to be recognized for the unique beings they are. They want me and you to listen to them, to say, "I see you, and I see your point of view. You are not just a body in the human race. You are a specific part; you have an irreplaceable role in the grand plan of God for humanity." I even loved it when I found out and believed that I was a part of the living church body. I have an important and individual role to play for the kingdom of God—His church. No one can be me! No one can be you! We have got to get our soul well and do what God has called us each individually to do for him! There is no time to waste. Time is a treasure we don't get back, and we can't buy it. Spend it wisely. Steward it. It's *time, now!*

Ways to get you on your way to *well* and *whole* in your *new* identity. These tools immediately helped me.

When I had to reinvent myself, I was so low in self-like that I couldn't say one thing I liked about me. I was too mad at me as a person. I had messed up; I was embarrassed and ashamed. I didn't know how I'd ever love me. So here is what worked for me. I took one step at a time with God's guidance. With His help, I would come to be a better new me. God saved me to become all that I always wanted to be and more.

I ran to heal. I prayed as I ran; I imagined my whole-body healing and growing stronger. From the inside out I was healing and restoring proper function and thought.

I journaled.

I did acrostics of all I wanted to be: loved, empowered, helpful.

I consumed the Word of God at will. Read the Bible and devotionals three times a day, minimum.

Car time and relaxing TV time were only Bible-based teachings. I watched no secular shows. What can I say? I had to rewire and submerge all my senses in Jesus's light and powerful words and teachings.

Faith It and Say So! I rehearsed scriptural prayer note cards, as needed. I needed it a lot!

I fought bad thoughts and desires to drink and smoke with the Word of God. I would say, "That thought is not useful" or *DELETE*. And then say Psalm 23:1 (NKJV): "The Lord is my Shepherd; I shall not want." I later studied a different version of that same verse that I would use a lot when all others seemed to be doing what I thought I missed. I'd say, "The Lord is my Shepherd, I lack nothing" (NIV).

I attended Bible-based twelve-step support meetings faithfully, no matter what. If I couldn't find a faith-based group, I'd go to a secular support group and ask the Holy Spirit to speak to me through the stories and people.

His Sacred Heart healed my hurts and helped me wait well until I felt better. He still faithfully does. In His love He is the one who healed my aches and longings. In Him, I felt tenderhearted but tough enough to stand firm in resolve.

Ways to *worship your way through*: It is in coming to know God and admiring Him, the Creator, that you learn to love and admire the creation, including yourself. You are God's masterpiece!

1. Apply the Word, apply the Word, apply the Word liberally. The Word never fails. Even when you don't see it working, it is working. Target your struggles with verses that address them.
2. Lift up His name. When you don't know what to pray or say, just say, "Jesus, my Lord." As you lift His name, evil flees.
3. Realize that your prayer is heard always. The Lord hears every word you utter; no prayers fall to the floor. In fact, the

Bible describes that our prayers are offered up in nonstop worship to the great Lord's throne. Furthermore, the Word never returns void.

4. Our faith never fails us; people do. Let us not base our faith on our experience. Instead, base faith on the infallible Word of God. Do not be discouraged by what you see or don't yet see. Faith builds what the heart believes. So take this to the core and to Jesus, and offer up to the Lord all that is in your heart. He gives us new and mighty hearts to believe in the good He died to give you and me.

5. Don't fret in the wait. In that slow growing process, there is so much growth happening you don't see. Think of a plant or flower and how much dirt it has to push through to finally be seen. Same goes for the seed of your prayers. Once spoken, they are planted. "Trust the process," as it has been said. In the supernatural or spiritual realm, God's work is being done, and unseen changes are happening. The Word always works.

6. Trust that the Lord's words have power and authority. In the meantime, choose to wait and walk by faith and not by sight. Stay in belief, and do not waver, the Word of God says, and you will receive your victory. Unbelief, pride, and sin are what blocks the receiving of your prayer. So repent of your unbelief, and ask the Holy Spirit to help you believe in the midst of your unbelief.

7. If you have a hardened or unbelieving heart, soften it by hearing the Word of God. Just like in cleaning, sometimes a long soak is necessary. Sometimes you need softening agents and paint thinners and buffers. The beginning to a tender heart is an honest heart cry to God. Listen to a Bible teacher that you really understand.

8. Read a beginner's Bible. I literally picked up baby devotionals and built my way up to teen Bibles, and now I read Bible commentaries written by theologians. Don't be too proud to turn on your childlike faith with children's songs and Bibles.

I did a YouTube search of all my favorite hymns growing up in church. It is in childlike faith that we can lean on the wonder of God.

9. Worship comes naturally when you think about things. Instead of doubt, think of wonder.

10. All who seek will find. There is no heart that God can't rescue. Pray for the lost you are believing to come home—even if that's you. In today's world this could be a badly wounded person who doesn't believe in good anymore. It could be a skeptical, analytical type with a low or undeveloped spiritual side. Either way, if they are meant to be a child of God, God will keep talking to them in different ways.

11. God will relentlessly pursue and call them, but the ultimate choice to believe is theirs. He takes ninety-nine steps to meet you; it's up to you only to take the one last step to unite with your heavenly Father. So if you are like me and your heart is heavy for a friend or a family member to come to know Jesus, just keep praying the Word of God over them. God is faithful to bring all His children home.

12. If you are a believer and find yourself lukewarm or drifted off in the heart toward God, warm yourself up! How? Soak in the warmth of God's living Word.

13. Repent, turn away from what is hurting you. First, make sure you aren't living in a recurring sin such as gossip, that you are not parked in unforgiveness or nailed up high and mighty with pride. Repent. Confession is how the sting of sin is removed from you.

14. Eliminate your kryptonite of fellowship with God. Then, just speak the living Word of God over yourself, and the Word promises that faith comes from hearing and hearing from the Word of God. Just as sure as a fire takes off when the right conditions and materials are present like oxygen, wood, and a spark, then your heart is sure to be set ablaze by the Holy Spirit's work on your ready and yielded, available heart.

HIS SACRED HEART FOR YOURS
END OF CHAPTER REFLECTIONS

A Glimpse at His Heart …

A Step into the Sacred Chambers of His Heart—His Holy Word

I will think on these things: whatever is excellent. You are excellent because He made you excellently.

But as you excel in everything—in faith, in speech, in knowledge, in all earnestness, and in our love for you—see that you excel in this act of grace also. (2 Corinthians 8:7 ESV)

Take a praise break. The Lord is the calm in your storm, just like the eye of a storm is stillness and focal power.
Song: "You Say" by Lauren Daigle, 2018.
"Tears to Diamonds," Apollo LTD, 2021.

A Guided Prayer for You

Lord God, Your banner over me is love. Your name Yahweh Nissi describes that I become the righteousness of God in Christ. That means that as I claim and confess, I am your child, you are my God, and I have right standing with God.

I love that as I accept my identity as Your chosen creation, I am because of who You are. I believe You created me specially for a good life and purpose. In You, God, I am justified; I have peace about my past and am hopeful about my future. My identity in You has heaven-sent wisdom and favor just because You love me. In loving and seeking You, Lord, I have infinite possibility. I can make peace with and appreciate how You made me and how my body and spirit change in maturity. Thank You for going before me and showing me that as I abide and remain in You, I can stay powerfully humble. Your grace is enough to develop me into all I'm meant to be. May I always point to You as the source of all the good I discover in me. I love You, Abba!

Never let me forget who I am in You.

Your white space ...

9

KING OF MY HEART

Once you have a new heart, you have to choose who is the king of it. Every word you say and every choice you make determines the kind of life you live.

So as I learned to rest in the peace that Christ died to give me, I could finally break out of that psychotic spin cycle of hating parts of myself and a continual approval addiction. Love broke through for me when I lived God's love as a way of life every day, not just on Sunday and occasional Bible studies.

How did I break this cycle of hate and break into a healthy self-love? *How* is how …. No, I'm not trying to confuse you. By being *Honest, Open, and Willing*; that is HOW.

As I allowed myself to be real and admit struggles and the need for help, God sent me into sweet surrender. I had a broken side to me that I had run from and covered up long enough. This was really hard, being real and honest with myself and God. Kind of like what we do on social media, I would only reveal and share the good part of myself and suppress or hide the darkness in me. But when

I allowed my heart, mind, and soul to be laid bare before my God, God covered me with all of His light. I met truer light—a balanced light, a light that brought clarity, a light in darkness— and it cast out all the dark in me, it cast out the selfish parts of me. A light shone in the rebellious and straying part of me—a light in the sinful desires in me, a lightness in the weight of being all that I am and am not.

Before I thought I couldn't face all that. I believed I didn't even need to. After all, it was all in the past wasn't it?

But if I wanted God's truth, power, joy, peace, and presence in my life, then I had to go back. Back where? To the unknown where I could barely remember, but which I quivered to face. He called me to boldly face with Him the place I had escaped from long ago. I said, "God, I buried that, to never revisit again. Why, God? Why would You, a loving and healing God, ask me to revisit all that hurts? You know how badly it hurts and what it does to me."

To which he answered: "No one can hurt you now. You are an adult, and moreover, you are a child of Mine. So with Me by your side, you will overcome this all. Do as I say."

And so I did. By going to the most badly broken places and facing this ugly, dark, messy storm with God, I would break the agreements I had made with the enemy. God would turn the mess I had made into His message. The love of God can break through any desperate situation!

In restoration, I broke up with the lies I believed. For me, the lies I was told and believed came from several moves and from feeling like an unliked outsider. The lies we believe are always complete nonsense. As for me, the most deep-rooted lie was that I was not good or worthy enough, and any favor or forgiveness from God or people had to be earned.

In case you don't already know this, a lie is defeated with truth. The living Word of God, light itself. It immediately casts out all darkness an lies by the nature of light and truth. Grace and truth are a person, Jesus Christ. His light and truth are a lamp unto my feet and a light unto my path. So little by little I washed over and cleansed the lies I believed with the positive Word of God. Write out the truth of God on notecards and sticky notes, and put them everywhere. Daily and every time a lie comes into your thoughts, you can rehearse the truth over you. There the dark lies burn off. Even dark memories fade. They can never win when put them next to the Light of the world, the Word of God. Just like my math book says that a product of a negative and a negative become a positive, so I can expect that the Book of Life added to my negative thoughts becomes a positive equation in my life.

I hope you can see so far that my experience was a process that happened step by step. In each faith-led step I hope you have seen how love redeemed me. Though my foundation was shaken literally and spiritually, you can see that it only happened to shake me into new places and to break off of me what was not useful for my life's impact and purpose. God's love broke through my foundation, and He led me to complete peace and restoration of a very wounded and dysfunctional past. In His complete love I was restored to know and walk in my genuine worth and my true identity. Which led to a renewed sense of perspective on my same life through God's lens. With a renewable and fresh outpouring of the Holy Spirit's power on my life, I received an eternal sense of secure belonging and an urgent sense of my purpose for God's kingdom. I would finally feel at home, secure and confident in God's plan for my life, my destiny both here and forevermore.

If we all truly allow God to take His place as the source of our life instead of just a part of our life, all of life's existence and meaning questions would be answered.

You might say, *"But I don't have the time*; I'll deal with my soul when I'm closer to dying." No. Salvation and heaven's promises are ready for you now. You have a work to do. Only you can do it; no one can want it or do it for you. *Excuses, be gone in Jesus's name!* The longer you stay away from God's closeness, the more hurt you'll cause for yourself and all your loved ones.

You can "do" life and fulfill all your responsibilities and still give God the number-one spot He deserves. God's will is to be your number one. His Word promises that if you put him in His rightful place, aka the King of your heart, then all other things will be added unto you. That means He provides the rest! So if this doctor and private practice owner, wife, and mom of four can tackle prayer, church, work, workouts, therapy, twelve-step meetings, volunteering, feeding and caring for us all in both school and extracurricular sports, attend and take kids to faith formation Bible classes, repair damaged relationships, reinventing marriage and family life, stay in relationship with God, stay sober and neither smoking nor pill-popping and anxious for *nothing, you can too*! Yes, I am well aware that that was the world's longest run-on sentence, but that is what the love of the Lord does for you. *He* is an *abundant God*. He helps us do what we could never do on our own. *He* is the time, energy, and resources we don't have.

God plus you in a surrendered and yielded and obedient heart can do all things! You + Jesus = Everything.

When Love Broke Through My Excuses!

I told you amazing grace was hard for me to accept.[1] So this was me, trying. Before my sweet surrender, I was white-knuckling sobriety and Christianity on and off. I was working on myself—trying to feel better about life and raising kids and choosing to do right, acting right, and hoping it would flow over into "feeling" right. The deep-seated problem was that you can't see or feel yourself right when your belief system is wrong. In other words, you can't live right if you see yourself wrong. You must come to know and accept who and whose you genuinely are. That came by process and slowly too.

Self-help, New age studies, chakra clearing, sage cleansing … I had done it all. It was all at the beginning of my sobriety, and at the rehab center they presented all the tools available to have people feel relief and wellness from the pains they held and had previously tried to numb away. Some people were on the other end of the spectrum:

they were so numb and far removed from what life had brought them that they would cut themselves and get high to feel something, anything. I was in complete shock when the girls I was in rehab with, while in rehab, were cutting themselves with paper clips and burning themselves with cigarettes. One girl was in sex addiction treatment and had sex in the shed with her treatment counselor. One told me she was in rehab for her sixth time already. A supervisor and group facilitator was caught with a controlled substance on her being and was fired.

I thought I had taken enough bad news until this bit hammered me. A previous client of my group counselor OD'd and died. When she told me the news, I covered my heart with my hand and my mouth with the other hand in shock. She said in her deep Southern drawl and a jaded matter-of-fact undertone, "That's the nature of the disease."

My heart was crushed in every sense of the word at that rehabilitation center. God had given me the eyes to see and the ears to hear through each one of those people circumstances. I listened to everyone who shared, I sat in their pain and saw each beautiful person underneath all the scarring and fear they felt. There was salvation. There is complete healing and restoration for each of them. I believed this and could see it in every part of me. For me and for them, there was JESUS! Yes, disease exists, and it is progressive unto death in nature.

But *with God,* the story line changes. Read on.

My story would have been the same. Remember, I was warned by my guardian angel in a dream. It was then I learned the "but with GOD" clause. It's mine and yours to have. Jesus said it Himself: "With man this is impossible, *but with God all* things are possible."[2] "Glory to God," in the most exuberant tone. I chose the *but with God* clause. My daughter's classmate lost her mother to a car accident at four in the morning on a holiday night. Substances were most likely involved in this one-car lethal accident. That could have been me. Believe me, I gulped; I felt a deep ache in my belly for the third grader left suddenly motherless. Then I exhaled a sigh of relief and said a prayer of thanksgiving that I had chosen to be made well, with God. Love truly broke through for me. Love called me out of my pit and hamster wheel. I'm so glad I answered. For that I will celebrate in thanksgiving eternally. I was saved from addiction but the process of recovery involved more healing.

I was back at my house in year two of sobriety when I got the call that a dear college friend, one of an inner circle tribe of girls from college, had committed suicide. I was in shock. She was so strong and so positive, enthusiastic and a pure lover of her family and friends. In her private world she fought a good bit of evil. Childhood issues arose with a vengeance, and they divorced. How do you invent a new life after many years of marriage? On the outside things were picture perfect, with wealth and great, beautiful kids. All of this caused her mental and physical health to decline. She moved to start rebuilding. None of us saw this coming. Another punch to my gut and deep pain in my belly. The kids were left behind—old enough to know, yet too young to understand.

As my girlfriend was working on loving herself and healing, she participated in yoga and outpatient trauma therapy intensives and hung out with friends to relieve the stress of it all. I knew what it was like to work through the process; it was deep and difficult to shake off internal work. Both she and I were in active struggle to get free of it all. She had suffered from addictions in a few forms and had been hospitalized for depression and possible bipolar tendencies. Only bits and pieces of her story would I come to know. She was private in her struggles. Sometimes she would let me in, so I looked to her for help.

I had reached out to her because I was trying to invent a new healthy life without drinking in the equation. We had been married for some years when my drinking became a huge family battle for me. She had reported that her family had gone through similar struggles. So I was looking to my girlfriend to help. She had already gone through a period of a focused wellness and sobriety for both herself and her husband and their family. So I called her, and she was great to talk to. She just listened and told me that we could and would adjust. She was a natural cheerleader and powerful optimist and encourager. After that hour-long chat, we just texted frequently, and I was cheering her on and trying to point her back to her faith in Christ as "the Source of hope and healing." I knew she could rise above her divorce and her pain-filled past. I had seen it before. She was a very strong-minded individual, that could easily write off a person or set of events that no longer served her goals. I would definitely call her resilient.

Over the years, we girls would text often. As many of us gathered annually for "girls' weekends," we were always close, no matter how often we talked or how much time had gone by. So when I heard how she died, I was infuriated. I knew the source of her demise. She fell victim to the lie Satan whispered to her in her darkest secret compartments. I mourned her death deeply as I prayed fervently for her surviving kids. I was crushed that she wouldn't be present for the important "first" events for her kids. I was deeply saddened that they would not know the amazing person their mom was. Though she died, that does not negate that she was a born survivor in spirit. She rose above much trauma and adversity. Yet most people would only look to how she finished, giving in to the lie that there was no hope.

Mind you, all this happened while I was in the nitty-gritty of "family of origin" and "adult child of alcoholic" therapy. What if all that darkness overtook me as it had overtaken her? According to my therapist, it was critical for me to make peace with my past to be fully present in the future. According to my Lord, it was critical for me to lean into Him and to trust Him to see me through my entire restoration story. With God in the center, His Word said that He has already overcome anything in this world.

Even in that knowing, I still felt bad. I was in the process of transformation and renewal, but I found myself missing the very behavior I was trying to change. I learned that it triggers one greatly to look at the bowels of your dysfunction and mistakes. I hated revisiting all the bad stuff. I can remember I would drink on the way to therapy, and after that I'd sneak cigarettes and chain smoke for a complete year, anything to escape or soften the blows. So even as I finally quit in rehab the drinking and smoking, I remained mildly triggered at all times. You could say that my mental internal chatter was raw and churned up, brought up to the surface.

So there I was, trying to do homework with the four kids, cook dinner, and set off to evening sports, my typical evening. It was hot out and dry, so I went out to clear my head and heart while watering my frangipani tree. There the father of lies showed up and whispered to me, "Don't you want your struggle to be over?" It was the spirit of suicide, coming to speak his lies to me. He tried to wear me down when I was hot, alone, and dry spiritually. He said, "You know you have the same thing your girlfriend had." Childhood trauma and addiction, struggling to raise a family, and trying to move on and "function and live successfully" through all the "therapy." It was horrible in every sense of the word.

There the father of lies, Satan, tried to have me take the bait. He said, "Don't you want all this to be over and done with? You wouldn't damage your children if you died; it would be all over, and you wouldn't be able to hurt them, like you hurt."

"Glory to *God*," I say, in my most Spirit-filled way. Thanks be to God, grace and wisdom in just right amount showed up to fight back those lies. The spirit of truth came to me. I immediately followed my Lord's example. I spoke aloud: "Get behind me, Satan," I said, while watering my tree. "Yes, I want the struggle and pain to be over. *No, I don't want to die.* Not in that way; that will not be the end of me. Not today, Satan! To God be the glory!"

I was floored. I had never seen that level of darkness, and I pray I never see it again. God faithfully delivered me out, but I was terrified that I'd even been approached in that way. I thought it was somehow indicative of the level of insanity I was fighting. I thought it was because something major was now wrong with me. But see, the father of lies has no new tricks. He uses the same lies on everyone. He wants you to believe you are the only one, and you are the worst of "lost causes."

I took that experience to pastors and counselors, and they helped me see the event for what it was: an attack of the enemy. He is after my purpose and future. He wanted me to end it to bring more attention to him. My therapist revealed that I have a "sticky brain," that trauma stories stay with me and are hard to shake off and not replay. It's the OCD part of the brain that looks at accidents, though you know you don't want to because it's hard to "unsee." This explains why Freddy Kruger, a villain in a nightmare film in the 1990s, still pops in my head on occasion . Ugh, high school win, not. I broke up with scary movies after that! Kids, youth, remember it's hard to unsee what you see! So choose carefully what you allow yourself to see.

Anyhow, it took months to shake off this loss. Here is the part where love broke through for me. I get into my van where the Christian radio station is always on, and the song "Love Broke Through" by Toby Mac, comes on. Through his song, God delivered me from that "sticky ugliness" that comes with that type of loss. There I was listening to the message of hope in that song. God came to meet me where I was, in the doubts and questioning of His goodness. I asked God, as I broke out in tears, "Where were You? Why didn't love break through for her? Yes, her, my girlfriend—she needed Your love too." God held me through my questioning, my anger about why she wasn't saved, and my tears of loss. He never gave me an answer as to why she had to go. But He did say the best way to honor the lost is to Live with a capital L. We can Live and Love for them. In the memory of their legacy, love never dies. Their love given to me can live on through me.

That is when I birthed my purpose: to let the love that broke through flow through me to others. So that *not one* more beautiful soul would ever fall victim to the liar and cheater of life. I was from that point forward living and loving for "the one."

Living and loving for the one is to be genuine and see and engage each person you see as the only person you see. Can you imagine this for a moment? Imagine the entire world has disappeared except for you. You walk for miles and don't see one human. Then one day, after months, you see a human. Tell me you wouldn't run up to that human and love on them, ask them questions, and listen intently to their story. Now, next time you are next to someone in the deli line, do you think you can treat that person as the first human you have seen in months? Now don't be scary eager, but just genuine, intentional, and fully present. I believe that if we treated each other that kindly and lovingly, we wouldn't have all the social and mental ills we do today. Maybe, my college doctoral level head professor and my two college friends (one of them my roommate) would not have felt so helpless and taken their own lives. As helpless as I felt to "save my girlfriend," I realized I can't heal all the broken or save every person. But what I can do is share my story and reveal how God's love broke through for me. And my brave becomes your breakthrough. My "yes, I will love on you" turns into your yes for loving on another. The ripple effect to God's very good commandment to love on one another outlives us.

I don't need to worry about the right words to say. Just be there. If I just stick to my story, they will see the experience, strength, and hope God gives. I don't ever claim to know all about the Bible or be an expert; I'm just a humble student of the Word. I stick to what God has done to me and then share that what the Lord does for one He lovingly would do for another. I encourage people not to lose hope but just keep talking to God in a true way. It is the Holy Spirit and Jesus Christ who do the saving and changing. My job is just to *love*—one person at a time with one story at a time.

Sharing this love is for me! Not for a tiny little insignificant part of a huge church body of believers, but just little ol' me, loving on and listening to one person at a time. Love given grows. Joy shared grows. Resources given grow. My gift from God is love, joy, and encouragement; the gift that broke through for me is now a faith-based nonprofit recovery from addiction assistance foundation. To date we are helping one life at a time become free of substance abuse. One day, it will be a recovery wellness center. Until then I keep "loving on the one."

What is your gift from God? How can you best give it away, so that you will be replenished with more? Everyone has a God gift; seek it out. Your purpose awaits you!

NOW I'M LOVING THIS JAM—
THE REDEMPTION SONG

I'm on the edge of my seat. You, Lord have opened my eyes. I can now see some of the fruit of my redemption and what it looks like for my family. I want it for everyone. I see the fruit of the sacrifice of prayer; worship, faith, and renewing my mind with Your Word has paid off.

Now, we wake on Saturday mornings and make pancakes and waffles and fresh fruit together, me in paleo versions. My husband plays chess, or most of the time they work on the Jet Skis or any of the toys, all while my daughter and I make barista quality lattes. The older girls tell me of high school life and tell me who is coming over by boat later.

It's the life I always dreamed of and more, unimaginably more— just like the promises God made to me when my heart was broken over and over in my formative years. Life may break it again. If you love, you risk, and I risk because I love people so deeply. People usually don't intend to, but it is naturally human to fall into sin, and sin breaks hearts, including God's. *But with God*, He heals. He is the Comforter and the Healer through the *Holy Spirit*. He moves you past and through the heartbreak and heals the heart to love even more strongly and deeply the next time.

It all sounds so cliché, the living amends and rewards I describe in my now freer life in Christ. But that is what I meant to every premise or path God leads us to, he will get us through to the promise. It's not that dreamy Saturday all the time, but it is enough to pay back a hundredfold the investment I made when I picked up that cross, breaking the chains of addiction. God led me to what He wanted from me. I chose to give Him my all, my faith empowered my recovery from alcoholism, and with that decision a family's chains broke off, along with all they ever hid in my family, my family before me, and the ones to come. The Word of God promises a life of healing and blessing that lasts a thousand generations, for those who follow Him. So every time I want to quit the call or the work it takes, I remind myself that this is for this generation and the future generations in my family and in the families of my community.[3]

FLYBYS – WHAT DO I DO WITH ALL THOSE PAINFUL MEMORIES?

We use them. That is what God does too. I truly wish that love had broken though for me and my excuses with a little more nobility, and I had the courage to be, say, the female version of Buzz Aldrin, one of the first two men to walk on the moon. But that is just not my story. We can only be the best at being ourselves and the story line we landed in. As I learn and grow with where I have been and where I want to go, I have learned that God wastes nothing, so we shouldn't either. Our story line may not have landed us on the moon, but with God we can outshoot any rocket to the moon. God uses all of our experiences and our complex backgrounds for our specific purpose. So, my rehab (aka jail experience) was very rich in lessons I'll never forget. They will serve as a platform to remember what I was saved from and to share to help people not end up there.

In fact, one lesson was a tightrope walk about two feet off the ground, which was very hard to balance on and navigate. One spot was the "relapse tree"; that one I fell off of and scarred myself, literally and soulfully. I didn't even know what relapse was until I went there; it is when you fall back to using a substance in active addiction or abuse. I also learned that for any human behavior there is a psychology term and a statistic to match it, and most of the time it terrifies you. Don't fret, if that happens to you. If you were labeled with any psychology term, there is Jesus's full healing for that condition and behavior. Believe me, I've witnessed a complete change and transformation on even convicted criminals who did time. There is no condition God can't heal, and if He does not, He gives the grace to represent Him through the situation.

At rehab we had a growth exercise somewhat like an escape room where you had to navigate an unknown territory and find a way out of the room. You had to stay on the rope that was waist high, and you would hold it between your hands. You could never let go of it and, but you had to find an exit to get out of the exercise/game. I was the second person to win this game, the second one out of the maze. I knew the secret because the minute I surrendered everything and did it God's way and went to rehab, I could see in the sense of the Holy Spirit. I could hear as never before, and the Holy Spirit told me the answer and I followed where He led.

The way out was to ask for help. You even had to say it a certain way: "I need help," That was the phrase that freed me out of the maze. Afterward, I sat and watched my bunkmates and even my husband get out of the maze (it was family weekend at the rehab facility), and these were the unifying and growth exercises. Anyhow, after the last person made it out, I went up to the counselor leading the exercises. I can't even remember what I needed to say to him exactly; it had to do with my wish not to affect my husband's quality of life with my recovery.

What pierced me was his response: "This is *your* cross to bear." It cut me. I couldn't bear that cross—no, not that; I couldn't do it *alone*. That burden is the one that took my dad down to an early grave. The same thing took his dad down. Couldn't I have a different cross? It was a painful realization. The biblical truth and lesson hidden in the cross is that the cross is light, so long as you don't deny the cross and the journey to carry it, Jesus shows up and gives you the strength to carry it. He Himself shoulders our burdens and sends help in community and family. Every time I start to feel burdened by "forever," I go back to the verse that in my weakness He is my strength and that His grace is sufficient for me to succeed.[4]

It turned out that my husband wanted to give up drinking too. He was given a similar vision, a new family life that was clean and wholesome and not muddied up with drinking. We both wanted to teach our kids to cope with life and relationships and disappointments with honesty and good coping skills instead of partying as a stress reliever, hiding, masking, and numbing the feelings away. I made peace with that cross I had to bear. The minute I had the courage to pick it up, the same God who died for me took the brunt of the weight off. When I humbly say, "I need you, Lord," He comes. To know and follow Jesus is to die to our fleshly desires and live with the Spirit leading. We get to live in the glory of His resurrection, *alive* and living free of the weight of sin.

THE PEARL OUT OF THE ICK

I found it fascinating when I heard that pearls are made out of the irritation in an oyster's little snotty environment. So bottom line is that God *uses our* yuck and ick to give us a beautiful and strong pearl, something of rare beauty and value and uniqueness. With our life's irritants, He builds a special strength and beauty into us, like a pearl. In our healing process, he purposes our special "pearl of pain" to impact others. As we show faithfulness and courage through the process, we inspire people that they can do what they are called to do, hard or not. In our broken and messy storms of life, God shows up to still our fear and show the storms who is boss. He told us that His grace is enough to get us through.[4]

It took a long time for me to learn to accept and live in God's grace; you can learn faster, I'm sure. It takes childlike faith. It takes embracing imperfect progress instead of perfection. It takes valuing the lessons and people you meet more than the goals you have in mind. It takes your agenda-driven taskmaster self off the track and puts more emphasis on journey and experience instead of destination and accomplishment.

If I find myself in a narrow state of mind, or processing life through wounds or filters of experience, I purge it out as quickly as I can. Then I fill my mind and heart with God's Word and rehearse the blessing of the renewed mind God has given me. Empty of my old self, I'm sure the Lord will fill and bless me in new ways every day! It's a promise; I just take it in faith, because the Word of God says that the Lord's mercies are new for me each day, fresh and catered for that day exclusively. If I'm overthinking a perceived problem of tomorrow in worry, I have just stepped out of that day's grace, and that's why I find myself not handling it well. I've overdrawn grace and am now operating in undue stress. I can't live a day or its grace any sooner than it comes. The grace I need for that day is not there for me yet. It's like manna in the Bible; if I try to collect more than I need on any day, then it spoils my day!

All of the good news messages and promises are way too good to be true. But they are. So take this lesson, and believe it by faith. You are made to grow in maturity naturally. You aren't meant to be a baby Christian all your life. We are all meant to grow in faith. What does that mean? It means you do this God's way; stay there until He says. Think of yourself as a seedling in the dirt, it just stays put, the nutrients and water come to it. The work all happens under the surface, behind the scenes and without the seed "trying" to grow. The seed just receives and waits well. Soon enough, it will spring forth; that will be our active part, so it's almost effortless, because growth is what it was made to do.

So if you find yourself in a life challenge that appears way bigger than you, do this. Call out for God's help through the Savior, Jesus; read and stay in the Word of God continually. Park there, meditate on it day and night. Sooner rather than later you will find that you yourself or the situation has changed (or both). It's just what God and the Word of God do. This formula is effortless change. You can't explain it; it just does what it does. Open your heart to belief and faith, apply the Word of God on it, and keep doing it. Then wait in expectant faith and hope. You will grow. I didn't say instantly; it takes time, consistency, and process to change. Don't grow weary in the wait. No word of God ever returns void; that means it always gets things done! The Word of God accomplishes its purpose.[5]

HIS SACRED HEART FOR YOURS
END OF CHAPTER REFLECTIONS

A Glimpse at His Heart …

A Step into the Sacred Chambers of His Heart—His Holy Word

I will think on these things; Whatever is worthy of praise. The Lord God is ever worthy of our praise. Elevate your small situation to a mighty God. He is a good God who is almighty.

Help me remember the battle belongs to You, Lord. God is worthy of being our delight and devotion and to be forever worshiped. It takes much spiritual maturity to praise God in terrible or hard times, but do it anyway. It's just a matter of time before He turns the situation around. His love never fails. Take a praise break. As you lift up the Lord's name in worship, your problems shrink. Praise Songs

"Lift You Up" by Ryan Stevenson, Oct. 2017.
"Proof of Your Love" by For King and Country, 2013.

A Guided Prayer for You

Almighty Yahweh Rapha or healer, You have put in me a new heart with new desires of excellence. It is in Your healing presence I can light up every dark chamber, balm up all the raw wounds, and mend up the tears in my heart. As I fully reveal to You and myself all my heart and the desires in it, You will wash it and mend it all new. You give me a tender yet resilient and strong heart. All my new heart is Yours. What shocks me most, God, is that though my heart seems too gravely wounded at this time, You are restoring it into vibrant life, little by little.

Never let me stray from loving You.

LOVE BROKE THROUGH

Your white space …

10

GROWING PAINS

Faith Is the Miracle-Gro –
A Matter of the Heart

A good environment, proper nutrition, healthful habits, right mindset, speaking the Word of God over yourself and your loved ones, and time—this is all faith in action. It acts like visible Miracle-Gro on your life.

We see in a healthful person a beauty and vitality like that of a garden. It is alluring and calming to most. When you see a health and wholeness, you see optimum results. Inspiring, isn't it? Yes, healthfulness depends on the elements. Proper care and attention directly affect the outcome. All this is pretty easy to understand and relate to. We all see what ideal conditions can do for us. So once God is in our lives, most of us truly pursue complete health so we can do the work of God and honor the temple of our body He lives in.

However, we have an enemy to that ideal growth and self. That also means he is an enemy of change. So he tempts us with our fleshly desires of quick fixes and instant results. We as a culture have technology and knowledge at our fingertips. We have no patience, quit or change activities often, or swipe away a challenge if it takes too long. Is it any wonder that patience is a virtue?

So if we want to make a difference in life, be our best, and grow, then we must overcome that tendency with our Lord. As I described before, being honest and open and willing makes our heart yielded to what God leads for us to be and then do. To be yielded in the heart is to allow your heart to be worked on, approachable and soft on all sides. Let's be honest; that does not describe today's culture. It doesn't take long for a cute baby who loves everyone to become a mistrusting and guarded li'l human. So what hope do we have? We have the hope of Jesus, the Word of God, and the power of the Holy Spirit. That, my dear, is the ultimate trifecta of power and ability.

So back to how this happened in my story. Once I prioritized a quality, God-honoring life over my comfort, I gave way to change. Once I valued the relationship over my need to be right, my relationship improved. I didn't want to write off people so that I could keep living an alcoholic lifestyle. My drinking was negatively affecting me and my family. That mattered more to me. When they all saw that I valued the relationship and wanted to work on a healthier way of life, everyone was supportive. The relationships I had with my husband, my children, and my family and friends deepened. I gave way to courage over comfort. I died to my selfish nature and become "born again" in the spirit.

I was able to claim victory and hope over my previous condition of being addicted to drinking wine every day. Yes, I could stop drinking for a month or two, but I didn't like it. I had all the telltale signs—blackouts, hiding or lying about how much I had drunk, and, worst of all, anxiety, depression, and sleeplessness. All those are side effects of excessive drinking and withdrawal from it. Bottom line, I depended on it more than I did God. I learned, once I gave up drinking, that all of that was symptoms revealing the sickness and condition of my heart and mind. I can't do right if I'm not thinking right. And moreover, anyone who drinks knows that after a few drinks, you are not thinking right or sober anymore.

So as I committed to God to grow and renew my thinking so that I could be more holy and sober, I taught my flesh how to submit to my spirit. The longer I did the next right and sober thing, the better I got being happy in spirit naturally.

I found that as I cut more and more away of my fleshly nature or pleasure and comfort-seeking self, *by the grace and power of God*, I could and would change to be a healthy and whole person. Instead of life being all about me, I started to be more Spirit-filled, peaceable, and genuine to people.

In time, with a continual practice of speaking and hearing the Word of God, I was filled with vitality and fruits of the spirit. I was happier, healthier, and more effective, and people noticed and said so. This time I could accept the loving compliment instead of letting it fall to the floor in shame. I showed more of the fruits of the Spirit—love, joy, peace, patience, kindness, goodness, faithfulness, gentleness, and self-control. I loved that the process was working.

God's Word said we will be known by how we love and by the fruit we produce. All fruit leads to and gives life—that is, prosperity and success. That's why Jesus was serious about whether or not a fig tree produced fruit. If it was not producing fruit or life, it was not worth its existence.[2] Jesus wants us to be fruitful and multiply; He has said so since the beginning of humanity. This abundant life was not just about populating the earth but about spreading abroad His loving principles, His way, and His love. All Jesus did on earth produced fruit, meaning life and multiplication by blessing and sharing what was already there. Jesus never made a child of His own, so this goes to show that He is not just about procreating but about sharing life. Picture a beautiful botanical garden; its whole life cycle serves to prosper itself. Even the ripening and death of the flowers and fruit gives itself to the thriving of the life and the youth in a producing garden.

So in our own lives, perhaps we had a disadvantage earlier in our lives, but it is of no matter. Once we start to think on or meditate on the Word of God day and night, over and over again, our heart is made fertile and described as good soil in the Bible. Jesus shared with us in the book of Matthew that with fertile ground in our heart we are able to grow the seeds of faith into God's good and prosperous plan for our lives. Growth happens in the fertilizing power of the faith. With faith in all God says, resurrection and life redeem what death stole. A seed must die to become a shoot and then a bud, and then so on and so forth. The Holy Spirit can move when He wants to but works most powerfully in a yielded, tender heart. It was in faith that I learned to recognize the promptings and leadings of the Holy Spirit.

If you get your healing and deliverance completely and instantly, *hurray for you!* Yet the Bible shows us time and time again that He heals us when we obey and do our part. That was the case for me; I received supernatural power to see and hear the Holy Spirit when I obeyed. I put that plug in the jug of wine and leaned in on Christ to teach me to live "high and dry."

When I stopped escaping what pained me and instead ushered my pains to the surface and gave them over to Christ, I could see differently, more soberly and wisely. The Lord knows, drunk people are rarely wise. So though the lens of perfect divinity, I'd process what was stressing me out. God made all that I eliminated in my life into fertilizer for the good stuff. He grew me and my fruit with all that nasty stuff that I had let pile up. Together, I've seen God raise up beauty out of ashes and pretty flowers out of the driest places.

In the terrible loss of a girlfriend, I made peace with the perfectionist in me and the Bible verse that always made me so mad. Through the lens of grace, Proverbs 31 women finally made sense to me. In the death and loss of my little butterfly friend, she gave life to me. The circle of life is naturally abundant and always gives life. No matter how death happens, if Jesus was involved for even one utterance or glance in His direction, He has them safe, in eternal paradise. You see even in a sad death, lost to depression, my friend was life to me. Will you, like me, take the challenge and be life to others?

My Prayer-Filled Words for the Legacy and
Celebration of my friend's Life and Friendship

I Don't Even See It

April 28, 2017

Dear Friends who have lost someone to suicide,
The message in the coffee cup changes.
I have a love for pretty and meaningful or inspiring coffee
cups. Today, I selected one that reads, "Many women have done
excellently, but you surpass them all" (Proverbs 31:29 ESV).
This message typically inspires me but in a way also deflates me,
because it describes one amazing, accomplished, loving, and patient
superwoman.
Sometimes—okay, every time, this inspiring message instead
becomes a reminder of the unachievable standard that exists in my
head and is so hard to emulate.
Yet this morning the message was met with love and compassion.
It did what *the Word* does and always will do: come alive for your
specific circumstance. This Bible proverb took on a different and
powerful meaning. See, this fateful morning as I still grapple with
the loss of a friend very dear to me, it meant something altogether
different.
If you take the time to read the Proverbs 31 message, as I said
before, she is one Wonder Woman, and I fall short time and time
again. It's a struggle I'm so tired of, because my inner critic is—well,
let's not put it lightly—an unpleasable witch! Yet with the love of
God, I'm deleting that virus-infested, useless malware to replace it
with the *truth*. I am complete, a beautiful, complex, wonderfully
made being, created in the very loving image of a supreme, good
and perfect, unfailing God. Yet I am in the process of believing this

truth, and I still beat myself up and get down on myself over not being or doing enough, not doing things well enough.

So here comes the transformation and compassion part. It was in this image of a coffee cup message, that God spoke to me about my friend. He gave me another morsel of compassion and understanding and goodness about her loss. See, when I read the passage on the cup, I immediately thought of my friend. She was and is one amazing Proverbs 31 type of woman. As I read this passage I said out loud, "my friend, you have done excellently, you have surpassed them all."

The inner critic, the enemy of a free soul, quickly blurted, "But didn't she do that thing?" Without a second passing, I silenced that lie with one divine thought, the message of God's love and grace. I said to myself, *I don't see that. I see all the beautiful, all the wonderful, all the soulful, all the sweet fun spirit; I see the inner soulful light that she was and is, because death cannot touch the everlasting light and love.* You see, with the eyes of truth, the unforgivable is erased, vanishes as if it never was. When I read that coffee cup message; I thought of my friend, the most excellent mother and woman. I didn't see any shortcomings or mistakes; I only saw the good and everlasting in her; that is the everlasting treasure that death can't touch.

So for the first time, in my three years of owning this bittersweet cup with the unattainable message bar of Proverbs 31. It became for me a message of excellence and worthiness. I loved my friend, purely and deeply, and I never even saw that dark place. I had heard that grace message before, that when one accepts God's forgiveness and love, they become justified, *just as if I'd* never done wrong. The huge gift me to me this morning was that out of this coffee cup marked with God's message of grace and admiration to women, the message had become alive, real, and understood in a new light.

Just as I had seen the Word say an excellent and surpassing woman and thought, *That is, my dear friend,* so does God see me and all His people. If I, being human, loved and could extend admiration and excellence to a woman fallen, then how much more does a perfect God see me, past my shortcomings. God does not see me or anyone miss the mark or say, "You are not good enough"; He only sees the excellence, the light in me.

I finally felt worthy of that cup; that deep message of the Word of God describing excellence was for me. That's what God is so good at; He turns a mess into a message. The loss of my friend and how I loved her through it all, past it all, as if she had never done it, drove home God's message for me. When I accept the message of the Good News, the Master Creator of all the universes doesn't see what I have done or not done, He sees those treasures and talents and gifts He placed in me to share with His favorite people. Who? Oh, everyone!

Today and every day remember, you and I can remember how to love well. We can love people through the eyes of grace and love within the space of knowing that we each are wonderfully made, excellent, and surpassing them all. Nothing we could ever do can separate us from this love and greatness in the eyes of the Almighty. With His transformative power I'll soon believe what He says about me, because today it became clear to me through my eyes of love for my friend. Our Lord understands; I was never really holding anything up or together, so I could never really let Him down if I should fall apart. He is the comforter and loves us so much more than we do Him on our best day. *He just loves us.*

Let's believe and receive that love and grace message, with much love,
Odilie Marie Bagwell Portocarrero

Proverbs 31:10–31

A little more faith talk never hurts. Faith really matters.

Faith is a bridge. It connects the unseen goodness in you to your future. Your current level of faith is creating the next environment you live in. Doesn't that make you want to rise up in your level of thinking and faith? In faith, amazing is possible. In faith, I could see myself grow into better, not bitter. In faith, I receive the hope that God could do for me what He did for all those heroes of faith in the Bible. I was ready see what faith could do in my life! I'll tell you just a few of my favorite redemption stories in the Bible. Maybe it will spark your heart, as it did mine.

Take the woman with the issue of blood for twelve years. This woman used her faith to go get her healing. She overcame being marginalized and ostracized, and she knew before she knew that faith in Jesus was powerful. Jesus not only healed her, but He felt her belief and then complimented her! "Woman, your great faith has healed you; go and suffer no more!"[1] (Adapted from Mark 5:34 NIV.)

The faith of the woman at the well told all (see John 4). She was thirsty for way more than water. Perhaps her past was weighing her down. She wanted a cleared rap sheet. Jesus knew all about her and absolved her guilt and shame. He gave her the will and power to go and tell all how Jesus had changed her life.

Then there is the faith of the woman with the alabaster jar. That one story it makes me come undone. This woman had unabashed faith; she walked into a private, highly respected and decorated all male meeting. Unannounced with no appointment or apology, she comes to Jesus and breaks an alabaster jar of expensive perfume and begins to worship Jesus in the most intimate way revealed in the Bible. She rubs his head with holy and set apart anointing oil. Her genuine and lavish gesture impresses Jesus and offends the religious officials. The cost of what she did was great but, she was willing to put it all on the line to honor Christ the Messiah. This account is in two books: Matthew 26:6–13 and Mark 14:3–9. Jesus Himself said that her worship was worth remembering and would be talked about for all time.

There is another impressive display of faith and deep repentance that involved oil and a whole lot of weeping, rubbing Jesus's feet with her hair and tears and oil. This woman was so repentant that she didn't care who heard her confession. She was so desperate for healing that she again would be publicly mocked by men, and Jesus would stick up for her too. So this really ignites my unashamed faith. If what I carry is heavy, I am willing to repent publicly and be undone so that God can heal me. This is told in Luke 7:37–50.

Then there was the time when a woman, completely unknown to all of history, gathered up all of her faith to make a bold move. She left all she knew and loved to seek Jesus at a rehabilitation clinic. She had never been apart from family and friends in her forty years of life. She had never lost faith in God, but she was so much in bondage to sin and addiction that she thought God wouldn't want to save her and that she would die young, as all the fathers in her family had done. She was publicly humiliated, and town whispers sounded like shouts to her. She never got to touch her Savior in faith physically, as another woman did in the Bible who was healed, but her encounter with an unseen God was sure. She even encountered her holy mother—all in the unseen spiritual realm, but nevertheless every bit life-changing. She has been telling everyone of Jesus since she was saved from her ultimate demise. That woman is me, Odilie Bagwell Portocarrero.

Without faith it is impossible to move and please God. I have hung on to that, though I thought my particular case was too far gone to be forgiven. I am ever grateful that my Lord Jesus saves all who come to Him, even the far gone. I'm glad I can revisit the times faith has paved my way to possible.

Faith is vastly powerful and has many abilities. I have loved exploring what faith has revealed to me. Faith has been my lifeline, and I hope it will be for you. I believe that faith grows with us until it gets us all into the arms of our Lord. Faith is limitless. It is infinite. Faith creates. Faith is an access point to the kingdom of God. Listed below are my interpretations of faith, with biblical evidence to support the applicational statements. These are each adapted affirmations I drew from the NIV translation of the Holy Bible.

Faith is a force (Mark 9:23).

Faith is a substance (Hebrews 11:1).

Faith is a currency in God's kingdom (Matthew 28:20).

Faith is a bridge (John 14:6).

Faith is the way (2 Corinthians 5:7).

Faith is a practice (Ephesians 2:8–9)

Faith is a stance (James 1:6).

Faith is sealing (Ephesians 1:13).

Faith fights (1 Timothy 6:12).

Faith discerns (1 Timothy 6:11).

Faith decrees (Matthew 21:22).

Faith delivers (Matthew 15:28).

Faith moves obstacles (Matthew 17:20).

Faith frees (Luke 7:50).

Faith refreshes (John 7:38).

Faith is a measure (Romans 12:3).

Faith produces (James 1:3).

Faith pleases *God*! (Hebrews 11:6).

I rest my case.

With great faith we make our own God marvel; without faith it is impossible to please God. Whoever would approach Him must believe that He exists and that He rewards those who seek Him (see Hebrews 11:6).

The Word of God says to be saved, or born again with a new nature, you must first believe in your heart and confess with your mouth that Jesus is Lord. In that soul-sealing and saving confession a powerful faith is born—the kind of faith that makes me a mountain mover and a water-walker. I could have had faith before, but what ignites this faith is putting the yielded heart (the heart's intention) and raising the voice in expression of biblical words back to God.

In that faith step, those two things that set us apart from the rest of creation are now honoring God. It is an active faith that creates godly work. It is faith that the apostle James describes as alive, when it goes to work for you and the will of God.

So think of it like opening up your Royal bank account. You are now a coheir with Christ and can draw upon your spiritual gifts and inheritance. This account is funded by the Lord's infinite storehouses (His glorious riches and resources—like a reserve). You are given full access to it by way of belief, which is faith. Faith is a currency, and the more responsibly you manage the faith you have and put it to grow, the more you get to use. Faith builds the life you've always dreamt of. God, being so generous and magnanimous gives us way more than our dreams: He goes beyond our wildest dreams. So again, by putting your full heart into the things that matter to God, and lining it up with an active faith and words, you build the bridges and travel the ways to your purpose. Your purpose is the most fulfilling and life-giving place for you to operate and live in. I'm still working on the stepping out in faith to live courageously in my purpose. Faith is the substance dreams are made of. So the saying goes that a dream without a plan is just a wish. So now you have a plan: your plan is to follow Jesus to where He leads. There He gets you to greater than you have ever dreamed. God's plan is always greater!

Don't be afraid to dream. If dreams have failed you before, it is just meant to lead you to a better or different one. Keep at it, one step at a time where your Lord leads you to faith over fear. That certainly inspires me to exercise my faith muscle, but for me the one that makes me quiver from working my faith muscle so hard has been to live in "faith without borders." It teaches me not to limit God. It was also the song I cried to and drank to, the song that accompanied my fervent prayers, that God would deliver me out of my bondage to drinking. Since then, it reminds me of what I was saved from and what I was saved for.

Exploring and implementing the little I've done to proclaim the

Lord's goodness to me has been expansive. The rich faith encounters I have shared with people have been above and beyond what I could have asked for, dreamed of, or even imagined. And I do believe the best is yet to come. This is what I was made for. Faith is never easy or cheap but always worth it!

Just as my bestie and tennis coach, Julie, said to me once when I complained to her. I had a serve and it more or less worked but mostly not; it lacked power and accuracy. As she coached me on new moves and I practiced them, I felt awkward. I couldn't do my old serve, and I hadn't gotten my new one down yet. I said, "I feel like I lost my serve, because you changed it all."

She said, "You didn't lose your serve; I gave you a *new* one." When I heard her say this recently, I knew it had way more meaning for me than tennis. God spoke to me about what God did for me. He didn't take my life; He gave me a powerful *new* one.

HIS SACRED HEART FOR YOURS

END OF CHAPTER REFLECTIONS

A Glimpse at His Heart ...

A Step into the Sacred Chambers of His Heart with His Holy Word

Oh, sweet child of God, that you would step into your own God-given potential. Stop doubting what I have said you are and have. I love it when you shine with confidence of what I put in you.

Verse:

Truly I tell you, if you have faith like a grain of mustard seed, you can say to this mountain, "Move from here to there," and it will move, and nothing will be impossible for you. (Matthew 17:20 NIV)

Praise Songs

"Oceans" by Hillsong, 2015.
"Give Me Faith" (acoustic) by Elevation Worship, 2018.

A Guided Prayer for You

You are Yahweh Shammah, which means the Lord is here at all times. You are for me and my ever-present help. You are faithful, and Your plans for me are always good. I know certain things might look bad to me right now, or my mind might wonder and say, *Where were*

You when this happened? Lord, I know that in the unseen spiritual world, You saved me in ways I didn't even know I could be saved. You are always working behind the scenes for each and every one of Your children. Forgive me if my faith is little sometimes; bless me with a great and mighty faith.

Almighty God, never let me lose my faith. Faith is my way to You!

LOVE BROKE THROUGH

Your white space ...

11

TRUST ISSUES

True love trusts.

The first Bible verse I ever committed to memory was on this topic. "Trust the Lord your God with all your heart and lean not on your own understanding. In all your ways acknowledge him and he will make straight your paths" (Proverbs 3:5–6 ESV).

If I'm honest, and I have been, I didn't want to talk about this. Why? There is still some remorse and shame on how I handled myself in my early dating life. But there is grace for that, so I walk in it, and I'll talk about it. But first, I preface with this: *Know your worth and identity before you date; if not, you'll be treated as worthless and nameless.*

So back to this verse and how I memorized it to heal and guide me. I was in high school and needed to trust in God in ways I never knew before. I desperately wanted to leave home to go to college and totally didn't see an inkling of a way. I also had made poor boy choices in both high school and college. I'm sure they are respectable men today, or so I pray, but I was needy and definitely broken inside, so I gave myself inappropriately to immature, hormonal boys. They betrayed my trust, many times over. So that verse helped me know that I needed to not trust in myself and needed to seek God first in everything.

This verse also helped me create a trust and reliance in God that He could work around, through, and past my brokenness and even my stupidity. Jesus, and the Word of life He is, could also help me get past all the blows and disappointments this season of life gave me: divorce, death, betrayals, lies. All that broken and human fallenness I had nothing to do with, but it had everything to do with forming poor opinions and wounds in me.

It was a tumultuous time in college; I lost the four dad figures I so adored to premature death and disease in a twelve-month period. Nothing made sense, not my behavior, not my family life, not my love life. The only good set of relationships I had in the early years of college were my group of girls who were the best support system. Yet inside I was still very unsettled. When I found my relationship with God again in college, I recited that verse often, and the Lord was faithful to help me. Yet, sadly, for many more years I had a far-off relationship with God. He was always there and steady; I was rebellious, clueless, and spiritually lost.

Let's just say that quite possibly this one verse, the Our Father, and the Hail Mary were all I gave to my Lord. That is pitiful, but my God is powerful! So He taught me and watched me through just what I was willing to give Him. Little by little, I learned how good it was to rely on and confidently trust in the God who gave me that verse. All that happened let me know *how much* I needed God to keep my paths straight, then and still.

Just as I write this, the Holy Spirit adds another layer to that Proverbs 3:4 (ESV) says, "So you will find favor and good success in the sight of God and man." How I hadn't connected those verses I've read before, I don't know. But it just goes to show that the Bible never stops coming to life. As I keep the Word of life before me, it continues to make more sense—or should I say, take on more meaning. The more I study, it may not make "rational sense," but I sure do grow in spiritual sense or knowing and trusting in what it says. What could memorizing a powerful verse do in your life? Lay the Word of God out upon your heart, and the Lord leads you on how to internalize it and live it out in new ways daily.

HOW DID THE MIS-TRUST GET THERE?

I ASKED MYSELF

Trust issues. I've had them. I have seen them. I'm not alone in this. I'm no psychologist, but I did do much graduate level college work and personal work in counseling. Trust issues can stem from many different experiences in relationship and during several stages of psychosocial development. Mistrust or lack of trust happens as a result of traumatic experience, low-self-esteem, trauma, bullying, rejection, abandonment, or any sort of witnessed or experienced abuse or lack of attachment. It is most commonly more deeply rooted if it occurred in early childhood.

For those of us who have worked through mistrust or want to, you know it takes patience to overcome. This chapter is not about interpersonal trust building but more *a taste of the hope and life that comes with a restored sense of trust mainly with GOD.* Then I'll touch on trust in the church and people of the church, including your family. Trust with God always overflows into wisdom and ability to trust people. Lastly, I'll trace out some important applications on trust and how to handle a breach of trust when that happens.

WHEN TRUST IS PRESENT, THERE IS PEACE

When trust is present, so is peace. So if you find yourself low on peace, you are probably high on control. You know the drill, trying to play God or, at the very least, saying to yourself, *Really, God? I would have done differently.* I've been there, and the good news is

I've left. Peace has His own way; it is The Way, The Truth, and The Life.[1] Notice this verse in the Bible doesn't say *a way* but *The Way*.

Together, let us clear out more of that pathway to Peace!

Peace is first a Person, a very important one, Jesus. His name is Prince of Peace. If you want more peace, you have to get more Jesus. Peace comes from Him.

I am married twenty plus years, raising four teens, and running five different business entities. When life throws me a wrench, I most definitely want to practice being more levelheaded, trusting, and staying in peace during life's harried moments. I would love to keep my mind fixed on peace. So much so I give it and I keep in it.

Can you imagine operating in a lifestyle so in communion with peace, that when you arrive on the scene, peace comes with you? We can have such a yielded presence of our Lord that we bring trust and peace into every atmosphere we go to. Think of it, Odilie just arrived, here comes peace and joy; Brad just arrived, here comes wisdom and peace. Isn't that fun? What arrives when you arrive? How do we tap into being what is already in and on us? We take our focus off this world and reside in another higher world or kingdom, Jesus. So what I mean by that is take your focus off the question or the problem in your world now, and fix your focus on the Lord Jesus. When you make your God mightier than your problem, the problem shrinks.

Now I'm not talking about living off in some la-la-land. My mind and entire being are living in today, fully present. The difference is, I live more fully in trusting my Savior. My perception of this world gets clear when I see it through the lens of a good God. Our good *God* is ever-present, all-knowing, and always going to make things work out for my good, even through bad things. I brought this up earlier, but we are to remind ourselves that our spirit is seated with Christ in heavenly places.

So I say to myself, as I process the chaos of this life, *This is no surprise to Jesus; He has the upper hand on this. I will sit back in peace and let my Lord speak to me.* If He wants to play a role in the solution in some way, He is faithful to reveal it to me. In the meantime, I do the most powerful thing I can: I pray into it. I trust that God is truly with me and for me, because a mind in Christ is a mind at peace. The Word of God promises that "You will keep in perfect peace whose mind is fixed on you, because he trusts in You."[1]

Are you starting to see what I see? Peace is an indicator or measure of trust. The degree I trust is the degree to which I get to live in His peace.

WHAT IS SO IMPORTANT ABOUT TRUST IN GOD?

I've lived on both sides of trust. First there was trust in myself to get through on my own plan and volition. Then there is trust in God where I say, "Jesus, take the wheel. You lead and guide me in big and small decisions of life." I hear God's leading, I trust, and I obey. I don't do this perfectly, but His ways are perfect. I keep trusting that He is leading me at a pace that I can follow.

This has made a major improvement in my quality of life. I can tell you that in my life, I lose fewer things, forget fewer things, and get in far fewer fights with people. In giving God the lead, I am wiser, I feel more in control of things, and I have even more positivity because I've given control to a God who can actually do something about what troubles me. I've also seen the good and blessings that happen in the lives of my Christian friends and mentors who display a lifestyle surrendered or yielded to the Spirit. There is just a good difference about them. I see it. It encourages me that a life given over to Christ is a better life. It is a life blessed beyond measure.

SO WHAT HELPED ME GET TO A HIGHER LEVEL OF TRUST?

A few obvious things: desperation and total wreckage in my state of being. If I was a car it felt like a complete engine failure and I totaled the car I had been driving. So in that analogy, I was so blessed to be alive that I would not return to a reckless and self-indulgent, self-serving life again. They call this the gift of desperation. It's the typical white flag moment. The situation is so bad that you surrender. I am finally well enough along in my redemption that I'm thankful for the crash that drove me into the capable and saving arms of Christ.

Surrender—most people hate that word. I've seen cancer-ridden, terminally ill "good people" still say, "I can't do it any other way but mine." The will or personal volition is the hardest thing to turn over. But once you do, you end up finding out that you are actually more effective and have a greater sense of independence by having full dependence on God. I hope that makes sense. I know it may sound odd. A vine analogy could help give it a visual. A vine can't grow on its own, yet fully supported, it grows healthy and travels far up and over anything in its way. Without a support, the vine either wouldn't be or it would be grounded for life. I don't want to be "grounded"; I want to rise up.

Okay, so maybe you aren't having the shakes if you don't drink, and sick if you do drink. Maybe your husband hasn't threatened divorce; maybe the people you love most aren't saying you are messing up your life, and you must change, or you'll lose it all. Maybe you aren't desperate the way I was. I had already seen how it all goes down. In my life I lost my family as a child to the dis-ease of alcohol and brokenness. Like I told you before, I couldn't relive all that dysfunction again; I would give it my everything to save this one. I had to do my part, but I knew if Jesus wasn't in it, I wouldn't win. I needed Jesus. When I surrendered to Jesus, I finally was empowered to do what I could never do before. I could *be* myself. I

ODILIE M. BAGWELL PORTOCARRERO AU.D.

would get the support of loving friends. I was living clean and felt good inside (no binging on eating or drinking). I even slept well, free of worry and anxiety, throughout the whole night. I was living completely substance free, no antidepressants, no antianxiety pills, no alcohol; just me, with Christ and *free* of it all.

For a person who literally didn't want to go on a mission trip before because they didn't serve alcohol, a person who couldn't stick to a workout and eating regimen for twenty-one days ever in her life, *this was my miracle.*

In God's power I was doing what I could never do before, with ease and enjoyment! I now absolutely trusted God. He gave me ability and the will to do good in my life! I saw that if I could do what I could never do before in my behaviors and choices, what could I be capable of if I turned my entire life over to God. I would give all of me and all I loved so that I could see what He could do through me. It was a raw deal for the Lord, I tell you; what would He do with my jaded and judgmental mind, my guarded and bleeding heart, and my messy relationship situations? I was angry and had no idea why. But with God's grace, I focused on what I wanted—all of God. Since I came to believe that He really did die just for me, then what He had planned for me must be good. It was the best choice I have ever made.

As I was saying, maybe you don't have desperation to that level in your life. But every person needs Jesus. That is written in the Bible too. "For all have fallen short." Short of what? God's best for you! Until you come to Him in a real relationship, you might have a dissatisfaction; you seek but don't get filled. You carry a level of discontent in the middle of a perfectly good life.

You are missing the very nucleus of your being. Your God-sized hole is meant to be filled. Until you put God in the center of your being, you will have everything or nothing and still not be content or happy. If you ignore this yearning, you'll die ho-hum and cold to all the good around you, unable to feel joy.

Or you might find yourself surrounded by all the things and

people you ever wanted and yet remain empty inside. I can't compel you to trust God. But I can keep sharing how it works for me, and I'll let the Holy Spirit lead you to the surrendered life. Then you too can live more completely and lack no good thing.

When I saw what trusting God with my present looked like, *I was utterly happy with the results.* Until then, the past had a firm grip on me. My therapies had me digging through my past mistakes, which seemed to take up a good bit of my mental real estate. I had lots of guilt and shame connected to my past. I had active struggles with wanting different for myself. I didn't want this for myself; I was still romanticizing my past and a good part of me wanted it back. Ugh, such an age-old human thing, to want things back the old way, because the new way was too unfamiliar and uncomfortable. I pressed on and saw that I wasn't alone in this. I would get past this adjustment period and learn to enjoy my new way.

I took comfort that my ancestors the Hebrews, freed from the Egyptians, wanted to go back to slavery, because they didn't know how to handle dependance on a good and providing God when they couldn't see a solution. I would say to myself, if God provided water to His people out of a rock, He would refresh me too. It was hard for me to deal with, but God saw me through. The Lord cares so deeply about what pains us. No matter how silly it may be to us, He cares for every detail. It was in my little daily insignificant struggles—like, say, homework time with four kids—that a calming and comforting God met a stressed and worrisome mom. I learned to trust God for my every need.

Sadly, my own way of handling life got me into major messes and a complete breakdown. So I surrendered to God, and He gave me a new self and a new future. But the enemy was now trying to keep me from my promised future. Given how much I was rehearsing my past, how could I possibly step into the best of my present or even the promise of my future? Most of my day I was in the wrong time frame. I can't be present, living in the now, when I'm mentally occupied by past pain or fear of the future. I feared what I could be capable of if I failed again. It was pretty bad; I was terrified to even buy a one-month calendar. I feared I would relapse. The only way I could be free to enjoy the time I had now, the present, was to give all of my days to God.

I gave Him my time—all of it, past, present, and future, to God. God is not bound by the constraints of time; He dictates all seasons and time. God has *all* the time in the world and eternity to work with. I knew if I gave my time over to God, He would do a good work in me to help me manage all the days of my life, even the fallen ones. He would be my only chance at peace with the past, my guide to fullness of living in the now, and my only hope for a good future.

God taught me a way to talk to my time and manage it, not let it manage me. Whenever the reminders of the past came, I put them in their place. My past is what made me as I am now. Without it I wouldn't have the strength, experience, and hope that I do now. All that I am now, I find to be invaluable and priceless. I wouldn't trade it for an easier way. If not for the past, I wouldn't have the depth and ability to remain in the trust in God I now know.

Christ's love for me came to be real and a part of everyday awareness. God wastes no pain or trouble. He uses it all to reveal Himself to us. The troubles and desperation of the past led me to the peace of Christ that reigns in my life today. That peace is priceless, and it does surpass all understanding. It's unexplainable, really; you just know it when you are living it.

I used to approach a full-blown panic attack when someone would say to me, "You know, you will have four kids in high school and college one day" (my kids were only babies or toddlers then). Really, people, you have to scare a new mom like that? I couldn't handle it even then. How was I going to handle vaping, underage drinking, and other kids picking on mine? Needless to say, that made me worry for the future too much—a future that didn't even exist.

The Word of God promises His mercies are new every morning, fresh and catered for that specific day. So if my head is outside of the day I'm living in, then I've just outstepped the grace of that day.

It's as if I have overdrawn my grace for that day. Just like, in a real economy, you shouldn't live on borrowed money, so in the kingdom you shouldn't live beyond the day you are in. I'm trying to live a day that I don't have grace for yet. That is why some future thoughts make us anxious. If you are like me, you might allow yourself to mentally entertain a billion terrible what-ifs. I would imagine or worry about my extended family, my husband, my kids, my health, their health, my job, and their future jobs. The scenarios I would try to prepare and control for were endless.

Living like that is giving my anxious thoughts the map of where I want to go; it's anxiety-driven. The future I had in mind was completely in defense mode. If I could think it up, I would try to buy some insurance plan or educational plan to protect for that. My future, though I generally imagine a good one, I would constantly try to protect from something ruining it. It was terrifying and exhausting to live in such a reactionary way.

I was doing it all wrong, too. If this was a game, I was playing checkers with life, reacting based on my enemy's move. Jesus, on the other hand, helps me play chess. He has me think through what I do first and how my enemy may use it to take my people or my territory. He showed me how to be strategic and plan my moves a few steps ahead by going on the faith of His leading. God said, "Let Me show you a better and easier way!"

As they say, the best defense is a great offense. The power of the Holy Spirit, through wonderful Bible teachers, showed me how to live faith on the offensive—you know, making winning plays, taking enemy territory, and scoring in life all the way to the win. For this inner Olympian, life was amazing to me. I love a win! With God I learned how to win the battle on my past, present, and future. You see, we all have an enemy for our affections, our attention, and most of all our future. It is fully trusting Jesus in my complete surrender that helps me *enjoy* today.

It is our own words and thoughts, actions and prayers that create our own future. That is why the enemy, Satan, is constantly distracting my present with reminders of past failures or fears of a failing or unsure future. Yet, anchored in Christ, I can remain steady through all the unknowns.

What is this preoccupation of the present? Why all the constant distractions, like notifications, instant news, and instant feeds on my phone? Yes, it is convenient, but it truly gets you completely off your day's purpose. All of us parents of teens need a check-in. How can we transition in life's seasons when we are too busy following our teens' every move on Life360? Come on, parents, let us let go and let the kids learn independence and consequence. Then you and I can be about the Father's business, instead of too much in our teens'. Then we can free up our physical and mental energy and serve who we really should be in our new seasons.

The enemy also wants to distract us from meeting that person or hearing that sermon to free or empower us. When I learned how to strategize a good offense on the enemy attacks, I won. The Word of God, fervent prayer, worship and praise, and out-loud affirmations let the enemy know that I know who the boss of my future is, *God*. Little by little I learned how to realize and acknowledge out loud to my Creator and in front of my enemy, that I knew my source of all that is good. I affirm that my Savior has never stopped saving me. I get to choose who I give my future to. I wasn't going to give the enemy my peace or future anymore. If I let the unknown and fears play out in my head, I've just sold out to the devil. *Check;* I just lost my tactical advantage, the upper hand. So now I would remind him of what God has said to me: that my welfare and well-being are sustained by my Creator. He alone is the source of all my days. God Almighty just bailed me out, *Checkmate*. Game over, Satan! Right there I submitted my worry to the Lord; I'm telling Him with all of my body and spirit, "I trust You."

The Word of God declares that as I submit to the Lord, the devil flees. I say to the enemy, "You will not have your way with me. You are a defeated foe. Move over; this is my territory to claim. Check*mate*.

"In fact," I continue, "God loves me so much, He promoted me. He gives me good places to claim for me and my family. He now trusts me with *His* kingdom. I don't live for just me anymore, devil. I do what I do to bring honor to God, So there! Begone!" And off he goes! God is faithful to protect us.

Little by little I was freed from my fear of the future. Suddenly, I could enjoy the simple things; for instance, I could buy a planner again. My fear was replaced with wonder. What was the wonderful future like that God was working out for me? That was a freeing moment. I even texted my girlfriend Jessica. I said, "You aren't going to believe this. I don't fear falling to alcohol anymore. I bought an 18-month calendar!"

That was a victory I'll never forget. You would not believe the amount of Jesus it took to overcome the fear I felt after attending and hearing all that is shared in ninety AA meetings in ninety days. I saw so much fallenness and so many broken people who kept making the same mistakes over and over. I didn't want to do that, but I had the same symptoms that led to those meetings, so I was very much afraid.

Think of it: rehab six or eight times, and still struggling. Yikes! Lord, please keep me from that mistake. Addiction is no joke, and it does not discriminate. Anyhow, the really good part of all this is that *by the blood of the Lamb and the word of my testimony I overcame these fears!* So when Jesus helped me overcome that, I celebrated!

Thanks to You, God, for freeing me to live each day in freedom. Only a prisoner counts the days, like in AA. I am no prisoner; I'm a free child of God. He capably holds my past, present, and future. So long as I remain in Jesus, I stay in Jesus's joy. I live each day with whatever it brings. Jesus said it first (John 14:1 NLT): "Don't let your hearts be troubled. Trust in God, and trust also in me."

If Jesus said it, I receive it when I believe it! I can handle all of life's blessings and disappointments, one day or even one moment at a time, in His presence. When I trust and accept what may come, I remain in Him. He has got me, and all of this—it will all work out. I know this. Amazing grace meets confident trust!

THE UNSEEN

The greater reality is unseen. Let me try to explain this truth so that your trust grows. As you know I'm an audiologist by trade. When I was in my doctoral training, what science revealed is that during a baby's development, if physical genetic marker happened, such as a malformation, then it was necessary to observe and study what else was forming at the same time and to check for the function of that organ. So if there was, say, a pit or tag that formed on the baby's ear, we needed to look a little more thoroughly into the hearing organs in order to rule out another malformation or hearing loss. The point is this: the seen can be an indication of what might be wrong in the unseen.

So why am I telling you this? Perhaps to recruit future hearing doctors—or perhaps to teach you to look deeper below the surface of what is seen. My external behaviors revealed that I wasn't coping with stress well. It was a visible marker of a deeper disturbance in function in my mind and heart. So before you go judging every fallen person in the world, investigate a little deeper. *The misbehavior is just a symptom or an indicator of a greater unseen reality.*

God knew all about my mismanagement and failures. He gave me the courage to face them. He had already set up people and finances for all of it to get straightened out. He set up the glory necessary to restore my story at this time and ahead of time. It was all ready when I needed it. Not early, just on time. This really encouraged me to trust in God. I fight a battle that Jesus has already set up for me to win. I was not alone. Neither are you.

There are more with us than you know. Whether you believe in God and angels or not, they are committed to performing God's will and plan. Irrespective of our own prayers or beliefs, God still has angels aiding us and getting us to where we need to go and away from other places. You don't believe me, you say. Read about a few of these Bible stories, and think about how God has kept and/or guided you.

An evil prophet, Balaam, was summoned by an evil king to come and curse God's people, the Israelites. So God sent a mighty angel to block the passage of this evil prophet. The mule wouldn't move; Balaam beat the donkey he was on three times to try to get him to obey. By a miracle, the donkey turns around and talks to him and says, "I've served you faithfully. Don't you see why I can't go." The Lord opens the prophet's eyes and he sees the mighty angel with his sword drawn and blocking the road. Balaam wanted to go, but God would not allow it.

Another story was when a group of prophets was overwhelmed by the high numbers of enemy soldiers in a battle. The prophet Elisha was with them and said, "Don't be discouraged. There are more with us than with them" (see 2 Kings 6:16). He prayed for God to show his companion the heavenly host protectors for as far as the eye could see. They were definitely supernaturally defended. So when I feel discouraged at some moment in life's battles, I imagine heaven and earth pulling for me to get it right. It is true scientifically, biblically, and in my life that the greater work and reality is unseen.

Peace is a promise you keep. If I'm honest with myself, I've been battling the same things for many years. I read my journals and prayers, and they floor me because they are still relevant to today's heartfelt prayers. Sometimes I let that dishearten me, but then I run that through the promises of God, and I see the prayers have gotten me through to better. No, not delivered, but I handle all those concerns better. I forgive myself and others faster, I ask for forgiveness sooner, I identify my part in improving the situation, and I remain in prayer about it. Just like the newest smartphones, my prayers may still perform the same applications; I just live in repentance, forgiveness, and grace better and faster. That is a good thing.

I revisit those prayer journals and give thanks for the prayers that

ODILIE M. BAGWELL PORTOCARRERO AU.D.

have been completely answered. I am so humbled. Who am I that He really makes time to answer my prayers? That definitely grows my trust. In sincere gratitude, I praise and reflect how far I have come. I even look forward to the point I'll reach when I have arrived! Even if I have to wait till heaven, He listens! That I even have His captive attention is mind-blowing. That I get to speak His name is alone a privilege. If I can somehow enrich your approach to a very holy, *holy*, HOLY, *almighty God*, don't forget that He listens to every word we say, but please remember who you are talking to. Give the Lord your God the reverence and adoration He is always worthy of.

It definitely grows my trust in God when I see Him at work in my life and in the lives of others. I constantly remind God that what He did for a believer before, He can do again for me. Then I trust and wait and remind Him humbly what I request of Him.

When I find myself struggling with motherhood, my most challenging role, I remind myself what He shared with me many years ago when I had my breakdown. He said, "Odilie, *I did not give you this challenge to take you down, but to show you what you are made of, to bless you. Seek Me for what I want to show you in all that makes you question or even run away from Me. Don't ask Me why. Ask Me and listen for What.*"

TRUSTING THE CHURCH –WHICH ONE?

If I could have the privilege of sharing with you my journey to find a church home, I'll start with my first experience with church.

The first time I felt peace and adored without condition was at the Catholic school and church, the Queen of Peace.

In this school we started our day every morning in mass. I can't even explain how much I loved going to mass. Imagine, a child with not too much good stuff going on at home and what seemed like to me a lot of unpredictable chaos. So as I walked into this beautiful sanctuary of God, there was peace, reverence, and the smell of incense, with soothing and peaceful music. The music had beautiful lyrics that soothed my achy, troubled heart. The unison, order, and structure of adoration and worship was fascinating to me.

At the age of eight, I fell in love with my faith, and it came alive in me. I remember, the day I received Christ as my savior it was my first Communion. It was the most holy of days to me. I still recall experiencing the presence, love, and peace of God that day. That day I knew I was His forever. I was saved and set apart for Him to watch over me and for me to come to know and please Him.

When I went to high school, all my faith and worship became occasional and obligational. I was working, distracted by friends, and consumed with making something of myself. I can remember writing God a prayer to help me find enough money to go to college. I knew God was powerful and loved me and would lead me. So I prayed. But sadly, I used Him to get what I wanted and then forgot Him and stored my faith in a closet. It would be a long time before my love and peace would reign in my heart again, but at least I knew the first time love had broken through for me.

I started going regularly to church again when I became a mom. I was raised Catholic, and I still consider myself to have a strong charismatic Catholic influence, but primarily I claim to be Christian. I dont like denominational splits, I can only say that I follow one Shepherd, Jesus Christ, and I worship Christ in any Bible-based Christian church. I love all denominations. I have visited them and worshipped in most of them all. I personally love that there are so many styles to worship God.

The most critical thing I have found as a family with young kids is to make church and youth group nonnegotiable. Kids' opinions come and go. But I love to see them plugged in and with friends and volunteering in the church. As the parents grow, the kids know of God's truths by just watching. Together we stay accountable that we are to put God before all. It is hard to practice, I know. It goes without saying that churches and youth groups have flaws too. We are all flawed people. But at least we gather in the hope that we are at the hospital for healing hurting souls, aka the house of the Lord.

I cannot do it perfectly: go to church and all the nights of worship, retreats, and Bible studies. Believe me, I have four kids, and all of them play competitive game-away sports. Yet I've seen more often than not that it is a family with Christ at the center that will remain together. So I pray for my marriage, my kids, and my kids' kids. I pray fervent, mighty, and strategic prayers for my extended family, the community, the nation, and the world. Once you learn to pray, you will find that it is easy to pray all night and day long, just as God asks of us.

Now briefly about people in the church.

The Relationship Failed ... Because You Handled *This* like *That*

How many of us suffer when it comes to relationships? In government, religious, corporate, organizational, parental, children/grandchildren, and neighborly relations, each have their own purpose and dynamic that make them work. It's all so much to juggle. Imagine how often in our day, a dynamic either changes or never even begins because of how we process the pandemic, politics, education, our health—all of it affects the dynamics of relationships that either strengthen, dissolve, or will never be. One person says to the other, "Because you choose to live in this manner, I can't respect you or trust you any longer." One person crosses a defined boundary the other person won't go past, and so it ends in division.

What is one to do when you have to stay in a relationship because you are blood relatives, married, or inseparable business partners? Or when you have known each other for years inside or outside the church?

One might say that person handled a particular situation in a certain way, and because they did, you've lost respect for them. It really is hard to live closely with people. Why does it seem that the closest to us seem to let us down the most? We let them down because we don't serve a need that they wanted from the relationship, or else they let us down. In the same way, what can you do when repeatedly someone you supposedly admire or study under finds ways for you to experience continual injury? It could be due to differing lifestyles or styles of managing risk. There is something we can do. Pray for unison, between families, communities, nations, and the globe.

Realize that we do not fight flesh and blood but dark, supernatural forces that influence our circumstances and our thought life. We are influenced by the need to be right, the need to have our point validated, and the need to protect our health and well-being. We feel the need to have self-expression and control for what happens to our body. Notice the focus right there. I'm not saying I approach anywhere near Jesus's status in this, but we are not to be so self-focused but rather to put the needs of others before ours. That is some maturity and Mother-Teresa-status living right there. Never tire of pursuing godliness or holiness.

Since most of us of don't live like our divine God-and-man Jesus, our holy mother Mary, or Saint Teresa, we experience a life less than holy. You know the drill: we put a wall up if someone is probing too much. We change the subject if it's a "touchy" issue. We say we need more boundaries in the relationship to avoid getting triggered or hurt. If it has to do with politics, race, religion, sexuality, and now Covid behavior, we avoid communication or even contact.

In love, war, and the art of communication, it all comes down to where you have placed your trust. In these instances, we protect ourselves. We deem this other person as unsafe in some regard or behavior, and we choose to fix the situation ourselves with self-protective mechanisms. In all honesty, *I've seen relationships work best with mutual vulnerability.* Honesty works to bridge villages; it works when given with transparency out of honor, love, and respect. God created us a colorful and complex and multicultural people. Once we realize that we all have the same needs and that we are more alike than different, we can meet and find commonality and mutual respect, authentic connections and enjoyment.

What would it take to unite us across denominations of religion? Is our biblical standard is to help and love a brother or sister as if they were a beloved family member or friend?

Honestly, I see us most united in tragedy and crisis. I don't want that for us, unwanted loss of life or property. But look at how we unite and help in response to 9/11 or tragic natural disasters. More than not, we do link arms well in tragedy. Let us not wait until the next disaster. It starts with me showing God that I am willing to live and learn and think about others. I can touch cold or weary hearts in radically kind ways.

If each one of us who reads this book then tells one person of this radically kind love, we can start to turn the tide. Start the movement, *Love Broke Through,* and spread this unity! *How?* First, we ourselves get healed and made whole by God's relentless and good love. In a living and active relationship with a *good, honest,* and *willing* God, I learn to bend and flex to keep peace above being right. Yes, this is radical, but it starts with each of us reaching across the faces of our phones and coming out from behind our Covid masks and connecting with people.

Recently, I asked a person at the car wash how he was. The conversation was easy, and he was willing to engage. So as we chatted, I asked if he had a prayer concern. He was so happy that I was interested in talking. We were visibly different people brought together in the hope of a brighter day! That is where it starts: you and me challenging ourselves in believing the best in people and their situation. Compassion, time spent sharing and caring—this is how trust grows for both God Almighty and people.

Ask yourself, "What is the most loving thing I could believe and do for this person?" Change and connection between very different people happen one interaction at a time. Couldn't both you and I do or think on and pray on *one* loving act? Tag it, do it, share it. It's contagious in an uplifting way. Ask yourself; visit my gram page @drodiliebagwell and @lovebrokethrough.thebook, and tell me about you and *what is most loving?* #WIML Let's give one another ideas on social media on how to bridge gaps and create loving unity.

Lastly on trust, can I ask you to place complete trust in God? You see, if a person in your life is challenging you, it's for a reason. The reason is always for your good and further sanctification in godliness. If that is true, and we know it is, because this is stated in the living Word of God,[4] then it is our job to rely on relationship with our triune God—Father, Son, and Holy Spirit—to reveal to us exactly how to navigate relationships with all people in our lives.

To preserve any relationship, we must value relationship. We have to overlook and forgive more than we would ever want to or thought we could. The Word of God says that we can do all things through Christ who strengthens us. Not necessarily all things we *want*, but probably more all things we are appointed and called to do. We aren't meant to do it all and be it all, just where God appoints and anoints us to.

Adding to that, Jesus instructs us to love one another; to forgive seventy times seven times. It's not easy, but with Christ we can do all things (yes, forgiving is for all times; it is for your good and a must in relationship with Christ). Realize that this person or this trying situation is in your life to teach you. Stop willing it away and praying it away. It's here to stay until you get with your Lord to get you *through it*. Why? To help you know your Lord better, to grow you in godliness, and lastly, so that you may glow or shine and reflect the goodness of Jesus.

To make peace with God's will for your life is to choose to trust God's knowing over yours. When we have our God with us, we can more readily accept His divine plan and trust He is allowing all this for more than what we know. No matter what our feelings say to us, when we remain with God, we can get through anything.

Would you, could you trust God, once more or for the first time? As I shared with you, trust grows one interaction at a time. It is one step at a time into further intimacy or rich quality time through one loving act of kindness. If doubt comes, and it will as you learn trust, you ask for affirmation. When I was rebuilding trust, I would say,

"I'm sorry for needing reassurance, but right now I do need it." God is *most* loving, and He will give you affirming signs to trust. This works for human relations too if there is mutual interest in building trust. But it is God who will get us through the difficult and the hurtful, the disappointments and the downright betrayals.

To remain in relationship means to abide in *Him.* When we trust God to develop us through and by way of the challenging relationship, we grow. We grow past the troubles and grow deeply and strongly in Him. Release the relationship or the trial completely over to Him. Some of my favorite verses say, "Be still; I will fight for you. Trust that I am good. Trust in Me, and lean not on your own understanding. I'm working this out for your good." Then we can allow the situation to play out the way it needs to be.

Don't let the wait or the questions block the gift of developing godly growth in you. Each time I find myself having a pity party, I flip the script from frustration to query. I say, "*What* is God trying to teach me through this person and situation?" In time and trust you will rise above. Every time you want to fix it or teach that person a lesson, sit back and trust. You have a mighty God working on that situation for you. Let go, and *let God.* God never comes off the throne, never sleeps or slumbers through your problem; never is He too busy with bigger things than your little problems. Sit back, and be with Jesus. Let Him take care of you, love you, and empower you.

The result: Faith works! God *gets you through!*

The devil's hand is always overplayed. He likes to create a scene and always has a scheme to throw us off our purpose and God's good plan for us. So beware. Use the Word of God to keep him off your tail.

This pandemic and all that it has done to our church, our families, our faith, this world—shoot, our waistlines! Can I get an amen, that this has been Lord helping us!

This too shall pass. Our Lord will not be mocked; when the time is right God, will arrest the devil's scheme.

Division is of the devil; unity is of God. It doesn't take a spiritual genius to see that Covid 19 is of the devil's work. From having to wear masks to cover our mouths, to stealing our breath, to prematurely passing away—it's pure evil. But evil will not prevail!

Fear not, God is on the move. In the meantime, I'm led to say, in word and in deed, do good for the common good. It is in protecting others that we ourselves are protected. It is in giving that we receive. Want more love? First receive it fully from your creator God; then you can give it. Do you want more trust? Be trustworthy. We can't give any more than what we first are and then have.

In love and war, remember these practical tips.

1. Trust in the truth of the Bible. It is not just a history book; it is your lifeline to wisdom. Trust in the faith that it is all true and does exactly what God says it does. Deny any doubt, cast it out, and *just believe!*
2. Honor God with your time, and your love and trust will grow out of that.
3. Listen more and talk less. Trust grows when we speak less. You can connect by listening.
4. Remember, your job is to love and forgive. God's job is to change people, us or them. We don't change ourselves or others.
5. Be all in.
6. Be patient.
7. Speak life. To speak hope into a person is to give life.
8. Set boundaries so that you don't enable bad behavior. For example, "When you choose that behavior, I won't be in relationship with you." Or "You crossed a line I couldn't meet you past." Regarding trust and boundaries, get with God and good wise counsel.
9. See the drawings after this chapter.

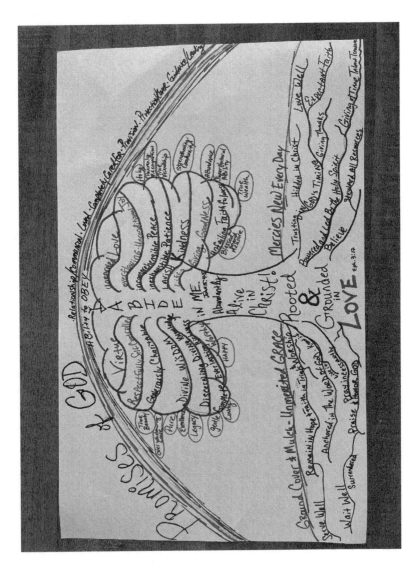

Image 4: Promises of God

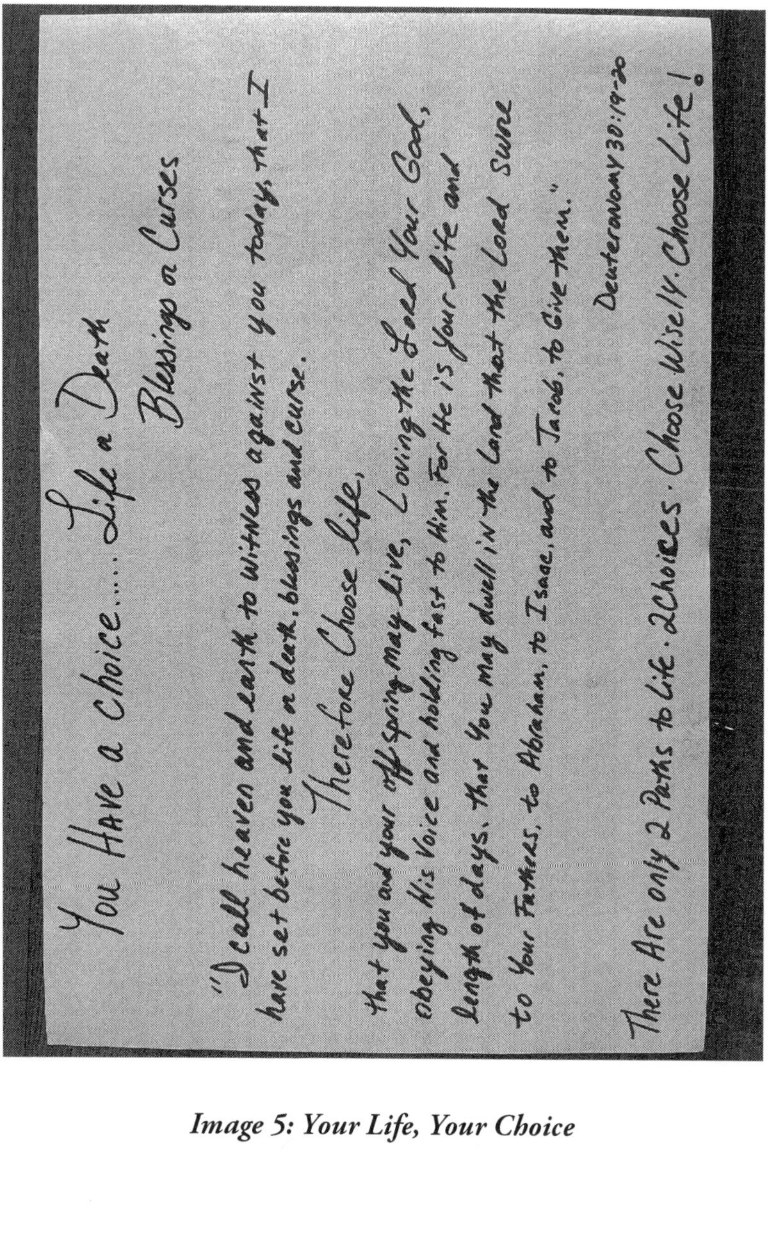

You Have a Choice.... Life or Death

Blessings or Curses

"I call heaven and earth to witness against you today, that I have set before you life or death, blessings and curse.

Therefore Choose life,

that you and your offspring may live, Loving the Lord Your God, obeying His Voice and holding fast to Him. For He is Your life and length of days, that You may dwell in the Land that the Lord Swore to Your Fathers, to Abraham, to Isaac, and to Jacob, to Give them."

Deuteronomy 30:19-20

There Are only 2 Paths to Life · 2 Choices · Choose Wisely · Choose Life!

Image 5: Your Life, Your Choice

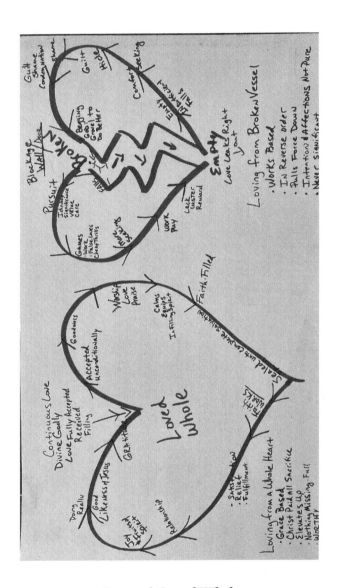

Image 6: Loved Whole

HIS SACRED HEART FOR YOURS
END OF CHAPTER REFLECTIONS

A Glimpse at His Heart …

A Step into the Sacred Chambers of His Heart with His Holy Word

But blessed is the one who trusts in the Lord,
    whose confidence is in Him.
They will be like a tree planted by the water
    that sends out its roots by the stream.
It does not fear when heat comes;
    its leaves are always green.
It has no worries in a year of drought
    and never fails to bear fruit.

(Jeremiah 17:7–8 NIV)

Song: "I'm Gonna Let It Go," Jason Gray, 2019.
"Sparrows," Cory Asbury, 2020.

A Guided Prayer for You

Thank You for changing my will and heart, so that I want what You want for my life. I trust that You are using everything to lead me to You. I trust that You will help me know that You are with me based on truth. Your Word says You will help me grow in all my life challenges. You make all things work together for my greatest good and Your glory. As You guide me through any fiery trial, I will radiate more of You. Help me become more aware of Your leading. I want to trust You with all of me. Thank You for helping me in this, Lord. You are so good to me! I love You, Abba Father!

LOVE BROKE THROUGH

Your white space …

12

THE PRACTICE

To practice means to stay at it. It is more of a lifestyle. A committed practice schedule is consistent. Anyone who has practiced knows that we can't let up at our practice consistency just because we are terrible at the skill. You keep at it to get better, no matter where you start off. A lifestyle does not pursue improving for just a season; it is for good reason and for life. In continued practice, I make amazing gains, and my confidence grows.

Sometimes practice is horrible, and I pull a muscle and shank a play. Sometimes I have to bench myself. But I stay at it, getting better all the time with continued practice. I play in the name of Jesus forever. So I have committed to be all in and at it until my last breath. Even when I fall, I will always get back up because God saved me for a reason.

In this last chapter I'll share what keeps me playing, running, and exploring how I advance in this race I run for Christ. I practice, and I have come to know that in getting to know more of Christ, I come to know my deepest and truest self. I have come to believe and allow myself to receive that I was set apart in love, by love, for love. So now I practice loving and knowing God better, and that makes me a better lover of people, too! I practice love; won't you?

Though God speaks to us individually and sets each one of us apart for a special and custom purpose, there are definite inalienable rights and privileges that belong specifically to you and me. These truths are intrinsic to all of us believers. My point in saying this is the following, what I have come to be blessed with in understanding God's wisdom is not just for me. It's for you, too.

So do not dismiss your call from God when it comes through a person. God sent that person who can speak to you in that certain way. They are tuned to your receiver; when that person speaks, you just "get it" better. That is a wonderful thing, and if I am that person for you, to *God* be that glory. I am just a vessel with a great mouthpiece and volume; this makes sense to anyone who has watched me online or met me in person. My volume control is permanently broken when I get excited, and God always excites me! —But I digress. Back up and running.

Please remember a few things when you seek instruction and understanding through a teacher of any sort.

1. Always use the Word of God as the ultimate say.
2. Never rely on a human as the sole source of your learning the Word and receiving encouragement. Inevitably, they won't be there when you are in a hard place. They are human and aren't made to take the place of your God. Only God is infallible, ever-present, and all-knowing. So give only Him the highest place of seeking and adoring. He is forever available to you and me as our source of good life and wholeness.

That being said, please take this fully in. Breathe it in richly and deeply, until every bone in your body is drenched in this truth at the cellular level. In accordance with God's plan and by His grace,

say this truth aloud: *Nothing I do or didn't do can let my God down.*
Now and forevermore,

I am ME—
    Dearly loved,
        Completely forgiven,
            Forever free *in Christ.*

Those, my dearly *beloved*, are the beginning of your inalienable rights or gifts as a child of God Most High.

As I continue to grow, strengthen, and mature in Christ, I find stability for my ever-changing feelings and moods. I receive a discerning ability that I only get when I've locked eyes on my Savior. When I do, I clearly see my next step; difficult decisions and hard conversations come easily by a grace that only comes from God.

When I stay in my new way, version 2.20, I truly feel in my spirit as though I've won the Lotto; I have in eternity. Secure in all I'll ever need for life and godliness, I trust. In a closeness to Christ, I can claim the set-aside blessings for me to discover and spoils besides.[2]

There is so much to discover in a life following God. He takes us strange places sometimes, and we can't seem to find Him in the situation. Think about it; when Peter was called to walk out onto stormy waters, Jesus said three things to settle his anxiety. Maybe this could serve to calm ours whenever needed. Jesus said, "Be of good cheer! It is I; do not be afraid."[3] Why would Jesus say that in the darkest hours of the night, in the midst of an intense, stormy time? I can see a lot I could use in my day-to-day off of this verse.

1. It must be that good cheer—also found as "be of good heart" and "take courage"—is great for a weary or worried heart.
2. "It is I," Jesus says; "I AM" in another version. Could it be that Jesus is trying to tell us that, no matter how dark the night is or how terrible the storm, *He is there* with us. Could

it be that He also says, "Look at Me, not the storm; I've got this and *you*." We could probably dig all day for what He might be wanting to reveal to us, but I'll leave you with this last one to consider. Could it be that Jesus is saying, "You might not recognize Me in your dark areas or times, but it's still Me. I won't leave you." Remember, Jesus works through people until He should return and we physically see Him again. So if someone good wants to help you in the middle of the storm, don't be too proud to accept the help.

3. Do not be afraid. Fear is a spirit, and it totally cripples us. So I believe that God is saying in these dark and stormy days of late, let His perfect love cast out all fear, and go where He calls us. In faith, with eyes locked on Him, we can follow Him onto oceans and live in a faith that walks on water. Isn't that amazing? He says, "Fear not, I am with you." This is found over and over in the Bible.

Think about my practice of love. If I'm forever on the team and have the best coach, Jesus, I know I won't lose my starting position in Him. He only made one of me. So I can never be replaced; I am completely approved. The way for me to get better or level up in my game is to stay close to my coach. He wrote me the best play sheets and workouts, and it is all in His living and active Word. He helps me stay clean and right-standing with Him—that is, righteous. In fact, in His Word, He gives me of Himself. He is the way for me to live free of sin.

In all this I share, I hope I can show you a personal story of a real person who can truly win at any battle of mental health. The truth is that if you have fought addiction, and I have, you have bought a lie somewhere. To fight addiction is to a fight a war within. The battlefield is in the mind. The bait of Satan is the lie. When you believe the lie, you empower the liar. If you are like me, you bought a whole lot of them.

So in Jesus, I took the challenge of fighting PTSD, anxiety, and depression. The story was rewritten. When you believe the truth, you empower liberty. The cure is Jesus. He is grace and truth. He sets the captives free, and whom the Son sets free is free indeed.[4] We know freedom is not free, but Jesus paid for all of us to be really free of mental trauma, turmoil, confusion, self-doubt, all of it, really. Yes, He did defeat darkness, so yes, He really can set us completely free.

I know it because I lived it. The Word of healing and life washed me clean, and the spirit came alive in me. The Word of God is life itself. With the Word, I was given the key to being made whole and well. It is well with my soul, and it can be for you too. Put your faith to work in obedience. Go where He calls. Do as He says, like holy Mary said when Jesus preformed His first miracle (see John 2:5).

Miracles have already happened for me, and I'm not done believing for more. You and I know there is a bunch of God's kids still out on the streets. I put my faith in the Lord. He knows some of His kids call Him Father God but aren't living like they are free. The Miracle-Gro of faith and love is to practice it.

Yet there are careful building elements to faith: repetition, obedience, and proper use of it (stewardship). I don't mean like a daily grind of "obey or else." That is a form of slavery, forced militant oppressive work. God's type of faith at work is without that forced burden—the kind when you have to sell a certain number of fundraiser tickets for your kids. Most of the time we have to buy them ourselves, all so we don't fail the school.

When God calls us to obedience, He empowers us to do the work. When he calls us to obey, it is a clear call, yet hard to see. Think of the time when Peter walked on the water. Jesus called in the dark and in the middle of a terrible time, stormy weather. Has God ever asked you to come do something for Him at a terrible and dark time? He has me, with a call to a war-torn and politically unstable area for a mission trip. There he said, *"Go."* I faithfully went, and it was worth it. Let's be clear here; He doesn't call us for His benefit. He already has everything. He calls us for our benefit.

When He calls, He usually gives one-word commands like "Come." Typically, only the bold go where He calls. Just like Peter in the storm, both visibility and reasoning seem poor at the time of the call. But in faith, you'll know to go! Trust in *Him*, and you will see after you've listened.

How do we get better at obeying? Just like practice says, it is in obeying more often, you come to better obey. To obey is to really just to listen to His leading. As I described, stewardship is mission-critical. Stewardship means being faithful or taking care of what you have been blessed with. This is God's type of responsibility. Think of it more like wealth management run through the lens of love and loyalty for the Lord. Love honors the giver of life. Stewardship honors the giver of the gift.

So when each of us are given a certain number of gifts, resources, and talents, it is up to us to grow them. Jesus really wanted us to know this. Allow me to share how this Bible truth became something I wanted to live in my life.

In this parable, Jesus tells of three of His people called to a certain responsibility. Each was given according to their own ability and not more. In the parable each was given plenty of time to manage their resource. Two of the three had a heart for pleasing the master, went to work, and doubled their resources. The last servant buried his talent for fear of losing it or displeasing what he thought was a harsh master. He gave it all back but had no growth. He did nothing.

Jesus described the two servants who grew the kingdom resources as good and faithful servants. The master would honor their stewardship and invite them to enter the joy of the kingdom. The last servant he casts out and scolds. He was told that he was slothful and wicked. Ouch! All because he left what he was given untouched. I hope this tells you that our God is serious about the command He gave us in Genesis 9 to be fruitful and multiply. Let's be clear: He rewards growth.

So as I grow in the courage to fiercely pursue life following Jesus wherever He may lead. I start noticing more and more that I am living in more of His blessings. I do work my faith and talent to enlarge God's territory and team. In fact, with this *Love Broke Through* book, I am now a talent scout and a corporate kingdom trainer. I am willing to put love and time into growing God's kingdom. I have a heart for making sure God's team *looks and acts the part of saved* by grace. On this Team *Lord Jesus*, I faithfully seek God so I can run the Holy Spirit's plays to prosper the Lord's kingdom. I want to seamlessly bring home the harvest of souls. Together, we will be sharply dressed in the Word of God. The Lord's holy fire purifies our hearts to want to do this, to seek and save the stragglers of the faith. I can see us now; what a good-looking and godly-powered bunch!

"DOING IT AFRAID,"
ONE MOMENT AT A TIME

Why do we wait to act on this faith already in us? Most of the time it's just the paralysis of analysis; we feel frozen by the enormity of the project. The feelings are the same whether it's tackling the clean-out of a garage or closet or planning a special event. Its bigness overwhelms us, and we freeze; we either don't sign up or procrastinate in carrying it out.

But the most important thing to remember is that one action at a time builds on itself. Inches turn into miles and minutes into years. For me it has been helpful to not make something forever in your head when forever is really only today. Make it a moment of choice. Just for this moment can I do this thing that God has asked me? I literally break it down to 26 seconds. We pretty much can do anything for 26 seconds. So I do it, and then I say, "With men this is impossible, but with God all things are possible" (Matthew 19:26 NIV). Hence the 26 seconds.

One second at a time, one step at a time, we get empowered by God to do it better, longer, and stronger. When God shows you a vision of where He wants you to go, but you don't know how to, it is on purpose. He reserves a spot for the two of you to do that thing together; it is your calling to be on a journey for a purpose with Him. When you fully surrender the design and outcome of all you are and all you do, He walks out your God's plan for your life with you, step by step. *God's* plan is way better than yours and higher than you can imagine The Bible even describes that you'll hear a voice from within that says, "Go this way."[8] It's on this path that you will see God move obstacles for you. For anything above my head is below His feet. It's at the end of me that the miraculous begins. It's His way of ensuring that we stay super close to Him.

I loved when God showed me this, because the God of the entire universe and beyond says, "Step with Me into something way beyond yourself." He says, "Believe in Me, and stay in the moment. There are great things for you in the 'present'; that's why they call the present a gift." We were made for greater things and receive them from our great God when we stay present in the right-now. Allow, surrender, yield to the greatness of God, so He can break through your own basic agenda into His extraordinary ways.

So almost, on a monthly basis a thought comes, the desire to comfort myself with a relaxing drink. Can I ask you what you run to for comfort? Is there a certain lifestyle God spoke to you about? I hope before you go back to your former ways, you give the Lord first place. I do now. In my weakness, in my despair, I say, "Lord, I want off this planet now. I feel cornered or tempted. Be with me to stay with You. I don't want to go back to a sinful or less than God-honoring way. Lord, You are the way and the life; help me. You want me fully present and sober in my whole being; this I know." He faithfully helps.

Remember, to be tempted is not a sin, so don't shame yourself or be saddened. Let it remind you that you need God to remain pure and lovely. It is a beautiful thing about God, He wants us to rely on Him. He is never too busy for me. It is He who saves me from death or sin and unto life at salvation and every tempting day along the way.

When obsessive thoughts come, I don't allow myself to entertain my former ways. I used to say things like "Is forever really forever? I can't have wine with my daughter when she is grown or have drinks with friends at a dinner like they do? Or what did I do so different or wrong that they still get to and I don't?" The Word of God says to hold those thoughts captive.[5] Now I just say to my brain, "That thought is not useful. Move on! I choose to live free of this entanglement." This train of thought can always drive by, but I don't need to get on this train of insanity. It's going nowhere. This will pass. Just for right now, *do* what is right and best for you. "Better *and* blessed *is the harder* road that will lead me to You, O Lord!" Then I think on what God says about my future. He says that He has begun a good work in me and that He is faithful to bring it to completion in Christ Jesus.[6]

When I was walking in my new ways, sometimes I said to myself, "Why do I feel so alone?" I grew up very accompanied. When you come from a big Latin protective family, you are never alone. Yes, we all love going somewhere, anywhere all together. So in this life struggle, it was very uncomfortable to be alone. In college was my first time being alone; I never liked it, and I quickly changed any situation so I wouldn't be alone. Now I know the difference between solitude, loneliness, and isolation. One is super spiritually beneficial; the other two are deadly to the soul.

Alone has a layered meaning. It can come about suddenly or happen slowly for some. It can be physical, or it can be spiritual or mental or psychological or emotional. Alone can happen in each of those facets of our being. What I most want you to receive is the truth that if you have God, you are never alone. God is with you even to the end of the age. But I didn't always know this, and the devil loves to get us alone.

So if you are like I was, I ask you to boldly face whatever it is you fear will come up when you are alone. For me there were dark, haunting, lurking bad thoughts. I felt as though evil came to bug me if I was alone. With God's deliverance I faced them all. Let me impress upon you that just because you have dark thoughts or darkness comes at you doesn't mean you are bad or evil. You get to pick whether you are God's or the devil's. When you were chosen to be a child of God and you accepted the call, you were sealed as His own. The devil and evil can't have you. Yes, they can attack or tempt you, but they can't have you unless you let darkness in. Unconfessed sin separates us from God's best. The other way evil has to be overcome is by purging out all the dark. You take out the garbage in your thought life and let Jesus's way and the work of the Holy Spirit cleanse, renew, and transform you all the way into your deepest, darkest wounds. As you know, to even witness evil and sin wounds one, deeply. But as a redeemed child, you are saved and have the authority to run evil and darkness out.

So, whether you witnessed domestic abuse or were a victim of any form of abuse yourself, you can be free of your visual memories and emotional wounds. As a young child, I feared. I feared evil, the devil, I feared sudden chaos, I feared emergencies, I feared fighting, and I feared getting hit. All that combined with the immense need to be approved and liked wreaked havoc on my spiritual, emotional, and psychological strength and development.

All of that is darkness. The Word of God declares that it must flee at the presence of Jesus and His most holy name. So you do not need to live tormented by your past. It was in worshipping God that I felt like my whole dirty and wounded soul was Roto-Rootered or completely flushed clean. I cried out and proclaimed the name of Jesus as my healer, and that He did. Declare who is Lord of your life, and the devil must flee.[7] My Bible tells me so!

So in the face of all that is uncomfortable to process or face and fear, I have three choices.

1. Avoidance, doing anything to distract or busy up one's attention. Avoidance takes up a lot of mental and emotional space; you won't be able to experience fully or store new life

in your mind and body, because this one takes up so much space. Your emotional and relational bandwidth is clipped and cramped. You are not emotionally available even if the offense or wound is under the psyche or subconscious.

2. Hide or escape. Leave, never to return. Geographical salvation doesn't result in new life. Your haunted past moves with you.

3. Face off. I say to the fear, "My Lord is bigger than you. He is the boss of me, not you!" Then I square off face-to-face with whatever intimidates or scares me. I take it to the root and offer it up to Christ to help me process it or cut it out and off. This one has never failed; fear, begone! Perfect love casts out all fear.

More on being alone. Here is the huge secret about aloneness. It's all about what you allow to occupy your head space. If you give the enemy the microphone in your head, he will target you when you are at your weakest. Hungry, angry, lonely, tired—that forms the acronym HALT, meaning take a pause. Don't do anything rash. You are currently vulnerable and cannot make wise decisions. So when alone, or in the lonely mind frame, the enemy will tell you lies and give you ideations that are not good for you. He will tell you not to bother people with your troubles and keep what burdens you secret. He will call you by your former slave names and tell you that you are worthless or incapable of change. *But with God,* you freely practice good and loving, disciplined choices! Amen.

What about isolation? This is a form of escape and is a poor coping mechanism. People who don't trust people hole up either by themselves or with the few people allowed into their circle of trust. Isolation will keep you from your best self. It is in concentrated community that you will reach your highest potential. In isolation, you'll become sicker and sicker. Depression, compulsive shopping, overeating, or any other mental health condition will manifest when isolating along with every other unhealthy coping mechanism.

Now here comes the healthy portion of "I just want to be alone"; it's called solitude. Here you refresh, recharge, rest, reflect, create, and innovate—heal, meditate, commune with God, and hear from Him. Solitude is how we rejuvenate and stay in communion with our Creator and Source. Here you are alone, but you have chosen to invite the infinite and mighty, divine *God* to join you. That is where the Holy Spirit's voice will be loudest to me as well as my divine leading and inspiring is found. It is a practice; I quiet my uncomfortable flesh and sit in the good company of God. When thoughts or the environment interject, choose to stay still, abiding with Jesus. He is the only divine Source that leads to the truth and healing.

Embrace aloneness. The truth is, if you live the narrow path that Jesus died to give us, you will find yourself more alone. Why? Because you are living counter to pop culture. But think of it as being "saved for" or set apart most especially for. For what? Only the choicest and best good that Jesus died to give you.

Living in the full abundance of Christ comes at a cost of standing out in common culture. You will act differently than the mainstream. You won't dress like the rest or act like the rest. God wants you to live in freedom, a freedom custom-catered for you. While we are in this mortal body, we won't have it all together. But God just wants us. He wants us to press on, keep on keeping on. When we take on our true identity in Christ, we know we are never alone or left behind. No, not ever. The steps necessary to press on are your Christian practice. You do get to customize your flow and your methods. But these five steps practiced continuously and wholeheartedly will bring you to significant growth, strength, balance, flexibility, and rich enjoyment in your Christian practice. Love will flow and lead you. God's love never fails.

Step 1. I Accept. I accept that I have been called chosen, forgiven, and free to live an abundant and purpose-filled life in a right relationship with Christ.

Step 2. I believe. I believe what God says about me, despite what I see or how I feel. I believe that if I keep following Christ, He will bring my life into alignment with His good future for me.

Step 3. I "faith it" until I make it. I live by faith, not by sight, not by my feelings. My faith is mine to use. If I feel I don't have any because I'm so low, I rest in Jesus. He called me, and that says I am valuable to Him. Jesus has a faith in me, or I would not have been called *His*. I continue to get closer to Jesus and He gives me faith that does so much.

Faith is a force. Faith is a substance. Faith is a bridge. Faith is heaven's currency. Faith is the way we see more of heaven on earth. What will your faith do for you? Only the Lord your God can show you. Don't tell me you don't have any or that He can't do it. The Word of God tells me we each have been given a measure of faith. So I know it is there.

Step 4. I trust. The kindness, love, and mercy God has for us is larger than life itself. I may be small and have no real thing to give our great God. But it is when I am fully yielded over to Him that He shows me His peace and strength and my significant worth and value! I trust that if I am fully me, empty, insufficient, broken, and longing, You, O Lord, can be fully you. You are overflowing, abundant, whole, and completely fulfilling.

The Lord says, "I've got you. Hold on, this ends well. If it's not well, it's not over. Trust in Me. You are in for the surprise of your life! Stick and stay with Me."

Step 5. I practice love. That is, my Christian practice. For God said that we will be known as His, by how we love. Over and over, I remind myself that I am fully known, fully loved, fully forgiven, fully kept, and fully healed and restored. That is my divine inheritance package. In this life each of us is created for the main purpose of "our Father's delight." So I am naturally wired to be loved by Him, then to know Him, and finally to make Him known.

As I live in the flow of love, I practice living out of that overflow. That is my main thing: my center, my grounding is knowing and living in Jesus. If I insist on the main thing as the main thing in my life, all else goes well with me.

I don't want to struggle and strive anymore. I want to live a life operating in the Spirit, where God leads, and I follow. There He leads me to pleasant places, and I find myself with more of God's people. But if I take back the "plans for my life" and live out of a fleshly agenda, I am in disobedience. In disobedience, I step out God's provision, blessing, and favor.

I'm more willing to live where and how God calls. I constantly pray and praise my way there. I lived forty years of my life my way, I royally tripped up. The story I was writing wasn't going to end well. So I gave God the pen. In these last eight years of the rewrite of my life's story, the story truly does get better and better. Even in all the world's chaos and illness due to the evil pandemic, I am blessed. If I find myself alone again, I know that I can tell the devil to buzz off.

My new story is a wonder! As He is, so am I. I am His ambassador in this world. Signs and wonders are meant to flow through me. I choose moment by moment to remain in the peace of Christ by complete intentionality. When the enemy wants me to gawk at the havoc he creates, I look away and remove myself. The enemy is a copycat and trickster. He always overplays his hand. He twists the truth into a perversion. A perversion is a twist on the intended use of an original creation. He can't create, so he just changes the Lord's original intent. He influences with media and pop culture, and rebellion. He loves questioning both God's authority, Jesus, and the authority God placed in you.

He consistently asks, "Are you sure?" and loves indecision. He plays off fears and insecurities to get you and me off our main purpose. Why so? Because when we delay obedience of where God calls the enemy has a field day with us. Take Jonah for instance. I totally pulled a Jonah—you know, the guy who ended up in the belly of a whale for three days. I ended up in the bowels of drug and alcohol rehab for thirty. I don't know which was worse. I was called, I ignored the call and ran in the opposite direction, and the devil had a field day with Jonah and me. The parallels were there: when I was out of God's will and instruction, I fought some battles that I wouldn't have needed to if I had listened to God's leading and timing in the first place.

I have come to realize that I must fight my battles by letting God fight for me. When I surrender the outcome and the method, God really does step in and make good things happen. I pray and stay with Him in worship, and He moves the mountains for me. In obedience and good relationships with God, I am blessed. Again, to be blessed is not to be free of trouble or trials; that state is reserved for heaven. I am blessed to know I have a big God with me all the time! That is what I call blessed assurance.

Draw a line in the sand today. Never go back to letting the devil twist your thinking. Come to know and trust that you have the blood-bought right to live free of the devil's torment. *We as children of God* have been given authority to silence the liar in our minds and environments. Silence the chatterbox from this day forward; if it's not building, edifying, or encouraging, it is not from God.

Peace and truth now reign in my mind. The renewed mind in Christ just keeps getting brighter and sharper. You aren't doomed to lose your mind. My Bible tells me that we have the mind of Christ.[9]

Lastly, practice getting away to pray in private, like Jesus. Just a few minutes are sufficient, I promise! You must have a way to silence distractions and excessive noise. In the stillness of mind and heart, I can hear the promptings of God Himself. It takes practicing discipline to turn off the other voices in your life like Netflix, in order to tune in to the still, small voice of God.

Practice obeying. I can't say it enough. It is one thing to hear God and another to obey. Obedience is the weightlifter of life. In obedience, burdens are lifted off us. Just like a muscle builder gets stronger by lifting more weights we get stronger at obedience and courage by doing it more often.

Thank God for the practice and the want. It is a gift to have time to practice and even play, all while seeking God with joy. He tells us that in rejoicing, our hearts are soothed with his peace.

The longing for more is the call from your first love, your Creator and Provider, God. Wait well in God's presence. Praise and give thanks that He hasn't overlooked or forgotten us, not for one moment. He is not angry, and you haven't gone too far to be forgiven. He says, "Come close to Me," and He will come even closer to you. Get with that good God, and He will take care of your every need and nature, both sinful and holy. He is God and has power over it all. He wants to give you love and life not rules and shame. On this side of heaven, I'll come up short every day. In Him I lack no good thing.

I thank God that I was given a heart that finally puts the love of God above my plans and pleasures. Jesus is over and in all. I say yes to You, God. Help me do the yes.

So I ask, what is the yes you need to say *yes* to?

Someone's breakthrough is linked to your yes. This is my best yes. Where and what are yours? Can you see that my brave is your breakthrough? My yes leads to your meant-to-be. We are all interconnected. This life isn't just about me or just about you. Put a different way, someone in the body of Christ is missing. Each one of our yeses and moments of bravery brings another member of the body back home.

Think of it this way. If you were missing your eye or arm and you heard it was in Australia, what wouldn't you do to get to your missing body part? You would want it. You need it to have your body's full capability and functionality. The same goes for the members of the church. The Bible describes us as each having a very important and critical role in the *body of Christ*. With missing members, we don't have full capabilities until all of our body parts are doing what only they can do.

Does that prompt you to be brave? All of humanity needs you! You are a hero of the faith when you show up to work in the body of Christ.

For love, for humanity, for your loved ones, would you be a hero of the faith?

So I ask, my beloved, have I moved you enough to move you *one step* closer to your purpose?

Where, may I ask, do you need God's *love* to break through for you?

God's love is present here and now. In these very prayed-over pages. He is with you, take your brave step, and receive your loving breakthrough.

Today is the day.

This is the day the Lord Has made just for you! Let us rejoice and be glad in it! Celebrate because all of heaven is celebrating with you. You are free!

Your Name; _____

Date; _____

Love broke through my _____

_____

My one step is _____

_____

Share for an added layer of freedom.
Tag me on IG @DRODILIEBAGWELL and
@LOVEBROKETHROUGH.THEBOOK
#WIML
#LOVEBROKETHROUGH
#LOVEBROKETHROUGHJUSTFORME
#Myonestep

A Prayer for My Unknown yet Thrilling Future—
The Lord's Blessing over My Today and All My Tomorrows.

Lord, sometimes I get tired and have pity parties that I never signed up for this. The sanctification process hurts. I know You are refining me with each fiery trial. I know You are cutting away the fleshly desires and indulgences so that I live more powerfully in the life of the Spirit. I want to believe and follow Jesus in a deep and immersive way. But the more I know You, Lord, the more I want to be with and know more of You. Keep me from ever falling away from You and faith.

I cast out and bind any ideation and or assignments that derail God's best for my life. Only You, God, can take me to my best days ahead. Help me treasure and give importance to Your eternal promises, the time You give me, and the people You give me to learn from and to patiently teach.

Lord God almighty, I thank You that for such a time as this I do desire to know and love You most above all. I ask You to rid me of any thoughts that would trip me from reaching my good future. Worry and fear melt away as I trust in You to be my current joy and strength. You are the same Lord who saves me day to day from my destructive ways. You are faithful to save each day in renewed mercy and grace and guidance and power.

Lord, keep me from hurting myself or others.

If I haven't told You enough times that I'm sorry—let me say it another layer deeper. I did it my way for so long. I ignored You, lied to You, and hid myself from You. If I ask You for forgiveness continually, it is not because I don't accept and believe You forgave me the first time I asked, but more because I can't believe Your immense goodness to forgive me. I can't believe You would grant me a full pardon!

Thank You for saving me and blessing me despite all of my wretchedness.

I can't help but wish that I had reached out to You sooner. I would have loved living this alive truth in godly higher and pure ways at a younger age.

But, forgiven, I press on with zest. All I could do from this day forward is to live life for You in a way You would be proud of. The best reconciliation to my past is to live fully, lovingly, in the present. In humble honesty, I can show anyone looking or listening what redemption and love look like. I can help encourage and give hope to the one who wants to see a real God heal a real piece of work, an imperfect person.

Perhaps I can reach one heart. May they have the courage to live a godly pure life sooner. My brave is their breakthrough. So I will keep sharing my story so that their way could be sweeter and less painful.

Life is always going to get better the closer and more surrendered I am to You. I'll stay close to You.

Help me, Jesus, to unashamedly represent the love and faith and healing You have taught me. It's so real in my spirit mind, my spiritual eyes and heart, but I lack the method to share it as powerfully as it is. Take and do with me as You will. I am not afraid. I just believe!

Keep my wandering eyes and mind fixed on You! I love You, Abba, for all eternity!

Lord God, not only did You give me a new life and ability to live it, but You have called me out into the deep. As I trust in You more, You give me a life beyond all that I could ever want or imagine.

Lord, I impart by the power of the Holy Spirit Your love to break through all barriers to this person's complete wellness. Bless every individual reading this with Your ability to overcome. It is with a deep knowing and resolve that You are what I long for. With Your love, God, I can live in Your love and pass it on to the level of overflow. Intentionally I choose the kind of days I live. I choose You, one day at a time. Okay, really, I need You every *moment!*

This Book's Final Praise Jams

But always keep your praise break jams *through* the *whole process*. I will keep praying and praising my way through!

"While I Wait" by Lincoln Brewster
"Promises" by Maverick City Music
"House of the Lord" by Phil Wickham
"My God Is Still the Same" by Sanctus Real
"Breakthrough" (live) by Rocks Rocks Worship
"Come Alive" by Dante Bowe
"My Jesus" Anne Wilson
"I'm So Blessed" Cain

REFERENCES

Chapter 3

1   Jesus was tempted in every way, yet sinless (Hebrews 4:15 NIV).
2   Indwelling of the Holy Spirit (Matthew 28:19 NIV)
3   Grafted into Christ and promise of His people (Romans 11:11; Ephesians 2:19; 3:6 NIV).
4   Saved for a purpose determined long ago (Ephesians 2:10 NIV).
5   Our new heavenly glorious bodies (Philippians 3:21 NIV).
6   Plans for a hope and a future (Jeremiah 29:11 NIV).
7   Iron sharpens iron (Proverbs 27:17 NASB).

Chapter 4

1   He is near the brokenhearted (Psalm 34:18 NASB).
2   All have sinned and fallen short of the glory of God (Romans 3:23 NIV).
3   He stoops down to us (Psalm 113:6 NIV).
4   His mercies are new every morning (Lamentations 3:23 NIV).

Chapter 5

1   God makes a way, even in the wilderness (Isaiah 43:19 NIV).
2   Do not be discouraged. The Lord, your God, goes with you (Isaiah 41:10; Joshua 1:9 NIV).
3   All things are possible with God (Matthew 19:26 NIV).

Chapter 6

1   Now faith is the substance of things hoped for, the evidence of things not seen (Hebrews 11:1 NIV)

2   So, faith comes from hearing, and hearing through the word of Christ (Romans 10:17 NIV).

3   Then Jesus said, "Come to me, all of you who are weary and carry heavy burdens, and I will give you rest" (Matthew 11:28 NLT).

4   Now to Him who is able to do immeasurably more than all we ask or imagine, according to his power that is at work within us (Ephesians 3:20 NIV).

5   The latter glory of the house shall be greater than the former, says the Lord of Hosts (Haggai 2:9 ESV).

6   The God we serve is able to deliver (Daniel 3:16–28 NIV).

7   I can do all things through Christ who strengthens me (Philippians 4:13 NIV).

8   Greater is He within me, than He that is in the world (1 John 4:4 NIV).

9   The latter glory of the house shall be greater than the former, says the Lord of Hosts (Haggai 2:9 ESV).

Chapter 7

1   Bearing with each other in love (Ephesians 4:2 NIV).

2   Knock and the door will open (Matthew 7:7 NIV).

3   Find me when you seek me with *all* of your heart (Jeremiah 29:13 NIV).

4   Seek first the kingdom of God and His righteousness and all else shall be added unto you (Matthew 6:33 NIV).

5   Behold, I am doing a new thing (Isaiah 43:19 NIV).

Chapter 8

1   According to Acts 9:1–2 NIV the early followers of Christ were called "disciples of the Lord" and "followers of 'the way'" (Wikipedia: https://tinyurl.com/43zzzbt6).

2   As iron sharpens iron, so one person sharpens another (Proverbs 27:17 NIV)

3   For the word of the Lord holds true, and we can trust everything he does (Psalm 33:4 NLT).

4   No foul language or idle words: and there must be no filthiness or foolish talk, or vulgar joking, which are not fitting, but rather giving of thanks (Ephesians 5:4 NASB).

5   But I say unto you, That every idle word that men shall speak, they shall give account thereof in the day of judgment (Matthew 12:36 KJV).

6   I tell you that in the same way there will be more rejoicing in heaven over one sinner who repents than over ninety-nine righteous persons who do not need to repent (Luke 15:7 NIV).

7   Issues of life flow from the heart: above all else, guard your heart, for everything you do flows from it. Adapted from Proverbs 4:23 (NKJV).

8   A new heart for you: I will remove from you your heart of stone and give you a heart of flesh (Ezekiel 36:26 NIV).

9   Our past: grace breaks through the regrets (Ephesians 2:1 NIV).

10 Made alive in Christ (Ephesians 2:5 NIV).

11 Our present is peaceful (Ephesians 2:6; John 14:27 NIV).

12 Our future is secured with good works (Ephesians 2:10 NIV).

Chapter 9

1   For it is by grace you have been saved, through faith-and this is not from yourselves, it is the gift of God (Ephesians 2:8 NIV).

2   Jesus looked at them and said, "With man it is impossible, but with God all things are possible" (Matthew 19:26 NIV).

3   Know therefore that the Lord your God is the faithful God, keeping his covenant of love to a thousand generations of those who love him and keep his commandments (Deuteronomy 7:9 NIV).

4   Three times I pleaded with the Lord to take it away from me. But he said to me, "My grace is sufficient for you, for my power is made perfect in weakness." Therefore, I will boast all the more gladly about my weaknesses, so that Christ's power may rest on me (2 Corinthians 12:8–9 NIV).

5   So shall my word be that goes forth from my mouth; it shall not return to me void, But it shall accomplish what I please, and it shall prosper in the thing for which I sent it (Isaiah 55:11 NIV).

Chapter 10

1 Woman your great faith has healed you (Mark 5:34 NIV).
2 Fig tree cursed for not producing fruit (Mark 11:14 NIV).

Chapter 11

1 The way, the truth, and the life (John 14:6 NIV).
2 Perfect peace the one whose mind is fixed on you, because He trusts in you (Isaiah 26:3 NIV).

Chapter 12

1 By love for Love … Whoever lives in love, lives in God … (1 John 4:16 NIV).
2 "Pursue," the Lord says, "for you will recover all" (1 Samuel 30:8 NIV).
3 "Be of good cheer! It is I; do not be afraid" (Matthew 14:27 NKJV).
4 Whom the Son sets free is free indeed (John 8:36 NIV).
5 In the same spirit we are all baptized into one body (1 Corinthians 12:12–13 NIV).
6 He who began a good work … will complete it (Philippians1:6 NIV).
7 Submit to the Lord, and the devil will flee (James 4:7 NIV).
8 You will hear a voice saying, "This is the way" (Isaiah 30:21 NIV)
9 I have the mind of Christ (Philippians 2:5 NIV).

APPENDIX A

This is a letter I wrote to help spread Christ's love on a spring break some time ago. I printed forty letters and selected people to give them to by the leading of the Holy Spirit along my travels.

YOU ARE LOVED

Your message from your Savior, Jesus Christ.

You are important in the very circumstances you are in. You don't need to wait till you finish that accomplishment you set out to get. You matter, and are needed. You are needed to be the light, be the kindness, be the generosity, be the friend, be the comfort, be the joy, be the help that you need and want at this very moment. I am here with you. I have selected you to make you aware of how much I love you and want to freely give you all that you need physically, mentally, spiritually, and emotionally, above all you could ever ask or think up. I am a way maker when there is no way, I am healer even when a lifetime has passed in a certain condition. I am a restorer for the little pains and for the unspeakable. I am the hope when you have none. I am *the only way, the only truth, and the only full life.*

Turn away from your fleshly ways, and live deeply in my refreshing and satisfying of wellspring of life. In me you will find true love and acceptance. You don't need to clean your mess up before you approach me or talk with me. You certainly have not strayed so far away that I can't reach you. I put in you an eternal message of love and a deep desire to know me and my ways. This is my thumbprint or Godprint pressed into your heart when I created you. Nothing in this world will ever fit in this God-sized hole but my *Word, truth, goodness, and love.* This is a message of love and speedy help for any and all your needs.

You have been called *chosen, free, forgiven, a child of the one true King.* When you decide to acknowledge me by asking for forgiveness for putting other people, places, and things before me, you begin a process of transformation. *In me, Christ, you have become a new creation* . Some of this will be an immediate change like the stirring in your heart and veins now. This change will touch all the rich parts of you, your mind, heart, soul, and spirit. This transformation will carry over into all aspects of your now blessed life. You will be surprised and refreshed by your new ability to do what you couldn't do before. The same situations or circumstances now suddenly become enlightened by God's work. I am sure to surprise you and give you pleasant adventures. As you choose my true light and love more in your life, you will find more peace, joy, and strength to do what life requires of you.

As you practice and learn how to remain in me, you can and will experience true joy, based not on circumstance but on assuredly knowing your Savior and your ultimate promise of a blessed life. You will be able to rest in the peace that surpasses your understanding and circumstances. You will love so purely that people who are difficult to love now can finally become lovable. This lifestyle of following Jesus will be the most fulfilling and most meaningful thing you can ever be and do. The joy of living out your very purpose gives you a smile so big, it's contagious.

You also will receive grace and mercy for each day's challenges. Keep pressing into spending time with Jesus by reading the Word of God. There you will find the power of healing and wisdom. Don't go back to living life your way and "on your own"; it's a harder life there. Daily, choose to put off your old self and put on your new ways. This is not by your own ability or by doing more right, but by grace; it is an unexplainable gift I freely give you. If you find you don't have enough of something in your life or your heart, rely more on me. Trust in me. I have placed eternal hope in you; nothing can snuff that out. Tap into it, by coming closer to me more. I fully know all about you, and I still absolutely accept and fully love you. I promise to meet you where you are at and go at a pace you will enjoy. You will be amazed by your growth in no time!

You won't get all my promises at once, because I'm protecting you and keeping you close to me. So do not despair when you fall short or don't see the changes happening quickly enough. *Trust in me! Never give up! Keep on trusting me. My love for you is everlasting.* Even through trial and disappointment, I'm working it out for your good. I'm developing you into a masterpiece with tremendous strength. If you should be brokenhearted deep inside, I am closest when you feel weak, and I am strongest in your life when you feel broken in the heart and crushed in the spirit. I carry you through this hard time.

You story will be beautiful, good, and enduring. Let this message prepared just for you serve as your formal invitation to know that I love you and want you to return love to me. Not a lukewarm love but a deep and alive love and relationship with me. I am not in a faraway place up in the sky, nor am I in a certain religion. I am alive and everywhere. Once you let me into your God-sized hole, I'll be with you, in you forever. Say, "Jesus is my Lord and Savior," and I'm sure to save. Talk with me as much as you want, share with me everything … *all* of you, for *all of me.*

I AM the great I AM.

I AM whatever you need me to be.

Now, and forevermore, *the Resurrection* today and each day with me! You were once dead, and now you have been born again in belief and in an eternal spirit.

You are now redeemed. Rejoice with me; all of heaven is praising you!

Faith develops as you use it. So stop trying to figure out everything before you believe. Just *believe.* All else falls into place as you do believe. So do believe in my ways; they are always higher and best for you. Rest in the peace of knowing I have already set aside your every need to succeed in life. Just seek and follow me. Be still and *know I am God.*

Celebrate the mystery and wonder in God the Father, God the Son, God the Holy Spirit—the holy Trinity—to be all that you need to succeed and live in peace, love, joy, and abundance. These are the riches that can't be bought or ever stolen from you.

Speak life-giving words over you and all you love, often. In my *living* Word of God I will help you, guide you, and will show you more to come. Look for me in the everyday, I'm here with you, *always.*

The word of the Lord:

> Christ will make his home in your hearts as you trust in him. Your roots will grow down into God's love and keep you strong. And may you have the power to understand, as all God's people should, how wide, how long, how high and how deep His *love* is. May you experience the love of Christ. Then you will be made complete with all the fullness of life and power that comes from God. (Ephesians 3:17–19 NLT)

> As for me, I call to God,
>   and the Lord saves me. (Psalm 55:16 NIV)

Feel free to write your thoughts about this call on your life. Your prayers to me are sacred, and I keep track of every tear, word you share with me. As you speak my power-filled words, I can release all that I have prepared and stored just for you. Glory be to God in the highest!

May the peace and power of Christ be with you!
Lovingly written by Odilie M. Bagwell AuD, DM, on Facebook Messenger or IG @drodiliebagwell
tag @lovebrokethrough.thebook

JUST ONE MORE THING!

Be in this world but not of it. Shine as the light I put in you. You radiate God's holy light and love now.

The world says,
> You are trapped.

The Lord Jesus says,
> You are free.

The world says,
> You can't ever change.

The Lord Jesus says,
> You become changed in Me.

The world says,
> You do you—boo.

The Lord Jesus says,
> In Me you are all you've ever wanted to be and more.

The world says,
> Follow your heart.

The Lord Jesus says,
> The heart alone is most deceitful; follow Me.

The world says,
> Find yourself.

The Lord Jesus says,

    Lose yourself, in Me.

The world says,

    To thyself be true.

The Lord Jesus says,

    There is only one truth; be true to Me.

The world says,

    Blend in.

The Lord Jesus says,

    Stand out—you are a light on a hill.

The world says,

    Admire creation—the God of your understanding.

The Lord Jesus says,

    Love only the Creator. Love no other thing above

    God—I am beyond your understanding.

The world says,

    You aren't enough.

The Lord your God says

    You are worth everything! I am your enough!

Affirm the following for you:

    In Jesus, I live above the circumstances of this world.

*

I love that I am not in denial of the real struggle and darkness, death, and division this world has, sometimes on me. I more-so choose to listen and believe that every word and promise God gave me to survive this world is *true* and *life to all of me and mine. His love is more than survivorship, but rather a life well lived, both here and in the eternal life.* It may look like I'm lost or down, but I pivot back to eyes fixed on my Jesus. He is always for me!

I use the Word of God to *live, to love, and to fight* for the abundant life God died to give me.

In Love … I press on!

In his kindness Jesus picks me back up from any fall of my bad choices, He then leads me to repentance, and He works *all* things together for my good and *His* glory!

I keep close to Jesus, eyes fixed on Him, until shadows heal ….

The rest is still unwritten ...
get to living with His glory
on your story!

Made in United States
Orlando, FL
15 November 2022

24570373R00163